George William Daniell

Bishop Wilberforce

George William Daniell

Bishop Wilberforce

ISBN/EAN: 9783743373327

Manufactured in Europe, USA, Canada, Australia, Japa

Cover: Foto ©Lupo / pixelio.de

Manufactured and distributed by brebook publishing software (www.brebook.com)

George William Daniell

Bishop Wilberforce

BISHOP WILBERFORCE

G. W. D...

Methuen & Co.
18, BURY STREET, LONDON, W.
1891

[All rights reserved]

CLAY & SONS, LIMITED,
 NDON & BUNGAY.

CONTENTS.

CHAP.		PAGE
I.	INTRODUCTORY CHAPTER	1
II.	EARLY YEARS AND TRAINING	9
III.	ARCHDEACON, DEAN, BISHOP	20
IV.	ORGANIZING A DIOCESE	38
V.	DIOCESAN DIFFICULTIES	71
VI.	THE REVIVAL OF CONVOCATION	109
VII.	THE BISHOP AND THE BROAD CHURCH PARTY	141
VIII.	RITUALISM AND CHURCH ESTABLISHMENT	168
IX.	BISHOP WILBERFORCE'S LITERARY INFLUENCE AND PERSONALITY	196

BISHOP WILBERFORCE.

CHAPTER I.

INTRODUCTORY.

DEAN BURGON, in his work entitled *Lives of Twelve Good Men*, describes and speaks of Samuel Wilberforce as the remodeller of the episcopate. It will be the aim of these pages to endeavour to present his life, work, character, and influence mainly from the point of view thus suggested. We owe a great debt of gratitude to those who will give us right and high ideas of the duties and possibilities that any important rank or position involves. The debt is increased when the true ideal, though once grasped and understood, has been lost, lowered, and obscured by the heavy pressure of unfavourable conditions, acting unrelieved over a long period. Since the Reformation, and more still since the Revolution, conditions of appointment, and the common opinion, had led men too little to seek the office of a bishop in the Church of England as "a good work." It was too much the reward of political service, valued for its secular rather than its spiritual opportunities, favouring an attractive combination of dignity and ease. A great apathy fell on the Church in England, partially deprived, under the circumstances just characterized, of her proper leaders. In a critical moment of awakening, the subject of this memoir will be seen, as Bishop of Oxford, to have been largely instrumental in putting a new life into the order to which he belonged. There was a truth in words written of him by his colleague, the Bishop of Rochester, towards the close of his life—" You have introduced such a system into the episcopate that one has time for nothing."[1]

Nothing strikes us more than the immense variety of talent and power that was displayed by Bishop Wilberforce in his life and work. Take in hand what he would, he might be relied on to face the public with success, and carry through his undertaking without the heavy disability that is incurred, especially in introducing apparent novelties, by seeming to fail. Other men, from timidity, or want of confidence in themselves or their calling, had hesitated to attempt all that their office and position really required them to do. It is not difficult to copy, or even to make improvements on, that which has once been done; and if it is, as Bishop Wilberforce's biographer says, "that his idea of true episcopacy is now a familiar one, and to those of a younger generation a matter of course,"[2] it is largely because his gifts enabled him to give a practical illustration of the way in which its many and various requirements might be met. There were few parts of the work that belongs to the episcopal office, on which he did not fearlessly and boldly embark, considering its

[1] *Life*, iii. p. 375.   [2] *Ibid.* i. p. 344.

relation, not only to his own diocese, but to the whole state of England, and the Church at large.

Thus it is, as it has been said, that the life of Bishop Wilberforce touches all the great ecclesiastical, and most of the great social, questions of his day. "No ecclesiastic within living memory—scarcely any Englishman—has enjoyed a larger share of personal celebrity than he. It would be easy to recall the names of men who eclipsed him by their achievements, or by the brilliancy of their writings; but it remains a fact notwithstanding, that as a public man, Samuel Wilberforce, by the general suffrage of English society, was without a peer."[1] In all parts of the country, and amongst all classes, he was known, not merely by reputation, but personally. His power of moving about was extraordinary; it was not uncommon for the morning of one day to find him in London, the afternoon in his diocese, and the evening at some house in the neighbouring county—the centre of great and important labours during the working hours, and the chief attraction of some social gathering at their close. We may say of him that he was amongst the first to show in railroad days how much might be made of time, and how little might be made of distance, by one who combined power to do what was suggested to him by a high idea of the call made on his energies by the office he held, with a really unusual capacity of mind and body for hard and continuous labour. He was often suffering from severe illness, and in his diaries entries such as "in much suffering all day," "the pain great," are by no means uncommon.[2] His domestic afflictions also were from many causes un-

---
[1] Burgon, *Lives of Twelve Good Men*, ii. p. 2.   [2] *Life*, i. p. 348.

usually great and painful. We find him, however, rising superior to these hindrances, and in the very midst of them, though obviously a man of deep feeling and keen sensibility, keeping stedfastly to work with an unabated courage and vigour.

We shall see that his ideal of what a bishop might be, and should be, was not merely left as a tradition peculiar to the diocese in which he worked. It has become the inheritance of the Church and the world; and gives a reality to the leadership under which it is appointed that the Church should work, such as has not failed to give a new enthusiasm and thoroughness to the labours of all subordinate ranks. Oxford, by position and circumstance, was, as Canon Ashwell has pointed out,[1] singularly adapted to make this new reading of a long otherwise understood story far-spread and widely known. The accessibility of London, the flood of thinking men constantly pouring forth from the University, which he could not fail to influence, made his personality and his ideas a power with many. Beginning his occupation of his see at a comparatively early age, he had time before him, and was able to start on needed changes and reforms without undue haste. We may then accept the estimate which speaks of his career "as offering an example of that which is too rarely seen—the concurrence of capacity and opportunity."

This career began at a time of crisis in the history of the Oxford diocese, and in the history of the Church of England. Dr. Pusey, in a letter written to the Bishop-elect, after his election by the Christ Church chapter, characterizes Oxford as a See which at that

[1] *Life*, i. p. 348.

INTRODUCTORY.

time most of all requires "supernatural gifts."[1] Dr. Newman's secession had brought about a time of intense anxiety, and a great unsettlement. In his letter, Dr. Pusey summarizes the position in these words:—"As far as I can see, what is chiefly at work is not attraction towards Rome, but despondency about ourselves." To the task of reassurance the new bishop was called. He has said of himself that "he could not have borne to be the bishop of a party," and very early in his career, while he was yet Archdeacon of Surrey, we find him thus expressing his feelings on this point in a letter to Sir Charles Anderson:—"Hook's letter pained me deeply. It is the very opposite of his own 'Call to Union,' and it seems to me really quite dreadful that he should avow that he thinks it a *duty* to split into a party. For this is really the force of his words, whereas it is our very blessedness in the Church to know no other party or leader, but to be content in her to take the good of all, and be followers of none beside."[2] He was keenly alive to the advantage that it might have been to him to be a party man. "You do not suppose," he writes in a letter to the Rev. C. P. Golightly in 1857, "that I am so blind as not to see perfectly that I might have headed the Evangelical body and been seated by them at Lambeth."[3] An ever-increasing number of imitators of his methods of government and administration, and of his principles, attest the correctness of the anticipations contained in a letter to the *Oxford Journal*, written by one of his old clergy just after his death. "No one," says that letter, "strove more than he to point out the true

---

[1] *Life*, i. pp. 300-1.   [2] *Ibid.* i. p. 197.
[3] *Ibid.* i. p. 360.

position which our Church occupies. No one resisted more strongly than he did the importation of doctrines or acts foreign to her spirit. Doubtless this feature of his character will come out more strongly as years roll onward; and the debt which Churchmen owe to him will be more fully acknowledged. The picture which by his life he has drawn of the Church of England, both in her adherence to scripture and to Catholic antiquity, will be felt to be a true one."

As regards the materials available for a sketch of his life and influence, a large number of his friends now alive agree in saying that there is little to add to the facts already collected and published in the *Life of Bishop Wilberforce*, issued in three volumes by Murray, and written by Canon Ashwell and R. G. Wilberforce. Their opinion also decides that "Dean Burgon's is by far the best short sketch." The Dean succeeds in making the great Bishop live again before us, and lets us see him as he was to those who knew him best.

It was originally intended that the three-volume *Life* should have been entirely completed by Canon Ashwell. He died, however, after publishing the first volume, and arranging the plan of the other two. He found that the Bishop's life naturally divided into three well-marked stages of different character and complexion.[1] The first of these, which exhibits Bishop Wilberforce "in the making," and in the full tide of growth, progress, and success, ends with the Hampden Controversy at the close of 1847, and the opening of 1848. The second extends from this date to 1860; in it the Bishop encountered a storm of opposition in his diocese, and outside it, as being "one who favoured the

[1] *Life*, Introduction, p. xxxiii.

unpopular school of the Oxford theology." At the end
he came out from the ordeal with success, and was
henceforth looked up to by Churchmen as "a leader
whose grasp of first principles was firm, and who not
only had the courage of his convictions, but the capacity
to give them effect." In the third period, from 1869 to
1873, "he stood out, not only as undisputed leader
among the English bishops, but also as undisputed
master of his diocese, and as something more than
either. He was no longer merely 'the Bishop of
Oxford,' and foremost among his equals, but he had
become the representative man of the English episcopate,
in great measure the representative man of the English
Church; and such as by this time he had become, such
he remained during the rest of his life."[1] In his diaries,
letters, and writings, his biographers have found an
abundant material for filling in the outlines thus marked
out. It was his custom to keep somewhat full
chronicles of his daily doings, and his thoughts of men
and things, as well as notes of conversations in which
he took part. These, with their revelations of his
inward and private life, have been drawn upon in the
last two volumes of his *Life* with a certain want of tact
and judgment, calculated sometimes to leave an unfavourable impression as to some of his motives and feelings.[2] The use made of them illustrates the dangers
of diary-keeping, when it goes beyond the barest record
of facts, and chronicles phases of thought and feeling
which were probably after all but transitory. The
Bishop's letters are a fruitful source of information
concerning him; he had a large private correspondence,

[1] *Life*, Introduction, p. xxxvi.
[2] *Quarterly Review*, No. 309, Jan. 1883.

besides his official one, and made time for very full
letters to his family and friends. Every one has heard
of him as writing a great deal in the train, or in
carriages; and perhaps, in illustration,[1] the story may
be quoted of the delivery at his address, Eaton Place,
of a letter addressed to "S. Oxon, Esq., Rail, Near Reading," in answer to one written on a railway journey, and
dated from the train. He liked, as far as he could, to
answer his letters himself.[2] In answer to the question
why he did not keep a secretary, he said once to a
clergyman, "that it would certainly be a great relief to
do so, but then so many people would be disappointed."
It was his feeling that a few kind words from himself
would lessen the annoyance of necessary refusals; and,
as a consequence, he has left in his many letters a
large material for his biography. From the sources
here indicated, the substance of the following pages
is mainly drawn. The *Life of Bishop Wilberforce*, by
Canon Ashwell and Mr. R. G. Wilberforce, and Dean
Burgon's sketch from the *Quarterly*, have been freely
used. Often, as in the case of the Cuddesdon troubles,
and the difficulties with Dr. Pusey, the writer has only
attempted to adapt to the limits of this little book the
work of the writers mentioned above. An old friend
of the great Bishop suggested the desirability of combining with Mr. R. G. Wilberforce's work Dean Burgon's
views; and this hint has been taken.

[1] *Life*, Introduction, p. xxxi.   [2] *Life*, iii. p. 409.

CHAPTER II.

EARLY YEARS AND TRAINING.

THERE is always an interest in the predisposing causes found in descent and heredity to any eminent and distinguished life. Next it is desirable to notice the circumstances of training and education that have contributed to the successful development of the opportunities offered by natural gifts. We will therefore glance briefly at the history of Samuel Wilberforce from these two points of view, and trace out shortly the genesis of the powers and ideas that made his episcopate such an era in the history of the English Church.

The family of Wilberforce, or Wilberfoss, can be traced back as far as the days of Henry II., and it is remarkable in its long history that no member of it seems to have entered Holy Orders till the generation to which Samuel, and his two brothers, Robert and Henry, belonged. The work of their illustrious father, William Wilberforce, in the emancipation of the slaves, is well known; and it is to him that the change in the family traditions which gave three of his four sons to Holy Orders may be ascribed. He was one of the little colony of Evangelicals who, residing at Clapham, were called somewhat contemptuously "The Clapham Sect." Here it was that on September 7th, 1805, his third son Samuel was born. We know very little of this son's childhood; but we can understand the atmosphere of thought and life in which he received his earliest impressions.

His father seems to have taken a special interest in his training and development. We are told how the elder Wilberforce was accustomed to make his son get up subjects of importance and deliver orations on them; and that it was in this way that he acquired his remarkable power of public speaking. He was never sent to a large school, or a public school; his father feared them, as likely, through a defective sense of honour cultivated in them, to cause a want of confidence between children and parents. "I know," he says in a letter to his son, "that this is often one of the consequences of a youth's living at a great school, especially if his parents are pious, that he has one set of principles and ways of going on in all respects at school, and another at home." Thus he was educated chiefly by private tutors.

There is still extant a long series of some six hundred letters, which his father began to write to him in his twelfth year. These bear evident traces of careful study, and had, as his father desired, a most important influence on his son's development and character. The results and nature of these letters are thus summarized by Canon Ashwell:—"Nascent faults carefully marked and checked, personal habits of upright conduct strenuously enforced, shrewd practical counsels as to social duties and conduct towards his equals constantly suggested, and all these strung upon the one thread of ever-repeated inculcation of the duty of private prayer as the one holdfast of life,—these remarkable letters

EARLY YEARS AND TRAINING.

exhibit the influences which formed that solid substratum of character which underlay the brilliant gifts and the striking career of Samuel Wilberforce." [1]

One or two practical suggestions, made about the time that he matriculated at Oriel, are worth quoting as having been so evidently acted upon. Thus his father impresses on him the following as a principle upon which he himself has often acted, *e. g.* the bringing together all men who are like-minded, and who may probably, at some time or other, combine and concert for the public good. He also advises him never to omit an opportunity of getting acquainted with any good man or any useful man. Other suggestions, such as that one should always pay ready money, should be hospitable but not lavish, that Sunday breakfast-parties should be avoided, all bear witness to the careful, wise, and sympathetic guidance that helped to ripen to a healthy maturity Samuel Wilberforce's many and conspicuous natural gifts.

In Michaelmas term, 1823, he followed his brother Robert to Oriel. During his Oxford career Oriel was almost at the height of its fame, and supplied, in its fellows, scholars, and commoners, a stimulating intellectual atmosphere, which had its full effect on Samuel Wilberforce's development. He took a leading part in the debates of the United Debating Society, speaking on the Liberal side, and being therefore often in the minority. His father supplied him with material for some of his speeches, warning him against being too much of a politician, and adding—" Watch, my dear Samuel, with jealousy whether you find yourself unduly solicitous about acquitting yourself creditably, whether

[1] *Life*, i. p. 3.

you are much chagrined when you fail, or are puffed up by your success. Undue solicitude about popular estimation is a weakness against which all real Christians must guard with the most jealous watchfulness." He was not at this time in robust health, and took his exercise chiefly on horseback; nevertheless he managed to combine steady and moderate reading with a thorough use of all the social opportunities of the University.

In the Michaelmas term of 1826 he took a first class in mathematics, and a second in classics. He tried once for a Fellowship at Balliol,[1] but about this time his engagement to Miss Emily Sargent was practically arranged after a long attachment, and his thoughts were taken up with preparations for his marriage and for Holy Orders. It was finally settled that his marriage should take place in the summer of 1828, at the end of which year he would be old enough to be ordained Deacon.

On June 11th, 1828, Samuel Wilberforce was married at Lavington to Emily Sargent. Through his wife at a later period the Lavington property passed to the then Bishop of Oxford, and made him, as he delighted to describe himself, a "Sussex Squire." On December 21st, in the same year, he was ordained Deacon in Christ Church Cathedral, beginning his work in the diocese that he afterwards made famous. His curacy was a sole charge—Checkendon, near Henley-on-Thames.

Just before his ordination he expresses, in a letter to Mr. Patrick Boyle, his determination to moderate his political feelings, which only, in his opinion, became a

[1] *Life*, i. p. 32.

clergyman when mildly shown. During his stay at Checkendon his political views underwent a complete change; he seemed to see in England, and almost all other Continental nations, a state of things foreboding some storm, and says of himself that, whereas he was once a Radical, he was now, with some exceptions, a very high Tory. He had already been offered preferment by Bishop J. B. Sumner of Chester, and had refused it; but some sixteen months after his coming to Checkendon, Bishop Sumner of Winchester offered him the pleasant Rectory of Brighstone, in the Isle of Wight, and he was inducted into it in June 1830. In his first curacy, with its non-resident rector, he had to work on his own lines, but there are traces of his work being well and wisely done; and he was thus fitted for the larger sphere to which he was removed while yet under twenty-five years of age. He left pleasant memories of his work and his personality among the simple inhabitants of the secluded Oxford village, who remembered him, even in the days of his greatness, as "our Mr. Wilberforce."

His first two years at Brighstone were mainly given to his parish work. Samuel Wilberforce always began with the thing nearest, and, when that was organized and well in hand, looked further for some new field for his energies. At the beginning of his incumbency the questions and circumstances connected with the passing of the Reform Bill of 1832 had brought the Church, and specially the Bishops, into great odium with the people.

Being then, as he himself says, gradually advanced in Toryism, he took a somewhat pessimistic view of the outlook, as he found an "infidel press, an ungodly people, and a scorning parliament, which knows not nor will hear the voice of truth except as a matter of ridicule." His remedy was found in using every possible means and effort, in spending and being spent, to make the Church, and its services and means of grace, very much of a reality to his Brighstone parishioners. It had been long an idea with many of the English clergy that rubrics were made to be broken and disregarded, and that it was not unworthy and wrong to consider how little might decently be offered of spiritual opportunity. The Rector of Brighstone plainly left no stone unturned to give his people every chance. He added a second Sunday sermon, a week-day evening service and sermon, a service and sermon on all saints' days, and a daily service during Holy Week. Besides this, frequent catechisings, cottage lectures, and communicants' classes were all parts of his parochial machinery. He interested himself in labour questions, then much to the fore among the agriculturalists; started allotments; wrote a small tract to try and correct the prejudices of the lower orders of farmers in the matter of tithes; and lived in close sympathy with the country life around him. He also published a hymn-book for his people, in order to give a new life and interest to the Church services, and to help to bring home in a most effective way the Christian's hopes and trials and aspirations. It is still remembered how his people sat listening with delight to his evening preaching, though he would sometimes go on till it grew dark, so that you could not see him. Being anxious to vindicate the value and usefulness to the nation of the parochial clergy, he put together a little volume, called *The Note-Book of a Country Clergy-*

man, which was meant to illustrate, largely out of his own experiences, the sort of influence a resident clergyman has. It was at this time also that he began with his brother Robert a *Life* of his father, who had died in 1833, and prefixed to *Henry Martyn's Life and Journals* a notice of the life of his father-in-law, Mr. Sargent, who died in the same year. Wishing also, as a stimulus to his own reading, to be a contributor to some review, he frequently sent papers to the *British Magazine*, which, edited by Hugh James Rose, was *the* Church organ of the period.

These years were marked by the issue of the *Tracts for the Times*, and we can see the beginning of the somewhat "peculiar relation," as Dean Burgon calls it, which Samuel Wilberforce held to the movement which led to their publication. He, unlike his brothers, stood outside it, and though "a High Churchman from the first,"[1] and "full of reverence for the personal holiness of certain of the leaders of the movement, had his eyes wide open to their faults, and, while he instinctively assimilated whatever he recognized in it as Catholic and true, whatever in it had a Rome-ward tendency he rejected from the first with unqualified abhorrence."[2] Thus it was that J. H. Newman declined further contributions from S. Wilberforce for the *British Critic*, on the ground that he is not "confident enough in his general approval of the body of opinions which he and Pusey held."[3] Wilberforce, in a letter to Mr. Charles Anderson, speaks of this step with regret as a mark of party spirit, and laments the policy that led Newman and Pusey to set themselves against the Martyrs' Memorial at Oxford.

---

[1] *Life*, i. p. 54.   [2] Burgon's *Twelve Good Men*, ii. p. 6.
[3] *Life*, i. p. 126.

It will help to the better understanding of the Rector of Brighstone's later work, to notice some of the ways in which, at this time, he showed himself a strong Churchman. The results of the Reform Bill, and the attitude of the Reformed Parliament towards the Church, had the effect of bringing clearly before Churchmen the necessity of asserting their conviction that, though the Church of England was established, it was something more than a mere department of the Civil Service. It was clear that the time had come when a protest must be made against the Erastian views that had prevailed during the Georgian period. Thus in 1834, and the years succeeding it, meetings of friends of the Church were being held all over the country, and Samuel Wilberforce took a prominent part in the Isle of Wight in these movements.

The general tendency of his thought and feeling at this time is shown by the attack he made on Lord Palmerston's remarks at a meeting held for the purpose of setting on foot a Diocesan Church Building Society. Lord Palmerston had taken a line which Samuel Wilberforce considered to be inconsistent with true Churchmanship, and which, in a letter to Mr. Charles Anderson, he afterwards said was "really speaking to his dissenting constituents." His success on this occasion shows us how his powers as an orator were maturing; and when the Duke of Wellington, who was in the chair, was asked why he had not checked the indignant outburst of so young a man, his reply was to the effect that he would only have diverted on himself the stream of eloquence; and "I assure you," he added, "that I would have faced a battery sooner."[1] He took a pro-

[1] *Life*, i. p. 108.

minent part in getting up an opposition to Dr. Hampden's appointment as Regius Professor of Divinity at Oxford in 1836; and, on going up to Oxford to vote for the censure passed against the new Professor and his views in Convocation, says in a letter to Mr. C. Anderson that "it was loose Churchmen against sound Churchmen, whatever were their politics."

It was only natural that the question of the importance of the episcopal office to a real and vigorous Church life should occupy men's thoughts. As early as 1833 the Rector of Brighstone preached a sermon on "The Apostolical Ministry," at the Bishop of Winchester's Visitation at Newport.[1] It called upon the clergy to prize at a higher rate that unbroken succession, "whereby those who ordained us are joined as to Christ's own Apostles," and it spoke strongly on "the danger of quitting the high vantage ground of Apostolical authority, to fight the battle out upon the doubtful level of Erastian principles." The author did not escape criticism, and was accused of bolstering up his Bishop into High Church notions on the subject. He kept, however, to his principles, and in 1837 was asserting strongly the importance of episcopal organization in missionary work. His work on the *History of the American Church*, published in 1844, illustrates his views on this point, and sets forth plainly how deadness and latitudinarianism seemed to him to arise in churches without bishops.

Wilberforce was always a great supporter of the Mission work of the Church, and a tour for the S. P. G. in the West of England, towards the close of his stay at Brighstone, did a great deal to make him widely

---

[1] *Life*, i. p. 67.

and favourably known. Part of it was arranged to coincide with Bishop Philpott's Visitation tour, and the Bishop was disposed to dread having to listen so often to the same speaker on the same subject. At the end, however, he expressed freely his surprise at the power which always found some fresh point of view from which to advocate the claims of Missions, and declared himself to have been by no means bored, but delighted and interested.

The Rector of Brighstone soon became a leader of the island clergy. He started a society amongst them with monthly meetings, and became a power in drawing them together and inducing an interest amongst them in public questions. Hurrell Froude writes to tell him how he had heard him described as "the μέγας διαλλακτής of the island," and had heard it said that if it were not for him, "all the parsons would be by the ears." His appointment presently as Rural Dean gave him further opportunity for such influence, and made him able to test the possibilities of an office which he afterwards made very important in his diocesan organization.

Amidst many occupations, and much bad health, the distance from Brighstone to London and Oxford was often traversed; the country rector never failed to keep touch with the great world, and found friends among men of every school of thought. While bringing out his father's *Life* he left his living in charge of his curate, and stayed for long periods in London with Bishop Sumner, and his relative Lord Calthorpe. He made a special point of listening to the great preachers of the day, and was brought by his inquiring spirit into intimacies with such men as Maurice and Bunsen, and also began his connection with men of mark in all schools of thought as a member of the "Sterling Club," so called because its members were expected to be free from the unrealities that cling around those who are fettered by prejudice and conventionality.

Several important offers of preferment were made to him, and declined largely because of his own health and that of his wife. It illustrates in some measure his theological tone to note that he was pressed by Mr. Simeon to take the Vicarage of St. Dunstan's. Sir Robert Inglis also offered him the living of Leeds at the time when it was taken by Mr. W. F. Hook. These openings were however declined, as well as an exchange to Leamington, in favour of his work in the South, from which the Bishop of Winchester was very unwilling that he should separate himself. There his reputation as a speaker and preacher grew rapidly, and Churchmen looked to him as a support and authority, more particularly in reaching practical solutions of the many questions then being agitated. He was prominent in an attempt to unite the Church Missionary Society and the S. P. G.; and took a leading part in the educational questions of the day.

CHAPTER III.

ARCHDEACON, DEAN, BISHOP.

It has often been a ground of complaint that the post-Reformation appointments to English bishoprics have given to the Church leaders with little or no practical experience; they have had a tendency to make bishops of men of academical and literary distinction, with a necessarily one-sided view of the position and difficulties of the clergy. Thus the clergy have not been drawn together into united action, and have been left to fall into the fault which Bishop Wilberforce did much to remedy, and which he characterized as applying, in their relations to their people, "not the Church system, but a man." It was, and indeed is, an uncommon thing that our English bishops should be those who have filled many of the subordinate offices in the Church before their promotion to the bench of bishops. Samuel Wilberforce had, however, within a short period served in almost every department of the Church's organization, and thus had a thorough practical insight into all parts of Church work. He knew exactly what was the nature and character of the machinery, rusty in places from long disuse, which he had to employ, and keep in motion, in an English diocese. His experience included service in a country village, and a town parish; he had been Curate, Rector, Rural Dean, Canon, Archdeacon, Court Chaplain, and Dean of Westminster, when the call came which placed him over the diocese in which he gave the striking illustration of his idea of the episcopate, which has quite revolutionized the notions that had previously obtained as to the value and possibilities of that office. Added to this he had, from his close intimacy with Bishop Sumner, a great opportunity of studying a good example of a vigorous and vigilant episcopal administration, of a type that we may perhaps be permitted to describe as belonging to the old school. His preaching and public speaking also made him much in demand on all occasions where Church questions and interests had to be publicly discussed and maintained. Thus he was *au fait* with all in the Church life of his day that was of importance and prominence. From his many friendships, both in London and Oxford, and from his acceptability at Court, he knew a great deal also of the mind and temper of the leaders in the political and social worlds, and could judge well of the lines on which it was safe and desirable to proceed. We shall consider in this present chapter his further growth in power and eminence from the time of his promotion to the Archdeaconry of Surrey in November, 1839, so as to see better what sort of man it was, that in 1845 was called upon to succeed to the See of Oxford, just in the doubtful and difficult times of Newman's secession.

At one time Samuel Wilberforce, his brother Robert Wilberforce, and his brother-in-law H. E. Manning, all filled in different dioceses the office of Archdeacon. There has always existed a certain haziness of idea as to the precise duties of archdeacons; Bishop Blomfield's wary definition of them in the House of Lords is familiar, when he defined them as consisting in the discharging of *archidiaconal functions*. Samuel Wilberforce, and his relations, gave a large and wide interpretation of their official obligations at a time when the general tendency was certainly not to make too much of them. His great idea was to take advantage of the reviving of ruridecanal work and chapters in his archdeaconry; to gather clergy and laity together in the rural deaneries four times a year, at the Ember seasons, for discussion and Holy Communion, and to be present himself as often as possible. His diaries show how on these occasions he tried to become acquainted with the character and tendencies of each individual clergyman, and how he made his knowledge and observations a link between them and the Bishop.

In his annual charges it was his habit to take a wider range of subjects than had been usual, and the six that he delivered during his tenure of office deal with all the more important ecclesiastical matters of the day. They were generally read over first to his Bishop, and aimed at giving the clergy of the county of Surrey, which took in the important district of South London, a clear view of what seemed to the writer, in the many movements of the time and the many anxieties of the day, their right attitude to their country, their Church, and their chief. It is worth observing that the novelty thus presented by his charges had not escaped friendly criticism, which fact perhaps, in some sort, illustrates the idea then prevalent that the Bishop was the clergy, and that any but bishops did best to be silent. Canon Ashwell quotes a letter from the Archdeacon to Mr. W. E. Gladstone, written in 1843, in which he says—" I am far from not perceiving the danger you indicate from non-episcopal doctrinal charges. But it is most difficult to know what at the present time to do in the sort of pseudo-episcopate into which so many causes have changed the archidiaconate. For so much is some expression of opinion looked for by the clergy, that its suppression would appear like a shifty evasion of difficulties." Scattered over these charges, besides the allusions to, and elucidations of, the greatest questions of the hour, there are discussions on many points, some of which deserve mentioning as indications of the general mind of the writer.

In 1844 he urged the restoration of the Diaconate, and the encouragement of lay agency in connection with the growing spiritual needs of South London, where, he says, amongst other things, " Church schools for 500 children to a population of 50,000 is the average provision we have yet reached." In his first charge he spoke at length on the proposals made by Government in reference to education, and the terms on which, as regards religious instruction, support was to be given to elementary schools. He had in the same year written a letter to Lord Brougham on the Government education scheme, and was strong in insisting that the Church must neither accept terms which would make it impossible to give to children definite religious instruction, nor omit to make arrangements for giving it in the best way. Two agencies are mentioned as likely to have great results in bringing about the desired end— training colleges for teachers, and the immediate and general establishment of diocesan boards of education. It was in the spirit here indicated that a little later the

Church took great advantage of the opportunity offered her of getting a strong footing in the field of elementary education. Government decided to meet with grants the voluntary efforts made by the various religious denominations for the teaching of the children in whom they were interested. The principle of preference for an Established Church was thus abandoned, and all sects were placed on an equality. Dean Burgon has described how Mr. R. Greswell started the movement, which led to the raising by Churchmen of so large a sum, through voluntary contributions, that they claimed from the State far more than all other religious bodies for the support of their schools. The Factory Commission's Report in 1843 drew special attention to the state of education in the manufacturing districts, and the charge of this year urges the necessity of the Church being to the fore. Letters that passed at this time between Archdeacon S. Wilberforce and the Vicar of Leeds, give us the views of the former on Dr. Hook's somewhat impulsive suggestion, that, since it was impossible to educate people in Church principles except out of Church funds, the bishops should voluntarily give up some two-thirds of their incomes for this purpose. "I do *not*," he says, "believe that the Church ought to strip herself bare as you propose. I do *not* think that this would be the way to regain a hold on the affections of our people. I *do* think that we want 'spiritual peers.'" He further gives it as his opinion that the rich laity are the people who ought to provide the needed funds. From the same source also he looked for aid in the work of church restoration, which he urged as most necessary.

But, besides his practical illustrations of what an archdeacon might be and do in the Church of England, in his incumbency of Alverstoke Samuel Wilberforce showed, like Dr. Hook at Leeds, what might be done on Church lines in a large centre of population. In his time Alverstoke, including as it did Gosport, Forton, and a new watering-place, called then Anglesey-Ville, offered a very varied field of experience and labour. He had representatives of all sorts and conditions of men in his flock, and sad instances of the social and moral evils that are so common in a garrison town. His first object was to provide fully for the thorough application of the Church's system, as set out in the Book of Common Prayer, by offering full opportunities for worship, instruction, and the frequent administration of the Sacraments. Living amongst his people, and making it his business to be well acquainted with their characters, circumstances, and wants, great as he always was as a preacher, he was at no time more effective than in his Alverstoke days, in this part of his clerical work. There is perhaps no relation more liable to difficulties, jealousies, and misunderstandings than that which exists between curates, and vicars or rectors. The Rector of Alverstoke added much to his power and influence in his parish by the men, such as W. Burrows, and R. C. Trench, who served under him as his curates, and by the intimate and happy terms on which he lived with them. He made a great deal of careful and systematic preparation for Confirmation, and drew up each week with his curates full notes of lectures for the candidates, regarding the time of the administration of this sacred rite as *the* great opportunity for effecting and establishing a true conversion.

A plan of regular district visiting was begun amongst the poor, and a great point was made of the district visitors' meetings, not as mere gatherings for business, but rather as means for uniting the workers, and inspiring them with an intelligent and devotional spirit. The thread of pastoral work was never, in spite of many outside calls and engagements, broken or lost; national schools were provided at Gosport and Alverstoke, and two new churches built. Samuel Wilberforce, at his Bishop's particular request, continued to hold the Rectory of Alverstoke during his short tenure of the Deanery of Westminster. This led to his being charged in the *Morning Post* newspaper with avarice, and the attack made him enter in his diary an account of his real financial position at this time. A short extract will fitly conclude this paragraph showing how the experience of vicars, curates, and clerical difficulties was gained, which led later to a most effective and sympathetic diocesan administration. The diary for Sunday, October 12, 1845, runs as follows:—" Croker sent me *Morning Post* with attack on me for avarice. God, Thou knowest herein my innocence. Upon reckoning up, I think I have hardly drawn above £400 per annum for myself, the rest having gone in charities, repairs, churches, schools, etc.; and I have been able to obtain or contribute to permanent Church objects in the five years £9,980. I am most thankful that God has suffered me to see the labour of my hands." [1]

The events of the years during which the Archdeaconry of Surrey was held by Samuel Wilberforce brought to a crisis the history of the Tractarian Party. We have already seen how he stood outside it, though admiring and adopting in his ministerial life the lost and forgotten traditions of Catholic practice and

[1] *Life*, i. p. 274.

doctrine, which had almost died out of the Anglican Church, till they were revived and brought forward by the earlier Tract writers. The Archdeacon of Surrey was one of those who had no sympathy either with foreign Protestantism or foreign Catholicism; he desired that the Church of England should be national, but by the power and assertion of true Catholic principles; he did not desire that she should be acceptable and tolerated by a wholesale sacrifice of these at the will and wish of the State. Holding such opinions, though a High Churchman, and one who rejoiced exceedingly in the revival of Church life in England, he was an active opponent of the later Tractarians[1] in their efforts to find within the Anglican Church a place, not only for the whole body of Catholic belief and practices which was not exclusively Roman, but also for some beliefs and practices which were. His votes at Oxford, during the various crises consequent on the publication of Tract 90, and Ward's *Ideal of a Christian Church*, were almost uniformly against the side with which the Tractarian party specially identified themselves, as in his voting for Mr. Garbett as Professor of Poetry, and for the condemnation of Mr. Ward's book and the degradation of the writer. He also expresses plainly his dissent from the most *peculiar* features of the teaching of the Tract writers. His mind was to secure for the Church of England, by degrees, a freer hand, as against the State, in matters that concerned doctrine and discipline. He was neither ready nor inclined himself to seek in the Church of Rome, as many of his friends did, a refuge from the perplexities, and perhaps the inconsistency, that attended the working out of his

---

[1] *Standard.* Letter, August 18, 1890.

ideal of a Christian and national Church in England.
It was clear to him, as it was not clear to the morbid
horror of papal aggression which possesses so many
religious minds in our country, that Rome is kept afar
off by the development, and not by the terror-stricken
suppression, of the true Catholic idea. The Jews once
destroyed the life and fire of inspiration to goodness in
God's law by hedging about the actual commandment
with a multitude of small precepts and observances of
their own devising; they hoped thereby never to come
at an infringement of the Divine precepts themselves.
Similarly, men in England thought that safety from
Popery could be found only by keeping very far away
from it indeed; they suspected efforts that aimed at
the reviving of a more real Church life, and a more
frequent and reverent use of the great means of grace.
Thus it was that many men who had no sympathies at
all with the later Tractarians, and their Rome-ward
tendencies, were assailed freely and fiercely as dangerous enemies of the Church of England. All through
his life Wilberforce was often attacked as a Romanizer,
and he did not escape even at the time in his life
which we are now discussing. The *Record* newspaper
had a good deal to say on the teaching that was found
in his allegory *The Rocky Island*, which it describes as
offering the "*soupe maigre* of Popery instead of the
sincere milk of God's Word." A short passage in a letter
of Samuel Wilberforce to his brother Robert, written in
1842, marks the position he at that time occupied in
the eyes of those inclined on either side to an extreme—
"As to Newman, etc.: day by day I am more confirmed and enlarged in my views; but I have no new
light. Dearest H. says that for three years I have

indulged in the most un-Christian bitterness against them. The *Record* says I countenance them."

The period which immediately preceded Wilberforce's accession to the episcopate is marked by the first activities of the now permanent Ecclesiastical Commission. At the outset it was acceptable neither to the enemies nor the friends of the Church; the one feared that it would largely increase her efficiency, the other that it would fetter her activity by making her more a mere department of the State. It was felt by Churchmen that the manner of appointing the Commissioners was hardly satisfactory, and that they did not sufficiently represent Church feeling and opinion. This defect was however remedied in 1840, when all the bishops and three deans were made Commissioners, and the clause which had hitherto made the Commissioners removable at the pleasure of the Crown was repealed. As Canon of Winchester and Dean of Westminster, Archdeacon S. Wilberforce had practical experience of the first working of the Cathedral Act. It was his opinion that though it was shown to be the result of good intentions on the part of Sir R. Peel, who desired to increase out of the cathedral endowments the funds available for parochial purposes, yet that it had really inflicted a blow on what constituted an important element in the life of the Church. Cathedrals and their chapters have a real function in the diocesan system; they are needed as centres of union, learning, and devotion. It was rather assumed in the new Act, that they had not this function, and it was in consequence wholly unsatisfactory on its constructive side. Since the Revolution, and more still since the Reform Bill, it has ever been the wisdom of the Established

Church in England not to repine at what she loses, or seems to lose, but to accept what she can get, and by making a good use of it, to justify a claim for more. The Archdeacon of Surrey in 1840 advised his clergy not to talk over what seemed to many of them the recent spoliation of the cathedrals; he reminded them that, now the matter was settled, they could have but one object, and that was to lessen the evils and secure the advantages of the new system on which they were entering. His words then precisely describe the temper in which he, in all his career, saw the opportunity rather than the drawback, and never allowed what might have been to deter him from using what was.

Other indications of the mind that was forming in the future Bishop of Oxford, concerning the importance and possibilities of the episcopal office, deserve and require a word of notice. He was one of those who had great hopes that the Jerusalem Bishopric Scheme, establishing a see there, to which the Crowns of England and Prussia were to nominate alternately, might lead to the gaining over of the people of Prussia to true episcopacy. He hailed with delight, as a mark of a more Catholic spirit in the Church of England, the decision that clergymen of Scottish or American ordination might officiate in English churches; and took a prominent part in the formation of the fund for founding Colonial bishoprics, and giving to the Colonial churches the necessary support, as he conceived it, of episcopal government and supervision. But, whilst he was eager to do all he could to further Bunsen's noble plan, by which he trusted that "on a back current episcopacy would flow into Prussia," and was one who made a point of wishing Bishop Selwyn "God-speed" on his departure for New Zealand, he was also mindful that the *vox Ecclesiæ* is not found only in the utterances of her bishops. In preaching before the Convocation of Canterbury in 1841, he was not, as a letter to his brother shows, without some thoughts of its revival into something more than a mere formal meeting to pass an address to the Crown.

In 1840 Samuel Wilberforce was elected a member of the Athenæum Club; and he became, by degrees, much sought after as a speaker and preacher. The growth of his power in these last respects was very rapid after his first great appearance in London, when he took a resolution at a public meeting for the S. P. G., held in the Egyptian Hall, on April 8th, 1840. He characterized it as "a hateful business," but felt that he had no choice in the face of a request from the Archbishop of Canterbury. The result completely established his reputation as a public speaker; and on June 1 he again spoke at Exeter Hall, on the occasion of a great anti-slavery meeting, at which Prince Albert made his first public speech in this country. This was his introduction to Prince Albert, who, some six months later, made him one of his chaplains. The close intimacy at Court which followed gave him, by bringing him in contact with great persons, the best education for being great and prominent himself. He was frequently summoned to preach before the Queen; and Lady Lyttelton, in a letter to her daughter, has given in the following passage a vivid description of the impression he made:—"The real delight of this visit is the presence of Archdeacon Wilberforce. I never saw a more agreeable man; and if such a Hindoo were to be found, I think he would go far to convert me, and lead me to Juggernaut; so it is hard if all who know him are not altogether Christians sooner or later."

There is a record of a discussion with the Prince on the Sunday question, the Prince complaining that the English Sunday was dull, and noticing the want of innocent amusements in England for the common people. Samuel Wilberforce also describes to his brother Robert the interest, in his visits to Court, of seeing the *dramatis personæ* near at hand, and of having an opportunity of speaking before such an audience on great subjects, "with the hope that God will bless His own appointment in the ministry of His Church to His own good purpose." It is clear that the writer felt at once the danger and responsibility of his high favour; and it is also clear that to his appreciative nature the intercourse thus enjoyed had a most important influence in fitting him for the right performance of the great work of his life.

In taking account of the forces which make a man, there is nothing to which we look with more interest and expectation than to the effect on his character of pain and sorrow. We should not be doing justice to the "Remodeller of the English episcopate," if we did not remember that he was not a robust man, and that he suffered several times, specially in the earlier part of his life, from attacks of illness that brought him near to death's door. However incredible it may seem, in the light of what he achieved, he confesses himself that he really loved quiet and privacy, and was naturally indolent, so that he had to flog himself into activity. His career, amongst other things, involved a triumph over bodily weaknesses and drawbacks, which have served to keep even greater geniuses and more shining talents than his, in the dead stagnation of an unworthy obscurity.

But, beyond this, the anxiety and sorrow of many bitter bereavements early laid their heavy hand upon him, and dimmed the brightness of his first remarkable successes as a public man. The scourge of many English homes, consumption, was in the Sargent family, into which he married; the steps by which the Lavington property passed at last, through his wife, to himself are the record of several sad partings, involving amongst them the great grief of his life. We know but little of Samuel Wilberforce's domestic life in the Brighstone days, when the family was together, before his wife's death, and he was himself not as yet called in all directions by his many engagements. There are little hints, however, of what it was for him, in the pleasure with which he returns in thought, and in fact, all his life through, to the scene of these his brightest days. Dean Burgon remarks on the happy relations that existed between him and his wife, that "we look in vain for anything which more conciliates our personal regard for Wilberforce than the many faithful references to this (evidently) admirable, as well as very delightful woman, which are scattered up and down his letters and diaries." Her birthday, their wedding-day, the anniversary of her death, never fail to remind us in diary and letter-book, of the life-long mourning of the husband, which nothing wore out. "Always, on returning to Lavington, the first thing was to visit the churchyard and to lay flowers on her grave; and after his last visit thither, on May 31, 1873, so near to his own departure, he wrote to his daughter-in-law, Mrs. R. G. Wilberforce, describing the occasion as 'one never to be forgotten. My dead seemed so near to me in my solitude, each one following another, and speaking calm and hope to me, and reunion when He will.'"[1] This is enough to show how terrible was the blow that on March 10, 1841, called away from him the sharer of "the sorrows and the joys of a twelve years' changeful life." That which is to be noticed now is the effect that the events of that day, which his diary describes as "one of unknown agony," had on his character, his ideas, and his activities. It is plain, from his own records of his feelings, that all came to him as a call to a more complete dedication of himself to the work of the ministry in the Church. He had long had forebodings that, as he expresses it, all that had "made life an earthly Paradise to him" might thus be at one stroke taken away; his prayer had been in the face of it, "that he might not so be scourged into faithfulness"; he speaks of his temptations to self-indulgence, covetousness, and vanity as the possible causes of his terrible bereavement. As one whose affections were very strong, who literally craved for love in his relations and children, and desired, even to the verge of weakness, to be liked and esteemed by his fellows, the keenness of the pang might well have paralyzed his energies and laid him aside, at least temporarily, from full and active work. He had the courage to seek in the faithful discharge of his duties the true and right relief, though he wished the departed back with him all his life through; and he tells how he cried out, as he lay awake at night, more than twenty years after, that "she would, if she might, show

[1] *Life*, i. p. 130.

herself but once to gladden his weary eyes." It seems almost strange how any one could unfold himself as he did in his diaries, on the subject of his great loss; but it was plainly his habit in that way to seek relief, and at the same time a better understanding of the real meaning and bearing of the events of life. At any rate we can gather from the records that he regarded this great affliction as a fire meant to purify him from faults and weaknesses, and temper him into a more efficient instrument in maintaining, against the worldly spirit and temper, the cause of truth. The following passage illustrates this for us in a pointed way:—"Oh, may HE enable me to lead a life more devoted to His glory and my Master's work! May the utter darkening of my life, which never can be dispelled, kill in me all my ambitious desires and earthly purposes, my love of money, and power, and place." The thoughts that governed him in the hour of his bereavement remained with him through his life. In 1846, on the anniversary of his consecration, he writes thus—"How perpetually is SHE before me! In business, in society, when I seem full of other things, how there is a constant underbase ringing secretly in my ears!"

With all this in view, while we admire the faith and courage that bravely looked for good in an apparently overwhelming evil, we are able to understand some of the force which made Samuel Wilberforce recollect so well a sentence, written by him in a book which had once belonged to his wife, to the effect that "God numbers the Bishop's absent or idle days."

In his visits to Court we find recorded that the Archdeacon of Surrey often met and conversed with Sir Robert Peel; he tells us that it had been said to him that he would certainly be called upon "episcopari." On March 14th, 1845, there came the offer of the Bishopric of Oxford, and the letter that offered it stated that the Queen had most cordially acquiesced in the suggestion, with very kind expressions on her part, and that of the Prince. A fruit of this was a very cordial letter from Prince Albert himself, containing his views on the right position of a bishop in the House of Lords. The letter suggests that a bishop ought to abstain completely from mixing himself up with the politics of the day, but that he should come forward whenever the interests of humanity are at stake, and give boldly and manfully his advice to the House and country. In religious matters, it advises also that the necessarily active part taken in them be that of a Christian, not of a mere Churchman, remembering that the Church does not exist for itself, and ought to have no higher aim than to be the Church of the people. Lastly it explains how, in the opinion of the writer, a bishop ought to be uniformly a peacemaker, and to watch jealously over the morality of the State in acts which expediency, or hope for profit, may tempt it to commit, as well in home and colonial as in foreign affairs. This letter shows us the interest that Archdeacon Wilberforce had aroused, and also gives us some of the lines on which he afterwards acted. Before his consecration he paid a visit to Cuddesdon, and records his delight in finding himself rector of the parish, and thus being able to keep up that pastoral character which our bishops are so apt to lose. A letter, in which he invites his brother Robert to preach his consecration sermon, indicates also the bent of his mind at this time, in its request that the preacher will remember how great evil anything, which just then raised a suspicion of a secret leaning towards Tractarianism in the new bishop, might be likely to do.[1] The few days before his consecration were spent in retirement at Lavington. His diary shows that the time was given to a calm and deliberate consideration of the possibilities of his new office in the matter of service to God. His own account from his diary for the day of his consecration, Sunday, November 30, 1845, will fitly close this sketch of his preparation, under a rare combination of favourable conditions, for showing during his long episcopate what a bishop might be to the Church of England, and what the Church of England might become under leaders who did not forget her spiritual position and capacities, or her Catholic traditions. The extract runs as follows—"*Up early and much in prayer. At 11 to Lambeth. The service very overwhelming; sometimes almost above my endurance. I trust that I did in very deed betrothe myself for ever unto my God, and that He mercifully deigned to accept of me, even of me. R.'s sermon, in parts very touching. Came home, and at night much prayer. Many friends round me, and full of sympathy and love.*"

[1] *Life*, i. p. 314.

CHAPTER IV.

ORGANIZING A DIOCESE.

WHEN the new Bishop of Oxford went down to Osborne on December 10th, 1845, to do homage for the temporalities of his See, it was just the time when Sir Robert Peel, beginning, in the face of the Irish famine and the Anti-Corn Law League, to accept free-trade principles, was compelled to resign office. The situation was a most critical one, and, to Samuel Wilberforce's strong Conservatism, not at all acceptable. Bringing as it did, however, into life, and activity, and influence, new men, new classes, and new thoughts, it went, with other events of the time, to bring it about that his episcopate should be specially connected with quite a new era in our national history. There was a distinct call for men of wider sympathies as leaders both in Church and State; there was a great opportunity for exhibiting the working capacity of new ideas; and the Bishop of Oxford, for all his Conservatism, was ready and willing and able to respond to the call, and listen to the voice of the spirit of the age. The following passage from a letter to Miss L. Noel shows how he felt and appreciated the stir of the moment—" I was down with all the reigning Cabinet on Wednesday. The

Queen was much agitated. When she held my hands in hers, as I did homage, her hands trembled greatly. No one has a question whether Lord John will be able to hold his ground, or Peel come in again." But the stir in the political world was equalled by the stir in the ecclesiastical world; the year 1845 was the year of final crisis in the Tractarian movement, when the Romeward tendency in the extreme section of it showed itself in many secessions, and above all in the secession of Newman. Oxford was of course the diocese in which all the agitation centred, and Dr. Pusey, in congratulating the new Bishop on his appointment, emphasizes the fact that he will find himself above all called to a task of reassuring those who had been shaken in faith and conviction by recent events. Dr. Pusey meant by this that he would have to reassure those who were fearful that they, like their leader, would find themselves drawn necessarily into the Church of Rome. But there was another and a more difficult reassurance to be effected by the Bishop of Oxford in his diocese, and indeed in the world outside it. The last developments of the revival of Church life, and the spread of Church principles, which the Tractarian movement had so successfully realized, served not unnaturally to arouse the bigoted anti-Roman spirit, which is so entirely unable to distinguish between that which is Catholic, and of primitive antiquity, and that which is really a part of the later errors and corruptions of the Romish Church. It was this alarmed and timid spirit that had also to be reassured, and induced, by reasoning and persuasion, not to cast away and neglect practices and principles of real, permanent, and sterling value in the maintenance and development of a spiritual life.

Recent political events had tended to aggravate this feeling in the country, particularly the decision under Peel's Government concerning the Maynooth Grant. The making of this grant certainly very much aggravated the anti-Roman feeling in the country, and increased the distrust of those who supported any of the practices, or theories, which the Oxford movement had brought into prominence.

It was long indeed before the new Bishop, in the Oxford diocese, and in the Church at large, managed to allay the alarm that was felt on this last point at the time of his succession to the See. He was himself fully credited with tendencies highly dangerous to the true Protestant character of the English Church, and the number of those who seceded to Rome from his own family added greatly to the prejudice that many felt against him on this score. Newman's work on *The Theory of Development* was published on his secession, and just at the time when Samuel Wilberforce began his episcopal labours. The part that this book played in the movements and controversies of the time is fully discussed in Mr. R. H. Hutton's *Cardinal Newman* in this series; but there is an expression of opinion upon it in a correspondence with Mr. Gladstone, which helps to show the attitude to Newman's latest utterances which Bishop Wilberforce had then taken up. The letter in question is dated from the Deanery, Westminster, December 6th, 1845, and runs as follows:—

"My dear Gladstone,

"Have you seen Newman's book? Acute as it is, perhaps beyond anything even he has written, I do not think, from what I have seen of it, it is calculated to overthrow the faith of many. For those who believe that the first divine afflatus conveyed to the Church, in the persons of the Apostles, all truth concerning God which man could know, and that the inspired Word of God is the written transcript of that entire knowledge, which it was but given to the Church afterwards to draw out and define with logical accuracy, as heresy created the necessity—for all such the book has no force whatever."

The difficulties of the position of the new Bishop of Oxford were not lessened by the *laissez faire* policy which his predecessor, Bishop Bagot, had pursued. It had been his desire to have as little as possible to do officially with the Oxford revival, and when at last it was reaching an acute stage, he was glad to accept a translation to the more peaceful field of Bath and Wells. In his time the See had consisted only of the counties of Berks and Oxfordshire. By the Act for the reorganization of some of the dioceses, passed in 1836, the county of Buckinghamshire might have been added; but the story is that it was declined on an inquiry as to the general character of its clergy, receiving from the Bishop of Lincoln the laconic reply, "Oh! topboots or Exeter Hall." It was only, then, under Bishop Wilberforce that the three counties were at last united, and thus he had an opening for a complete recasting and reorganization of the whole diocese. His work in this way had really to begin from the very bottom; and the arranging of the Palace at Cuddesdon, so as to make it a real centre of diocesan life and work, was his first care. The night that the future Bishop spent at Cuddesdon, when he was first nominated to the See, was disturbed by discordant noises. He was told by his host next morning that it was only the Garsington men going home from an alehouse, which actually stood in the grounds of the palace. This was speedily taken away, and a chapel built, and more bedrooms added to the house, so that it might be possible to take in, on occasion, a large number of guests. There is a passage in a sermon preached by the Bishop at the consecration of Cuddesdon Chapel, in 1846, which gives us his ideas of what his house ought to be to the diocese and the Church. "For as," he says in it, "the Bishop's dwelling-place is not his private house, but the common property of all his diocese, held only in trust by him for them, to be the common centre, at which from every part the scattered pastors may meet together with himself, for counsel, thought, deliberation, and united action: so is the Chapel at this place theirs as well as his." His occupation of Cuddesdon illustrates the working out of the ideas here expressed on the three lines of devotional intercourse, business intercourse, and social intercourse; in each and all of which he was well able to take the lead with unrivalled and conspicuous success.

A passage in the sermon just quoted gives also a suggestive summary of the preacher's ideas of his responsibilities as a bishop. He is unfolding the reasons why he has such great and deep need of his brethren's prayers, and expresses himself thus—"How great a burden to bear lawfully, honestly, is that care of all the churches! how fearful the condemnation if it be not borne! If indolence, or self-pleasing, or covetousness, or ambition, or worldliness, or sloth, be found in the seat where the Apostles sat, how great must be the Church's loss! how horrible the faithless pastor's condemnation! And yet, to bear it all how much is needed—what tenderness of spirit; what unwearied patience; what open-eyed vigilance; what resolute fortitude; what unflinching courage; what unfaltering sympathy; what an absence of selfishness; what a love of truth; what jealous hatred of error; what love of him who errs!" It is needless to quote more, as this illustrates sufficiently how high was the conception that Bishop Wilberforce brought to Oxford, of all that was involved in his duties, and their discharge. Wilberforce's idea was that you did not really have the Church without the bishop, and it was this feeling again that made him support the extension of the home episcopate, and enter warmly into Chevalier Bunsen's idea of making the Jerusalem bishopric a means of bringing back the primitive form of Church government to Prussia. One of his first speeches in the House of Lords brings out prominently his feeling about the character and necessity of the office he had just assumed. He pleaded against the then proposed abolition of one of the Welsh bishoprics, and advocated the immediate formation of the See of Manchester.

Bishop Wilberforce valued highly the opportunities that his position as a Bishop of the Established Church gave him in the House of Lords. His gifts as an orator and debater enabled him to make much of them. In a letter to Dr. Hook he expresses his plain opinion that the Church needs her spiritual peers, and that their rank and worldly position could only be given up, or taken away, with real loss and damage to her national influence and her spiritual power. He was certainly desirous of thinking and making a great deal of the "fatherhood" that belonged to his office; but at the same time by no means disposed to forget, or think little of, the power and advantage which belonged, in the Church established in England, to its "lordship." In one of his Addresses[1] to his candidates for Ordination, he speaks strongly of the relation of obedience that ought to exist between the ordained and the person from whom they received their Orders. He was always inclined to make much of the bond that the conferring of Orders made between a bishop and those whom he sent out; and when men had left the Oxford diocese, he still considered that they had a claim on him for advice and counsel if they cared to seek it. His dealings with his clergy make it plain that he always regarded himself as related to them on the principles and understandings that had governed the relationship between bishops and their clergy from earliest times; he desired to make these the rule of his own episcopal actions, and the basis of his government of his diocese. There is a simple solution of many difficulties, if the theory set out in the following passage might find a ready acceptance amongst the clergy of the Church of England; but, unfortunately, a bishop's acceptability is much complicated by the system which gives no real voice in his appointment to any one but the Crown and the Government.

"Primitive Church custom," says the Bishop, "proceeded on the rule that the priesthood and diaconate derived their authority from the apostolical commission given to the episcopate. Accordingly, following up this principle, the bond of duty by

[1] *Life*, i. p. 225.

which the ordained was bound to the ordainer was so strict that it could be released only at his own will and by his own act. No bishop was allowed to take from the diocese of another his priests or deacons without his entire concurrence; whilst within his diocese the bishop's rule over his clergy was subject only to canonical restrictions on its exercise, which presuppose its authority, and by the appellate jurisdiction of the metropolitan or provincial synod. All of these details, therefore, lead us back to what was then the universal estimate of the bishop's office, namely, that it was derived from the direct appointment and mission of Christ Himself, and so was the fountain and head of the derived authority and mission of deacons and priests. Thus in each Church the presiding bishop, as one member of the undivided episcopate, was held to be the depositary of ecclesiastical power and right for that diocese; whilst the priests and deacons, and other ministers of the Church, were in their several grades, offices, and employments, his deputies. To him in his office, it was then believed, had been committed by Christ all the powers of the ministry which He had founded; whilst from that office, under the leading of the Spirit, had been derived by the Apostles, first the diaconate, and then the priesthood, the holders of which orders were entrusted severally with certain parts of the bishop's office, which they were in his behalf, and in his stead, to exercise under his direction in the different districts of the diocese in which they were placed, and so to multiply by their ministrations that service which it was impossible for him to render everywhere in his own person."[1]

[1] *Addresses to Candidates for Ordination*, p. 243.

This long extract helps us to see the point of view from which Bishop Wilberforce, in his diocesan administrations, tried to break down the isolation in which the English clergy had lived and worked. It was their desire each jealously to guard his freehold from all encroachments, and to do by himself his own work, in his own way. The old idea set forth above that they were the bishop's representatives, and that they were responsible to him, was a new one indeed, when it was first revived and applied. The bishop was to most of the clergy little more than a confirming and ordaining official, whose interference might be expected in cases of grave and scandalous derelictions in conduct and duty. That he should regard them as only representing him in their cures of souls, and feel himself under an obligation to interest himself personally in their parochial labours, as Bishop Wilberforce did, was a novelty that some indeed welcomed, but some resented as an unnecessary, or even an unwarrantable, interference.

In his addresses to his Ordination candidates, he dwelt on one occasion on a clergyman's duties as a peace-maker. As we all know, it requires not only tact and resource, but great courage, to intervene in other men's quarrels. Bishop Wilberforce always felt that quarrels, especially between his clergy and their people, were in a special sense his business; it was his joy to end them, and bring the once divided into union and fellowship; and the moral courage that in Alverstoke days had rebuked Lord —— for profane speaking, stood him in good stead here. He dared to begin a mediation; he dared to persevere in it till all was well.

We have thus seen something of the idea of his sacred office that nerved his arm, and guided his action. We have now to notice the means and methods which he specially employed, and to observe, in the process, how much which is a matter of course now was used by him almost for the first time, and was of his devising, or his reviving. "No man," says Dean Burgon, "ever got more *out* of his clergy than he. They did whatever he bade them do; and he bade them do as much as he thought they were capable of doing. If any disliked him, it was the timorous, the secular, the obstructive. As for the men who neglected their parishes, their churches, their work—they hated him with a cordial hatred. Few things, *nothing* perhaps, was more remarkable than the art he had of screwing up to concert pitch (so to express oneself) men whose traditions were lax and unsatisfactory, but who, in his society and under his influence, became really very respectable Churchmen."[1]

Now we have already noticed his habit in any new work, of beginning from within, and gradually, as it were, extending outwards. Thus it was natural that, in order to get a body of clergy ready to his hand, he should at once make the very most of the opportunity offered in his Ordinations. This was obviously his very first thought. Witness an account of his intentions in the matter set forth in a letter written to Miss Noel less than two weeks after his consecration—"The Ordination has hitherto been conducted thus:—The Archdeacon of Oxford managed all about it, and examined the candidates in his rooms, as a student of Christ Church, and settled who was and who was not

[1] *Twelve Good Men*, ii. p. 47.

to be ordained. The Bishop came on the Saturday to Oxford, gave a charge to the candidates, and next day proceeded to ordain in the Cathedral. My wish has been, to bring all the candidates as much as possible under my own eye, and to secure all opportunities of social, friendly, and spiritual intercourse. Accordingly, I mean to hold the examinations here. I shall lodge as many as I can in the house, the others in the village round."

It is necessary, in order to appreciate what this then meant, to remember how Ordinations had been conducted in many cases before the establishment of our present ideas in the matter. No attempt at all was made by many bishops to inquire into the characters, modes of thought, and motives in seeking Holy Orders, of their candidates. Examination was only a test of the knowledge of certain books, bearing more on mere scholarship qualifications than the subjects needed to be studied and understood in ministerial work. It is wonderful indeed that, considering the number of men who have at all times sought Orders in the Church of England to take family livings, the standard of clerical life and capacity was even as high as it was; and that men in charge of parishes were not more prone than they were to be carried away with "every blast of vain doctrine." A large dinner, given by the Bishop, often closed the Ordination Day, and represented the sole personal intercourse between him and the ordained. On the days preceding the Ordination, the candidates, without supervision, discipline, or aids to devotion, were lodged in the hotels of the cathedral towns, meeting each other in the evenings for social enjoyment. The debt of the Church of England to the man who finally broke down all this, and made the Ordination hour solemn and serious, crowned with a full realization of the momentous issues involved in it, is simply incalculable. There can be no thorough Church work without an earnest clergy, and no effective preaching of the Gospel save from lips and lives of those who have considered, unto a true knowledge, how they were called, and why they were sent.

The system by which Bishop Wilberforce effected so much for his Church and diocese by his Ordinations is fully set out in a letter from the late Bishop of Ely, Dr. Woodford, who, as one of his able body of examining chaplains for many years, is well qualified to speak. The main points in it require a short attention, so important an instrument has it been in making the history of the Anglican Church in the nineteenth century a story of life and progress, and not rather one of death and decay. It is told of his first Ordination, that one of the candidates, who was then offering himself, voluntarily withdrew, and gave up for ever the idea of taking Holy Orders. The tendency had been, and often is now, to take a merely professional view of the clerical calling, and therewith to accept, as a matter of course, that any one may be sufficient for the things involved in it. All Bishop Wilberforce's efforts at Ordinations were directed at dispelling this false notion —at preventing men from blindly assuming a great burden of accountability without full help to bear it, and himself from "laying hands suddenly" on any one. But the voice that was eager to tell the danger, was eager also to indicate the encouragements, and hopes, and privileges which belong to the sacred office. On the Saturday evening that closed the Ember Week, the Bishop was accustomed to give a written charge to those about to be ordained. A volume of these is published on the questions put to priests and deacons in the services for Ordination. They mark the speaker's anxiety to make each man he addresses real in the present, and hopeful and efficient in the future.

But, besides these final charges, each day of the Ember Week the Bishop himself, at the morning and evening services, spoke, generally from the lessons for the day, on the work and life which was then beginning with those who heard him. It is not wonderful that under these influences an increased devoutness settled on the candidates as the week advanced, and that some, in deepening sense of their unfitness, voluntarily withdrew for a further preparation. The great principle that governed the arranging of these seasons, was first the securing of a bright social intercourse among all brought together by them. Every meal was taken at the palace with the Bishop and his chaplains, and the Bishop was unwearied in his efforts to make all at their ease, and to promote a pleasant, all-including conversation. Spiritual preparation, rather than the mere examination, was made the dominant idea outside the hour of necessary recreation. The questions were never printed, but given out orally, as the result of a previous consultation with the chaplains, each of whom came prepared with a complete set on all the subjects from which selection was made. They aimed at bringing out not mere intellectual knowledge, but the principles on which the candidates would be likely to administer their parishes, and to teach their flocks. All, and especially the question always put to those seeking Priests' Orders, and answered for the Bishop's view alone,—"What difficulties from within and without have you experienced in the exercise of your ministry?"—led up to the private interview which the Bishop had with every candidate. This was the time for a close searching into character and motives; for words of rebuke or encouragement; sometimes for rejection. There are records of men who, vexed at the time, have thanked the Bishop for thus putting them back; and the story is that, on such occasions, he would suggest that the rejected should leave him by the window opening on to the lawn, to spare them the mortification of a return to the examination room. All this was new then; it is old now, it has been improved upon; but it has been the means of making men much more informed as to what Ordination really involves, and much more ready to act upon that information.

It was only natural that he, who laid such stress on the right use of the time of Ordination, and its opportunities, should also be anxious to secure, for his candidates, the greatest possible amount of previous special training and preparation. Several theological colleges had been founded about the time when Bishop Wilberforce came to Oxford; and the foundation of the College at Cuddesdon followed naturally on his new arrangements for Ordinations, as described above. He wished by it to secure, as it were, a longer Embertide for those wishing to take Holy Orders. Cuddesdon was intended, as a rule, for graduates who desired, and could afford, a year's special preparation for the ministry after taking their degree. The course there provided for a happy combination of intellectual, practical, and devotional training, and has done much, with other similar institutions, to improve the education of the clergy of the Church of England for their work. That work has suffered not a little from the fatal fallacy that a man may be a good and efficient clergyman by the light of nature. Theological colleges have done much to remove this wrong impression, and to help men to correspond with the improved standard of ministerial life which Bishop Wilberforce did so much to introduce.

There was another part of the work of his office also, which the Bishop of Oxford felt gave a great opportunity for establishing a permanent and wide-spread influence over many people in many places. In the past, in Confirmations, as in Ordinations, the bishops had too often preferred to consult their own convenience rather than the edification of those placed under their charge. They held but few Confirmations, and those only in central places; so that the mob of candidates, the long journey to the place appointed, the rite hastily administered to whole rows of candidates at once, the short, perfunctory, and ill-heard address, destroyed altogether for many the solemnity of the occasion, and scattered to the winds all serious thoughts. Thus *the* great opportunity of life's most impressionable time went too often for nothing, and, instead of being a great source of good, became a source rather of harm. The prevailing sentiment in the matter is well illustrated by the story of the inn-keeper who sought for compensation from the Bishop of Oxford, because the candidates had given up staying at his house, as they had been used to do, for a ball in the evening of the Confirmation day. A passage from a letter written in 1847 describes well the feelings with which Bishop Wilberforce was possessed in his Confirmations.

"There is," he writes, "so much of deep interest in a Confirmation, that it takes a great deal out of one. The *present* interest is intense: the single opportunity of making, if God will, a dint in a character; the gathering in, if the candidates have been watched over and prayed for, the fruits of past weeks; the raising them to something quite new, if they have been neglected. Then all the old interest of Brighstone and Alverstoke wakes up. I remember the deep anxiety with which I presented one and another, the fear, the doubt, the trembling hope, the joy with which I saw one and another come forward, and the after fulfilment or disappointment."[1] It was in this spirit that he set himself with untiring energy, and no disposition to spare himself, to hold Confirmations in every part of the diocese; so that all might see and know the rite, its meanings and blessings, and the young might not be exposed to the peril of dangerous excitement in long journeys. In the town and in the village, in the school, the asylum, and the workhouse, he would give all their chance of making in this way their open confession that for them Christ and His ways were best. There was an endless variety in what he said on these occasions, based partly on his own observation of the place and scene, partly on the answer to his request, that the clergy, at the place where he was going to confirm, would tell him if there was anything they wished him to say.

His sympathy with the young, and his intense appreciation of the possibilities for good which lay before those presented to him, lent a fresh force and power to his earnest words. "His addresses," says Canon

[1] *Life*, i. pp. 401-2.

Ashwell, "at these times were the result of preparation of himself, rather than of that which he was about to utter." But it was not only what he said, it was also what he did, that gave a deep sense of the importance of the occasion. It was his custom to repress firmly and sternly any apparent levity in the candidates, even to the extent of making one or other of them a public example before the rest. "His way of doing it," says Dean Burgon, "was inimitable: the effect was astonishing. It *made* the rite a great success, even if the issue of the day had before seemed trembling in the balance." The whole service was concluded by one more short and stirring address, calculated to leave, as it did leave, a lasting impression on many of those who heard it.

Our day has seen a great deal of efforts to stir up a more vigorous and thorough spiritual life, by means of missions, in districts and parishes. Bishop Wilberforce made use of them in his episcopate, though hardly in the form in which they are too often used now, with certain "un-English characteristics" which appeal unduly to the emotional element in human nature. These Oxford missions—the first of which was held at Wantage, Farringdon and Banbury in 1850—occupied some nine or ten days of the Lenten season every year. The Bishop, with a chosen band of preachers, took as a centre some country town where, by daily addresses, frequent Communions, and a stirring evening sermon by some conspicuous preacher, he tried to rouse the inhabitants and neighbourhood from the dull slumber of formalism, or the more fatal torpor of indifference and neglect. Meanwhile, with the co-operation of the neighbouring clergy, services and sermons were arranged in all the surrounding villages. Each evening, gather-

ORGANIZING A DIOCESE.

ings of workers were held at the centre, and, under the guidance of the Bishop, the phases of the work in hand carefully and instructively discussed. With him all went well; without him such efforts must have been failures, and therefore better left alone. It was his custom to hold his Lent Ordination, and sometimes Confirmations also, at the place of the mission. What he desired was to make it possible for every part of his once much neglected diocese to see the Church at work with all her appointed methods in activity, and so to bring her system really to bear, in one united effort of Bishop and clergy, before the eyes of men. As to the effect for good of all this, it is to the point to quote from the Bishop of Oxford's charge for 1860 his remarks on one of these missions recently held at Reading:—"The last of these missions was recently held at Reading, and manifestly moved, to its centre, the population of that large town. I have yet before my eyes the sight of the great and deeply attentive numbers who listened in its churches to the Sermons, which set forth the sufficiency of Christ for man's salvation, and for every want of man's heart; I seem still to see the large bodies of devout communicants who every morning gladdened our hearts; and the brotherly assemblage of clergymen and laymen for mutual conference and edification with which the meeting closed. Some days after the mission had closed I had the great pleasure of receiving a deputation of some of the principal inhabitants, bringing with them an address from a considerable number of the laymen of all the parishes of the town, bearing witness to the blessing which had been given to the mission, and asking for a future repetition of what they had found to be such special opportunities for growth in grace.' The Bishop's diary for 1869 shows that time increased rather than diminished the effect of these missions. In that year the mission was at Maidenhead, and so much did the people then appreciate the efforts being made for them, that all the shops in the town, including those belonging to the Dissenters, were closed at seven every evening, in order that all might go to the evening services.

Closely connected with this attempt to make known what the Church was, are the courses of Lenten sermons by the greatest preachers of the day, organized by the Bishop at St. Mary's, and afterwards at St. Giles', Oxford. Several courses of these were published, and they served as an evidence that the revival of a more thorough and systematic application of the Church's system neither weakened nor disparaged the power of preaching, and the importance of the pulpit for instruction and exhortation. These courses of sermons the Bishop always introduced in person, and often hurried from important and pressing engagements, in London, and elsewhere, to do it.

We have already observed how it was part of the Bishop of Oxford's plan to make his palace at Cuddesdon a place of meeting for the clergy, for social intercourse, for business, and for devotional purposes. As regards the first, Canon Ashwell observes that " it was no small element in the hold which he established over his clergy, that to his palace at Cuddesdon he would constantly summon them to meet such celebrities, alike from the clerical and non-clerical world, as might from time to time be visiting him—occasions when his own wit had free play, and drew out corresponding brightness from others—a token of consideration which all men feel, but which to his younger clergy was especially valuable." His social gifts made Samuel Wilberforce a most welcome guest in the greatest houses, and amongst the best society in the land; but as a host he was inimitable, unwearying in his efforts to bring all into the conversation, or making interest and entertainment by his own brilliant talk, his stories, and his *bon-mots*. We can imagine the dining-table at Cuddesdon on such an occasion, hushed into sudden silence by a great crash, and the voice of the host reassuring his guests with the remark that " it was only the coachman going out with the *brake*."

Once every year it was his custom to gather together at Cuddesdon all his rural deans, to discuss the affairs and arrangements of the diocese for the year. His experience in the Isle of Wight had taught him what might be made out of the office of rural dean, and its opportunities. The ruri-decanal chapters were directed to be held at least quarterly; and were to include sometimes the laity as well as the clergy of the Deanery. Bishop Wilberforce's letters show the use he made of his rural deans, and how much he looked to them to keep him informed as to the affairs of the parts of the diocese immediately under their care, whilst he paid the greatest attention to their representations and their complaints. There is a story told of a brief interview between him and a clergyman who was taking charge of a difficult rural deanery, as the Bishop was passing in the train through a station, on the platform of which the clergyman in question chanced to be standing. The Bishop called to him in loud tones— " Mr. T——, I am very glad to have an opportunity of speaking to you. I hear great things of your zeal and success as rural dean." "Well, my lord," was the reply, "I believe some people are under the impression that I am somewhat mad." "All I can say then is," replied the Bishop, "I wish you would *bite* all my rural deans." If this may be taken as illustrating his appreciation of a really zealous man in this capacity, the suggestion by which he extinguished a clergyman, who was claiming at a conference a distinctive title for these officials, must in no sense be thought disparaging to them. On that occasion the Bishop reduced the speaker to silence, by suggesting " Rather Reverend " as a suitable title.

The charge for 1860 records how there grew out of the deliberations of the rural deans at Cuddesdon in that year two attempts to quicken the life of God in the souls of the clergy. Retreats and Quiet Days have grown to be comparatively common as a means of helping and strengthening that devotional element in a clergyman's character, which must be developed if his ministry is to be effective, and is to enable him to get a real hold on his people. These two meetings, both of which were presided over by the Bishop himself, respectively suggested what is now understood by the Retreat and the Quiet Day; the former perhaps may be said to aim at deepening the spiritual life of the individual; the latter at bringing out the fraternal bond of mutual helpfulness which ought to exist between the assembled clergy. The Bishop's comment on the experiment is this—"From these days, I believe, all went back to their work quickened, refreshed, strengthened and united; and I gladly assented to the expressed wish that such opportunities of mutual edification should be again secured amongst us."

As the rural deans were annually gathered together for conference at Cuddesdon, so also were the inspectors of schools, a body of voluntary workers at one time as many as forty in number. The Bishop's words about them in his last charge may be quoted as showing his sense of the value and efficiency of their work—"The various parish schools have been raised to a new level by the care and labour of the diocesan inspectors. Alas! for me, that I shall lose the strengthening, exhilarating meetings for which they were accustomed each spring to gather at Cuddesdon Palace." Those were stirring days in the field of elementary education; the Government was beginning to take it up, and no longer to leave it to voluntary efforts; as a consequence the question had to be faced as to the conditions under which Government aid could be given to, and accepted by, schools in which a definite religious teaching was given. The general policy of the Government of the day was to meet voluntary efforts, on the part of all religious denominations with pecuniary help proportioned to the voluntary contributions given. So vigorous were the efforts of Churchmen that their schools made claim to by far the largest share of this help. The giving of it was of course saddled with certain conditions of inspection and management, and the high "Mountain" party, as Bishop Wilberforce calls them, led by Mr. G. Denison, were for getting it accepted that no plan of receiving Government grants on condition of any management clauses could satisfy the clergy. A motion to this effect was brought forward at what proved a very stormy meeting held at the National Society on June 8th, 1848. The Archbishop and the Committee requested the Bishop of Oxford to move an amendment. "I never," he says, "since I addressed the Newport Radicals, spoke to so hostile an audience, but through God's help and the truth of my cause, I so won them over that the motion was withdrawn." The diocesan board, the inspectors of schools, and the training college at Culham were the instruments by which the diocese of Oxford sought to do all it could, on Church lines, under the elementary educational policy of the day. But the educational work of the Oxford diocese did not begin and end with elementary education. Schools for the middle class, under Church auspices, sprang up as at Cowley and Littlemore; and schools also were founded at Radley, Bradfield, Bloxham and Stony Stratford, where the children of the gentry and clergy might, to use the Bishop of Oxford's words, "be trained in that blessed union of true religion and useful learning, which has ever flourished and abounded in Church of England schools."

As the annual conferences at Cuddesdon, particularly that with the rural deans and archdeacons, brought the principal clergy of the diocese into contact with the Bishop, and with one another, so did the meetings of the diocesan societies do the like for the leading laity. Both helped to draw together men of various shades of opinion, to which they were encouraged to give a free expression. Both alike served to give them all a sense of a large field for common and united effort, which claimed their whole energies, and really left no time or opportunity for party strifes. The diocesan societies were at first three, the Board of Education, the Spiritual Help Society, and the Diocesan Church Building Society. Later on a Society for Augmenting Poor Benefices was added.

The Spiritual Help Society was intended to increase the number of clergy, so as to meet the demand for more services, and for a more thorough visitation of the sick and whole. In his last charge to the diocese of Oxford, the Bishop records that this society, with an income of £1,200 a year, had made it possible to supply to some of the most needy and populous parishes forty-one additional curates. "There are," he adds, "few cases as to which it is more true that *two are better than one* than in the spiritual charge of a parish. For nothing more tends to correct that great evil of our parochial system, the isolation of the parish priest, than the presence of a second clergyman."

The Church Building Society was organized to promote the building, rebuilding, and restoration of churches and parsonage houses. It started its work in 1847, and, at the time of the Bishop's translation to Winchester, had been enabled to grant £32,172 to this object. Its principle always was not to accumulate an invested capital in money, but to invest from time to time in increased Church accommodation the funds it had raised.[1]

The Society for Augmenting Poor Benefices was founded after the Visitation of 1860, with a view to increasing the endowment of the 223 parishes of the diocese which fell below £200 a year, and the 72 which did not come up to £100. The Bishop in his charge for 1863 mentions that, if all the calls on the clergy of these parishes were fully estimated, it would be found that they received less than an ordinary skilled labourer. He calls attention to the way in which this extreme poverty of remuneration of the clergy must tell with a disastrous influence on their position in

[1] *Charge*, 1866, p. 11.

society, and on their future supply. One great object in founding this society was to meet grants offered by the Ecclesiastical Commissioners, who were setting apart at that time £100,000 a year to meet equal benefactions for poor parishes. In 1866 it is recorded of it that it had, in this way, added £16,000 to the endowments of the diocese; and the charge of 1869 states that it had then raised many parishes, from furnishing a merely nominal income, to one which secured for the incumbent just a bare subsistence, and so maintained among scattered populations the separate ministry, the Church and altar.

It is clear that the Bishop of Oxford had it in his mind to secure for his clergy a diocesan synod. A meeting was held at Oxford on Friday, November 22, 1850, to protest against the Papal Bull establishing a Roman hierarchy in England. It was a time of great excitement, and the Bishop writes before it to his brother—"I hope to make Friday's protest a sort of diocesan synod. I have some apprehension from the Low Church party." A conversation with Mr. Wyndham Portal in 1871, given in the third volume of the *Life of Bishop Wilberforce*, explains the Bishop's opinions on the now almost universal diocesan conferences, which were then beginning to be held. He expressed his strong disinclination to institute them, "at present." "I know how it will be," he said; "the Bishop must always attend every meeting, while you laity may do as you please. When all goes well and smoothly you will say, 'See how well we have done it.' When there is a failure from any cause, it will then be said, 'See what a muddle the Bishop has made of it.'"

The Bishop of Oxford shows in his charges how great was the interest that he himself took, and that he desired to induce other Churchmen to take, in the missionary work of the Church. He took steps to secure systematic support, in his diocese, both for the Church Missionary Society and also for the Society for the Propagation of the Gospel in Foreign Parts. In his view taking an active interest in the spread of the Gospel was the mark and indispensable condition of a real true life and progress in any individual, and in any Church; it was the natural corrective to selfishness, to indolence, and to prejudice. Thus, in a speech at Cambridge on behalf of the Universities' Mission to Central Africa, he pointed out the danger of mere religious study untempered by works of Christian charity. He said also that for the Universities to be called often from their deep studies, and from their polemical maintainings of the truth, to the practical action of spreading Christ's faith in the world, was a most wholesome and blessed discipline.

There exist certain private notes made by the Bishop of Oxford after some of his consultations with his rural deans, containing a list of things that in his opinion ought to be done. Amongst these are two entries on the subject of his patronage—one to the effect that the patronage of the See needed to be amended; and the other to the effect that Chancellor's livings in the diocese and extern livings ought to be exchanged. When Bishop Wilberforce succeeded to the See, as Canon Ashwell has pointed out, not only was the number and value of the livings in his gift very small, but the local importance of the benefices was even less. When he left the diocese in 1869 he had obtained the presentation to most of the important town livings, while the total number of livings in his gift was one hundred and three as against seventeen; and of these ninety-five were in his diocese. Thus he had secured the means of promoting the more deserving of his clergy, and was able to choose whom he would place in the most important parishes and spheres of work. At the same time he had provided opportunities for putting into livings many of the curates of the diocese, whose number in his time was largely increased by the successful operations of the Diocesan Spiritual Aid Society. In the *Quarterly Review* for 1867, there is an article by Bishop Wilberforce on "The Church and her Curates," showing how small their prospects were, and how, in the many more opportunities of other careers, this would be likely to prove a source of weakness to the Church. A passage in this article shows us clearly what the Bishop had in view, amongst other things, in so strenuously setting himself to increase his patronage. "Many are those," he writes, "to whom preferment never does nor can come. That to which the poor hard-working curate may most hopefully look, the preferment administered by his bishop, is utterly insufficient to supply such claims. Even where the episcopal patronage is most fairly administered (and we know cases in which none but curates of the diocese are admitted to share in it), a very small proportion of the curates can ever attain preferment from its resources."

Amongst the instruments, methods, and organizations by which the Bishop of Oxford tried to give his diocese the full benefit and help of the Church and her system, it remains to say a few words about his use of Sisterhoods. They are now a most important part of the machinery of the Church of England; and the labours of Sisters do a great deal of her work among the fallen, the sick, and the poor. The wise and sympathetic management of the Sisterhoods at Wantage, Clewer, and Oxford, by Bishop Wilberforce, established them permanently, as recognized and allowable institutions, in the Anglican Church.

In 1848 at an unfavourable moment in some respects, owing to the outcry raised against some unwise peculiarities in the management of Miss Sellon's Devonport Sisterhood, a Sisterhood was founded at Wantage. The Bishop of Oxford saw in it a form of zeal that might be made of great and conspicuous use in the Church work of the diocese. "I have," he writes of this foundation, "the deepest interest in its welfare, and would do anything in my power to help its progress." But he was very strong that he, as Bishop, should have a control in the government of such establishments, and that they should be managed on lines thoroughly in accord with "the system of the Reformed Church of England, as it is to be found in Bishop Andrewes, Richard Hooker, and many more of like views with them." "It is on this scheme alone," he says in a letter to the head of the Clewer Sisterhood, "honestly, heartily, and completely adopted and maintained, that I can have any share in organizing and promoting Sisterhoods." In accordance with these principles he laid it down that "the sisters could not be allowed to practise continual confession to, or erect into directors, the warden or chaplains of the house."[1] He also stated that they should not use Roman Catholic books of devotion, or wear openly, or exhibit in their rooms, images

[1] *Life*, iii. pp. 326-7.

or representations which the Church of England discourages. On the question of the unlawfulness of perpetual vows he was always clear. The attitude that he took up towards Sisterhoods is thus described by Canon Butler, in a passage quoted in the third volume of his life—" Nothing could be kinder, wiser or more large-hearted, than the line which he adopted; and it is certainly not too much to assert, that to him our English Sisterhoods owe their present position of usefulness and acceptance. Instead of standing apart and waiting till they had made their way, he, with his characteristic determination to be the real ἐπίσκοπος or overseer of all religious movements in his diocese, took the matter into his own hands, without in the least quenching or thwarting the zeal and the ideas of those who gave the first impulse. At least once every year he visited the Sisters, considered their rules, sometimes spoke to each separately, weighed difficult cases, and received into the community those who had been elected." This policy it was that secured for the Oxford diocese, and then for the Church at large, a great power for good, and a vast amount of zealous and devoted labour.

But the greatness and weight of the Bishop in his diocese was much increased, throughout his career, by his position outside it. He made many distinguished appearances in London during the first year of his episcopacy, and at once gained a brilliant reputation in the House of Lords, where the influence of his oratory and his power as a debater made his support of consequence to the Government, or Opposition, as the case might be. This made him able to get a hearing in matters that affected the interests of the Church at large; and the estimation in which he was held abroad, made it the easier for him to get his clergy at home to accept his reforms, and give his methods a fair trial. A letter to Miss Noel gives a description of his feelings when he took his seat in the House of Lords, in January 1846. "You know," he writes, "how all such real business interests me. But I feel as if I should never take any part in debate; though some day I shall. The impediment of the lawn sleeves must be very great and entangling." It is obvious that his character as a bishop did act as some check on him as a speaker in the House. He was by nature gifted with an unusual power of repartee, and very much inclined to take advantage of it, and thus to put in those "sparkles," as he calls them, "on which the animation of a debate so much depends, but which must be continually regretted." Mr. Anson, writing about his speech on the abolition of the Corn Laws, speaks of the use he had been then tempted to make of this power as follows—"If I had your talent and your facility of sending home a *personal* shaft, when justly invited, I could not resist taking advantage of it, but I think it a little dangerous. Those men like the protectionist Duke and the insane —— will never forgive the way you showed them up, and made them the laughing-stock of the House. The subtle man on the Bench, too, will watch his opportunity of revenge."[1] It was doubtless the feeling that this was "a little dangerous" that made him express his intention "never to *debate* again, if he could help it;" though at the same time he could not consent to be, as bishops had been too much, no more than "a graceful appendage to

[1] *Life*, i. p. 368.

Conservatism, a mute in a great assembly, while the social and moral evils of his poor countrymen needed to be witnessed of before princes."[1] At first Bishop Wilberforce simply attended the debates of the house, and observed its usages; then he broke silence, and by his speeches on four subjects in the session of 1846, showed himself conspicuously capable of combining the rôles of statesman and ecclesiastic, and so playing successfully the somewhat difficult part that falls to the lot of a bishop in the House of Lords.

Thus at the end of his first Session the Bishop of Oxford was established in the House of Lords as a man to be listened to; he had also shown that he was of independent opinion, and could maintain and defend the line of action which appeared right. He was always eager to play a prominent part in securing legislation that seemed needed for the benefit of the working classes. Accordingly in 1847 he spoke strongly in favour of the Ten Hours Factory Act, which aimed at bringing relief to the excessive labour exacted, specially from women and children. He pointed out the doubtful gain, which was probably really a loss, in the last two hours of a more than ten hours' day, saying that "when exhausted nature failed to give that quickness of eye and rapidity of movement, which were necessary to keep pace with the machinery, the work then done became a sort of drawback to the work done in the other part of the day." An address was presented to him by the workmen of Bradford in 1858, showing how deep and abiding was the impression made on them by the Bishop's successful effort on this occasion. A passage from the address in question runs as follows—"Your Lordship, as a

[1] *Life*, i. p. 371.

patriot firmly attached to your country, and as a man possessing keen sensibilities for the welfare of your fellows, will not listen to these assurances without unmixed feelings of pleasure and satisfaction. You will rejoice that you bore a part in obtaining that great boon to our manufacturing population, 'THE TEN HOURS FACTORY ACT,' for which we, on behalf of ourselves and others, beg most respectfully to tender to your Lordship our most grateful acknowledgments."

But it was not only in the House of Lords, but also in other places outside his diocese, that the new Bishop was making his mark. In the meeting of friends of the Colonial Church on the day after the consecration of the Bishops of Capetown, Newcastle, Adelaide, and Melbourne, the Bishop was one of the chief speakers. So again he preached at Oxford just at this time, at the meeting of the British Association, a sermon which, Canon Ashwell says, "if it were not his really greatest sermon, was certainly that which attracted the largest amount of admiration." In the festivities that accompanied the installation of Prince Albert as Chancellor of the University of Cambridge, he was also a prominent figure; taking his *ad eundem* D.D. degree; preaching several times in Cambridge, and, in the University Church; advocating the due training of the teachers of our National Schools in the teeth of the old ideas that considered anything, or nothing, good enough here. It was all a brilliant opening to a brilliant career, which, in spite of private griefs and troubles, in bereavements, and the first secessions of some members of his family to Rome, had hitherto been in public one uninterrupted success. The next period of Bishop Wilberforce's life shows us, however, that the man who remodelled the English episcopate was not merely a fair-weather sailor, but one who could face a storm—and that too a storm whose severity was aggravated by his own not altogether skilful seamanship in the events which marked its beginning. The same circumstances, as the next chapter will show, which deprived him of the support of many friends, exposed him to attack from those who disliked his reforms, and suspected him of favouring principles that were, in their eyes, dangerous in the highest degree.

CHAPTER V.

DIOCESAN DIFFICULTIES.

In Bishop Wilberforce's diaries a saying of Lord Aberdeen's is quoted, in which he expresses his opinion that "the Church of England is two churches, only held together by external forces." This allusion is to the differences of doctrine and idea that seemed, in his day, to cause an irreconcilable antagonism between the members of what are most commonly known as the High and Low Church parties. Now, it is stated that "the fingers of one hand would suffice for numbering those who received promotion, from the Evangelical section of clergy, in the Oxford diocese during Bishop Wilberforce's long episcopate." This is remarkable from one who so clearly had, to use Dean Burgon's words, "an inherited claim on the friendship of men of the Evangelical school." The fact is, that, though the Bishop had no sort of sympathy with the Romanizing tendencies of the Tractarian party, he had a very strong sympathy with that "asking for old paths," and that claiming of Catholic rights, privileges, and methods, which its earliest aims and utterances had induced in so many of the clergy and laity in the Church of England. Bishop Wilberforce was strong in his insistence on the continuity of the Church established in England in going back, behind the Reformation, to the primitive Church of Christ of Apostolic days. He was entirely at variance with those whose views and inclinations led them to prefer to consider that this same Church of England was a new creation of Reformation days, and a child of the State. Thus he was active and eager in giving life and expression to the ideas that the Tractarian teaching first brought forward, after they had been long disregarded, as to the divine origin and commission of the Church. This was not acceptable to the Low Church party as a whole, and their inclination was to resist the new, and to defend the old, without considering enough the necessities of growth and progress in Church life. In speaking of his Ordinations held in 1851, it is curious to find Bishop Wilberforce noting, as a satisfactory point, the absence of Low Churchmen amongst his candidates. The fact is, that their apprehensions of a speedy return to the bondage of the Papacy caused the members of the Evangelical party to look with distaste and suspicion on much that Bishop Wilberforce started in the diocese. Thus he did not seem to find in the men of this school, in general and in the same degree as in men of the opposite school, that zeal in developing and extending the work of the Church on which he set a very high value indeed. A really conscientious opposition was apt to seem obstructive; and the Bishop often plainly expresses his opinion that the doctrines held by many men of this party were those of the Puritans, and not, as he desired, those that he held to be "the doctrines of the Church of England as expounded by R. Hooker."

Under all these circumstances the diocese of Oxford was for some twelve years a divided diocese; and the present chapter seeks to unfold the steps by which the opposition was gradually overcome, and the Bishop left in a position to exhibit, in harmony and progress, the value and efficacy of his methods. In some cases the very zeal, which he esteemed so highly in those whom he employed and trusted, was in itself a fruitful source of trouble and misunderstanding. The Bishop's wonderful and rapid advancement, his great personal gifts and endowments, his power of dealing with men, made him trust too much to his ability to check and restrain the exuberances and extravagances of some whom he was induced to place in important places. His men would sometimes altogether exceed their commission, and perhaps deliberately, as with his sanction, start on lines which they almost knew he would disapprove. The information would come to him after the event, when the mischief was done; and Dean Burgon speaks with some humour of "the explosion in the diocese which was sure to follow the dreary discovery that some of his lieutenants had in this way compromised him, been wanting in honesty, or played him false." Moreover, in his dealings with those of his clergy, whose principles led them to fear all real or apparent innovations as coming from Rome or leading to Rome, it had to be remembered how much the many secessions to Rome, from the Bishop's own family gave some sort of a reason and excuse for such alarms. These secessions certainly went to hinder his further promotion, and increased, more than he perhaps was inclined to admit, his difficulties with the Evangelicals in the diocese of Oxford.

In addition to these considerations, personal to himself, there were other events that occurred between the years 1847 and 1860, which went a long way to increase the dislike and alarm with which the Low Church party in his diocese regarded his administration of it. First, there was the Gorham case, which led Churchmen to put forward very distinctly the Church's doctrine of unconditional regeneration in Baptism, on the right holding of which Bishop Wilberforce was very strong. Secondly, there were the secessions to the Church of Rome which followed Mr. Gorham's establishment, by the decision of the Judicial Committee of the Privy Council, of his claim to institution to his new living, in spite of his opinions and the Bishop of Exeter's objections to them. Again, the Low Church party were also disturbed by the attempts to revive Convocation, which were prompted by the feeling in the minds of Churchmen, after the Gorham judgment, that an authoritative voice and a body more acceptable to the Church than the Judicial Committee, were needed to propagate declarations on faith and doctrine in the Church of England. To all this must be added the excitement caused in London by the ritual extravagances, as they then seemed, practised by Mr. Bennett at St. Paul's, Knightsbridge, and in the Church of St. Barnabas, which he had built for the poor of his parish in Pimlico; and, above all, the papal bull of 1850.

By this last, Pope Pius IX., encouraged by the secessions from the Church of England to Rome, sought to re-establish in England the papal hierarchy with local and territorial titles to the sees. A letter from the Prime Minister, Lord John Russell, to the Bishop of Durham on this subject went to inflame to the utmost the Protestant feeling.[1] He denounced the movement as being a pretension over the supremacy of England inconsistent with the Queen's supremacy, with the rights of our bishops and clergy, and with the spiritual independence of our country, as asserted even in the Roman Catholic times. But this was not all; he declared that he did not fear so much the claims of the Pope from without, as the treachery within the Church of England itself. These remarks were directed against the Tractarian body as a whole, and not only against the extreme section of it; and the same letter describes them as "unworthy sons of the Church of England," and "men who were leading their flocks to the very verge of the precipice." All this went to make the Bishop of Oxford's work, in a transition period of the Church's history, much more difficult, and to excite against him much opposition, more particularly as the truth to him lay with the then unpopular side, and with principles, which were the distinct outcome of the earlier Tractarianism.

Before showing how his policy was worked out, and how, after passing through many waves of opposition, the Bishop at last found himself able to command in his diocese a fairly general and unanimous support, it will be necessary to say something of his conduct in a matter which laid him open to much misunderstanding and obloquy. In November 1847, Dr. Hampden was recommended by Lord John Russell, then Prime Minister, to succeed Bishop Musgrave at Hereford. Lord John Russell had been looked on as a friend to the Church, and Bishop Wilberforce had

[1] *The Church in England from William to Victoria*, A. H. Hore, vol. ii. p. 353.

particularly expressed his own conviction that he was honestly determined and disposed, during his Premiership, to do what he could to increase its liberty and efficiency. But, as we have noticed, he had been angered and scared by some of the late applications and developments of Tractarian principles; he thought that these "tended to confine the intellect and enslave the soul," and was inclined, therefore, to do what he might to infuse into the Church a greater liberality of thought. He was moreover strongly disposed to resent any expression of Church feeling on the subject of an appointment to a vacant see, as being a most unwarrantable interference with the royal prerogative and supremacy. Dr. Hampden, at the time he was nominated to the See of Hereford, had lain for eleven years under the censure of the University of Oxford, for opinions expressed in his *Bampton Lectures* of 1832, and more particularly in his *Observations on Religious Dissent*, 1834.

As a first step, thirteen of the bishops, amongst whom was Bishop Wilberforce, addressed a remonstrance to Lord John Russell; and Dr. Longley, of Ripon, and Archbishop Howley, also wrote to him to the same effect. As we have to consider somewhat fully the Bishop of Oxford's personal share in all the controversy that arose over Dr. Hampden's appointment, it is to the point to establish, by a quotation from the letter to Lord John Russell, the ground that from the first was taken up by those who regarded the Premier's action as at least most injudicious. The letter urges particularly the point of view from which Churchmen must regard the nomination, and contains the following passage—" We are persuaded that your

Lordship does not know how deep and general a feeling prevails on this subject, and we consider ourselves to be acting only in the discharge of our bounden duty both to the Crown and to the Church, when we respectfully but earnestly express to your Lordship our conviction that, if this appointment be completed, there is the greatest danger both of the interruption of the peace of the Church, and of the disturbance of the confidence which it is most desirable that the clergy and laity of the Church should feel in every exercise of the royal supremacy, especially as regards that very delicate and important particular, the nomination to vacant sees."

In seemingly unfit appointments, however, nothing remains for the Church but to protest, and to minimize, as far as possible, the evil consequences that are at any time apprehended from them. Now, in the case of Dr. Hampden, this was the policy that Bishop Wilberforce tried to support and pursue. The letter from the thirteen bishops was unsuccessful, as the following extract from Lord John Russell's answer to it plainly shows. "I deeply regret," he writes, "the feeling that is said to be common among the clergy on this subject. But I cannot sacrifice the reputation of Dr. Hampden, the rights of the Crown, and what I believe to be the true interests of the Church, to a feeling which I believe to be founded on misapprehension and fermented by prejudice."

As Bishop of the diocese in which Dr. Hampden's charge, the vicarage of Ewelme, was situated, it was clear that the Bishop of Oxford would have to be the instrument by which any process in the Church courts, with a view of obtaining a decision as to Dr. Hampden's opinions, could be begun. Clergy in the Oxford diocese had already given their diocesan to understand that they meant to move him to that end. The Bishop was anxious to avoid this if he could, though at the same time clear and determined that the Church should have some definite assurance as to Dr. Hampden's orthodoxy. An extract from a letter to his friend, Miss Noel, shows us one of the considerations that, reasonably enough, weighed much with him at this time. "This whole Hampden business," he writes, "is *very* painful to me. It is so like hunting a man down that I am at times sick at heart, and feel I could do anything to show I hate persecuting him. Then it is painful to me to feel how probable it is that it will cost me that kindly trust of the Queen which for no *end*, but for *itself*, I do, now God has given it me, value highly. But one cannot *act* on these things." Under these circumstances, relying as he sometimes did too much on his own personal influence, not being sufficiently alive to the Premier's peculiar feelings in the matter, and presuming on Dr. Hampden's desire to clear himself publicly from the imputations made against him, he himself wrote a letter to Lord John Russell containing these words—"Will your Lordship apply to Dr. Hampden the rule you laid down for Dr. Lee, and require him to disprove, before a competent tribunal, the truth of these charges? This would satisfy the Church." In his reply Lord John Russell writes thus—"Turn the matter which way I will, I cannot see that the course pointed out by your Lordship would act otherwise than prejudicially." "Thus," to quote from Canon Ashwell's very full account of the whole matter, "the Bishop's first effort to promote the peace of the Church failed utterly."

As regards the next act in this painful business, the Bishop's well-meant endeavours to secure the peace of the Church not only cost him his Court favour, but caused him to be much misunderstood by serious and conscientious men of all parties in the Church. Worse still, they gave his enemies a real handle against him, and impeded very much the growth and extension of the new and wholesome influences which he was calling into activity in his diocese.

The Bishop hoped that Dr. Hampden's "Letter to Lord John Russell," promised at the time when he received his own answer, would prove to be "a prescribed publication," in which he was to ask for a trial. It proved to be nothing of the kind; it made no request for a judicial investigation, but complained bitterly of Tractarian persecution, and asserted strongly the writer's faith in all the fundamentals of Christianity. Upon this the Bishop of Oxford, at the instance of certain clergy in his diocese, signed the letters of request instituting a suit in the Court of Arches, which would determine whether Dr. Hampden's views expressed in his *Bampton Lectures*, and especially in his *Observations on Religious Dissent*, were in accord with the doctrines of the Church of England or not. But here, in his desire to avoid litigation in the Arches Court, whose judge, Sir H. J. Fust, he pronounces to be, in his opinion, "the most unsatisfactory pronouncer possible of a judgment," he made a very false step. In his final letter to Dr. Hampden, he explains that at this stage of the business it was suggested to him by he promoters that, the matter now being in legal train, it was possible that Dr. Hampden might be willing to render to his private suggestion, as Bishop of the diocese, the satisfaction which would otherwise be sought by a more painful process through the Court of Arches. Thus it came about that, with the assistance of the promoters of the suit, he drew up eleven heads of enquiry, which he invited Dr. Hampden to answer, and so to give a formal assurance of his orthodoxy. There was added a further request, that Dr. Hampden would withdraw, for the peace of the Church, his two objectionable books—"not as admitting their language to be unsound," but because, in the judgment of his Bishop and that of others, they did contain unsound language. The result was that he got from Dr. Hampden, with a protest against being asked to answer these extra-judicial questions, "an unhesitatingly affirmative reply" to the queries on his belief, and no answer at all to the request for the withdrawal of the books. At the same time Lord John Russell, to whom the Bishop also explained what he had done, wrote back what Dean Burgon calls a "saucy comment" on the letter to Dr. Hampden, wondering that a Regius Professor of Divinity "should be interrogated upon articles formed, not by the Church, but by one of its bishops, as if he were himself a young student in divinity," and refusing to interfere any further with "Dr. Hampden's judgment on his own position." Thus Bishop Wilberforce had made the great mistake of constituting himself at once accuser and judge, and gained nothing from the unfortunate position into which his good intentions and strange want of judgment had put him.

It would seem that now at any rate the suit must

proceed; but just at this time the Bishop learnt, through a letter written by Dr. Hampden to the Provost of Oriel, that the *Observations on Religious Dissent* were not being sold or circulated with his sanction, but against his wish, and that he had never reprinted the pamphlet since the second edition was sold.[1] A note of Canon Ashwell's explains how this had a very important bearing on the matter. The second edition had been published as far back as 1834, and, as being more than two years old, could not be made the subject of a charge under the Clergy Discipline Act. This discovery induced the Bishop to urge the promoters, in accordance also with advice received from Archbishop Howley, to drop the suit. He had now, moreover, made a careful study of the *Bampton Lectures*, and convinced himself that, when read in conjunction with certain explanations, which their writer had furnished to the public since their first publication, they did not warrant those suspicions of unsoundness to which they had given rise. Besides this, further consultation with lawyers had made it clear to him, that, as he expresses it, his action in transmitting a suit of the nature of that now before him was more judicial, and less purely ministerial, than

[1] In F. W. Newman's book entitled *The Early History of Cardinal Newman*, there appears what the Bishop of Newcastle describes "as the most complete vindication yet published of his father's action in the Hampden Case." Mr. Newman writes thus—" In my belief this very clever Bishop never did an honester and braver deed than his acquittal of Hampden. Any pressure from the Court is quite a false idea." He then goes on to show (pp. 85-88) how Bishop Wilberforce was induced by Dr. Hawkins to read Hampden's lectures, having previously "only read Newman's elucidation of them." The result was that he felt unable to blame Dr. Hampden, and at once explained to Mr. Keble and others that this was his conviction, and that at all costs he should act upon it.

G

he had thought. He felt that in transmitting it he was supposed to express an opinion that there was a *primâ facie* case. From the outset he had said that it would not be right for *him* to *promote* a suit; and he had now convinced himself that any charge made could not be sustained. As the result of all this, he wrote to the Provost of Oriel saying, "I have withdrawn from the promoters of the intended suit the Letters of Request." At the same time he still tried, through Dr. Hawkins, to get from Dr. Hampden certain assurances that he would alter, or explain, some of the causes of misapprehension in a future reprint of the *Bampton Lectures*. All this negotiation failed utterly, as Dr. Hampden by this time would only see in the Bishop of Oxford an antagonist, and, acting now on legal advice, would no longer say anything, or answer any questions. To quote from Dean Burgon, "the Hampden business in this way certainly reached a singularly lame and impotent conclusion," and ended, as far as the Bishop of Oxford was concerned, by a published letter to Dr. Hampden announcing his final resolution on the matter, and the steps by which he had come to it.

The question, however, was not one that concerned the Oxford diocese only, but the whole Church. The proceedings connected with it had been discussed and published in the public press; and there was very strong indignation felt amongst the large body of earnest and conscientious men whose feeling Bishop Wilberforce had appreciated, and tried—though not successfully—to represent, at his final withdrawal from the business. The assurances that had been indirectly won from Dr. Hampden seemed to them by no means adequate, and did not indeed amount to anything very definite. It was probably true that the opposition raised did prevent any further dangerous appointments, and did go to make it clear that the mind of the Church must not, in the appointment of her bishops by the Crown, be left out of all account. This, however, was hardly felt at the time, and the Bishop of Oxford was inveighed against by all parties for his efforts to give due effect to his desire to maintain the divine and spiritual character of the Church, and at the same time not to endanger in a critical moment its connection with the State. He had wanted to obtain legitimate satisfaction for those who honestly doubted Dr. Hampden's orthodoxy, and also to set Dr. Hampden right with the Church by getting from him some public and satisfactory explanation of his real views. Perplexed by other considerations, such as the likelihood that he would lose the Court favour, which had been so conspicuously his, and the fear he had of bringing vital Church questions before tribunals that were not satisfactory, he tried too much, and seems to have relied unduly on his personal influence, and to have been altogether too fertile in expedients. The outside world could not credit him with disinterestedness; and while the *Record* referred to his proceedings as "courtly," his friend, the Bishop of Exeter, expresses his surprise at the wonderful want of "judicial discretion" that he had displayed. It is plain that he felt all this very deeply, as he speaks of "the pelting" that he had to endure, and ends a letter to his brother Robert with a half-playful request, that he will write soon and tell him he is not a rascal.

The whole matter weighted him very much in his task of using his office to give a fresh vitality to the

Church; and the circumstances might well have influenced a less determined man to give up the effort to bring out the good in the Tractarian movement, and have made him acquiesce in the old as inevitable, while he floated into favour and power as a supporter only of the more Puritan element in the Church of England. It is to be observed that his conduct of the Hampden difficulty was all loss to Bishop Wilberforce, and no gain; it made his enemies bolder against him; it awoke in his friends a certain distrust; it did lose him the friendship of his Sovereign, and gave force and colour to other misrepresentations made against him at court. It was only natural that the Queen should have disliked his first action in the Hampden case; it came perilously near what might easily be twisted, or construed, into an interference with the royal prerogative. His later proceedings in the same matter were, though genuine and honest enough, easily capable of a sinister interpretation, and caused an unfavourable construction to be put on other of his sayings and doings. The change in his relations to the Queen closed up for the Bishop of Oxford great channels of possible usefulness, and deprived him of a prestige, which would have helped him certainly, with much less friction and misunderstanding, to win acceptance for the view of the system and position of the Church of England, which, amidst much earnest and conscientious opposition, specially from the Low Church Party, he felt bound to maintain.

After the Hampden trouble, and the Gorham judgment, circumstances brought up in rapid succession in the Oxford diocese many of the questions which involved a decision—how far there was a *via media* in the Church of England, and how far it could be made to hold both parties (High and Low) within its pale. As regards the Gorham judgment, Bishop Wilberforce says of it, that it only affirms that the Evangelical body are not to be expelled, and in a letter to the Rev. W. Butler thus summarizes his opinion of it—" This is to be treated as a mere State decision. It practically leaves the matter where it found it. It only decides that to hold infants need some preparatory grace, analogous to that which works faith and repentance in adults, for them to be due recipients of the grace conferred in Baptism, is not so plainly repugnant to the Church of England, as that the Court would be 'rigid' in excluding the holder of such a view. Now I do *not* see that this leaves us *in any way* tainted with heresy. It is very likely to mislead, and we must, of course, strive for a better state of things."

We have already had occasion to observe the way in which Bishop Wilberforce tried to do justice to both of the great parties which exist, and which are meant to exist, in the Church of England. In times of religious apathy, they have gone on quietly enough side by side; but his lot was cast in times when men were not apathetic, and he had to hold the balance between them when the adherents of the two, seemingly antagonistic, but really complementary, views, thought honestly that they must, for safety, cast one another out of the established Church altogether. In the charge given to the clergy of his diocese in 1860, the Bishop clearly states his point of view in the matter; and it was that which, up to that date, he strove hard to establish. He employs a luminous phrase to express his position in the matter, protesting against the commonly received theory that the state of things meant to exist in our Reformed Church is rightly called a compromise; "it is," he says, "rather indeed a combination than a compromise." He then gives as follows his account of what, on this principle, the Church of England is— "Both before and since the Reformation, the sacramental and anti-sacramental view has wrought strongly on the religious mind of England. It was a mighty and anxious problem, whether the favourers of these different views could be combined in one Reformed Church, with articles and formularies free from dishonest ambiguity of diction. This problem God gave to our fathers the grace to solve. To a marvellous degree the Church of England did combine all the men of both sections of thought, who possessed any moderation of character. The struggle indeed was long and often renewed; but, upon the whole, the fusion was most happily accomplished, and a rare inheritance of peace and purity was bequeathed to English Churchmen. The matter had been wrangled out; and we still enjoy the good fruits which have grown over the graves of controversies as old as those of Hooper and Ridley, of Travers and Hooker. This has been possible, because our common formularies contain all the positive truth which is needful for each class of minds, with no such contradiction of what either holds as would make subscription to them dishonest."

It was this that the Bishop of Oxford had to maintain, and being, as he states in a letter to Lord Ashley written in 1850, "a distinctly High Churchman," he was a champion of the sacramental view, rather than the anti-sacramental. This drew down on him the opposition of the other side as encouraging

Romanizing opinions, more particularly in a time when the Englishman's natural horror of Roman errors was intensified by many secessions to the Church of Rome, and by an increased activity in the propagation of Roman Catholic doctrines in England owing to improved Roman Catholic organization.

In the letter to Lord Ashley, to which reference is made above, the Bishop makes allusion to the fact that his toleration of Mr. Allies had been alleged as a proof that he (though of the school of Andrewes, Hooker and Beveridge, and opposed to the revival of a system of auricular confession, sacramental absolution, the sacrificial character of the sacrament of the Lord's Supper, the denial of justification by faith, etc.) was a Romanizer. A few words on the difficulties between Mr. Allies and his Bishop will bring out clearly some of the principles on which the Bishop desired to act with those who, though in the Church of England, were yet not of it. The Rev. T. W. Allies, Vicar of Launton, had from the first shown in his charge more zeal than discretion in his advocacy of advanced High Church principles. In 1849 he published a book, about which Bishop Wilberforce wrote to his friend, Miss Noel, as follows:—"I am reading Allies', of Launton, *Journal in France*. *Very* painful, very interesting. I am studying it to see if I must notice it. It is the most undisguised, unblushing preference for Rome I almost ever read." The result was that the Bishop wrote to Mr. Allies that his language as to the Eucharist seemed to him to contradict the teaching of our Church, condemning, in the 28th Article, the Roman dogma of Transubstantiation. He also complained of his tone as to the Church of which he was a minister, as depreciating and even insulting, implying alienation from her, and addiction to the Roman Communion. The Bishop's conclusion is that, unless there follows explanation or unqualified retraction, he will feel bound to call upon Mr. Allies to discontinue, as an honest man, that ministry which he exercised on condition of holding articles of religion, which he now publicly contradicted. Mr. Allies made but evasive answers, and, as the Bishop puts it, wished to make out that he might hold all Roman doctrine except the Pope's supremacy, and remain in the Church of England. The Bishop, on the advice of Dr. Lushington (who, though he felt reluctant to recommend the prosecution of a clergyman, thought it was in this case desirable and likely to succeed), determined, with the concurrence of the Bishop of Lincoln, to bring Mr. Allies to trial, on his further refusal to submit himself. This intention was abandoned, at the intercession of Baron Alderson, who also obtained from Mr. Allies a pledge that he would withdraw his book from future circulation, and would teach and preach in future in the plain literal and grammatical sense of the Articles. The Bishop then took steps to circulate this submission among the clergy, through the Archdeacon of Oxford. Thus the matter dropped, much to the dissatisfaction of the Evangelical party, particularly as Mr. Allies the same year joined the Church of Rome.

Bishop Wilberforce's views on the observance of Sunday ought to be mentioned amongst things that made him distrusted by the more puritanical members of the Low Church party. The matter had come into prominence because of the Post Office Arrangements (Sunday) Bill. As early as 1846 the Bishop had been thought to be lax in the matter of Sunday observance, because he had been present when Prince Albert played at chess on Sunday, and, not considering this in any way a breach of the law of God, had not protested against it, though he had asked to be excused from playing himself, on the ground that, in the state of English feeling on the subject, it would be highly inexpedient for him to do so. In a letter written at the time to Professor Walker, he defends the Prince in these words—"The Prince, you must remember, has had a Continental education; he has been accustomed to regard Sunday as it was regarded, I believe, over all Christendom, until the English Puritans altered the English feeling—not as 'The Sabbath,' but as the great Christian Feast of the Lord's Resurrection, much as we keep Christmas." He goes on to say that the Prince is a "thoroughly sincere Lutheran, and, not feeling our mode of keeping Sunday to be essentially religious, does not feel bound to conform to it; whilst he does feel that, as our mode of keeping it is now associated with all our religious feelings, he would on no account violate the religious feeling of others." In the matter of the Post Office Bill, Bishop Wilberforce took up the same line, explaining in a letter to the Rev. C. Barter that he could not promote any petition resting the obligation of Sunday observance upon the Fourth Commandment, as he did not think that Commandment applied to those in the Christian Church. Thus, the question for him was whether our English Sunday is to be a day of rest from labour, and of religious exercise, or a day of amusement; and he desired, as his father had, to assert its spiritual character, believing the preservation of this to be a main defence of religion and morals. His conclusion is that he could not, therefore, consent to the opening of museums or other public exhibitions on that day, though he says that at the same time he is "very sensible of the mischievous exaggeration of the puritanical view of the subject."

In September, 1849, came the papal bull, establishing a Roman hierarchy in England, and creating Cardinal Wiseman Archbishop of Westminster. The secessions consequent on the Gorham judgment, and the fact that the Government had conceded titular rank and precedence to Romish ecclesiastics in Ireland and the colonies, coupled with this "papal aggression," as it was called, threw all England into a ferment, and excited Protestant feeling to a high pitch of alarm. Bishop Wilberforce's dealings in the matter within his own diocese, and his speech on the Ecclesiastical Titles Bill, against the assumption by Roman Catholics of any titles taken from places in the United Kingdom, show us how he attempted, not unsuccessfully, to curb dangerous and fanatical panic on the one side, and unwarrantable assumptions on the other. The Bishop presided over two great meetings in the Oxford diocese— one at Reading, at which he says, in a letter to his brother, "he rather expected to be blown up," and the other at Oxford, in the Sheldonian Theatre. A form of protest was there solemnly adopted, in a not altogether friendly gathering, against the late usurpation of the Bishop of Rome, and the schismatical character of his act in intruding a rival Church into ground already occupied by the Protestant Church of England as by law established. The claim made in the protest, that "We are THE Apostolic Church of England," was considered objectionable. The Bishop writes on this point thus—"This is the ground taken by all our Reformers, and I am not afraid of sharing it with them... We are the Apostolical Church of England, holding the truth as contained in God's Word, and explained in primitive times by the Universal Church." In this way the Bishop of Oxford made the question of the moment a means of clearing away some of the misapprehensions concerning the origin and position of the Church of England, which were likely to mar her efficiency, and limit her comprehensiveness.

But Bishop Wilberforce's efforts to persuade the Church at large, through his work in his diocese, to remedy some omissions and defects, as it seemed to him, in her use and interpretation of the true Catholicism, by no means exhaust the story of his efforts to find in the Church of England a *modus vivendi* for the two great parties that have always, since the Reformation, existed in her. He also struggled to repress dangerous and un-Anglican excesses, where they seemed to him to involve theories and methods that tended at that time to lead men on to the adoption of the Roman system, and theology, with all its errors. All this then, as now, centred round the doctrine that men held about the sacrament of the Holy Communion; and, before briefly discussing the Bishop's action in dealing with some whom he conceived to exceed the Anglican teaching in this matter, it may be well to establish by one or two quotations from his writings, what, in his opinion, the Church of England position was. In his charges he often alludes with great satisfaction to the increase of the number of celebrations of Holy Communion year by year in his diocese. This following passage from his charge for 1857 gives us his idea on the subject. It runs thus—"The more frequent administration of that Holy Sacrament is another means I would mention to you for raising the tone of our ministry. The system of the Church of England plainly supposes a weekly Communion in every parish, where three or four communicants can be found to receive with the minister; and whilst such a frequency of celebration would probably diminish the numbers present at each time of administration, and so diminish the evil of the length of the service at each time of celebration, it would, I have no doubt, increase the total number of communicants." In 1869, however, he takes occasion to express the apprehension with which he regards the tendency, unquestionably manifested in certain quarters, to change the idea of the Holy Eucharist from a communion of the faithful into a function of the celebrating priest. "Such a change," he says, "is, in my most mature judgment, no lawful progress in increased reverence for that great sacrament upon the lines of our own Church. For in strict agreement as we believe with the words of Holy Writ, and with the teaching of the primitive Church, we do not regard the Communion of the faithful as an accident of the Holy Eucharist, which may be added to it, or separated from it, at will, leaving the great function of intercession untouched by the omission, but as of the very essence of the sacrament." As marks of this mistaken idea, the Bishop calls attention to the desire with some to make the celebrations at the principal Sunday morning service gorgeous as a display, to the multiplication of choral Communions, and to the growing custom of inviting the congregation to remain through the service as spectators, but not to partake of the sacrament as communicants. There is, he states, no ground known to him for supposing that prayer offered up by those who are present at the celebration, but do not partake in it, is one whit more prevailing than prayer at any other time, or in any other place; while to him it did not seem that a surrounding crowd of non-communicants added any honour to the sacrament.[1]

His views as to the Eucharist underlay the Bishop's dealings with Dr. Pusey, in the period during which the latter was not allowed to preach in the Oxford diocese. Dr. Dallas, a leading Evangelical clergyman, writing in 1850, reproaches Bishop Wilberforce for forsaking the Evangelical party, and throwing his influence into the opposite side; the letter suggests that if the Bishop would only inhibit Dr. Pusey from preaching in Mr. Marriott's church, he would thereby show that his sympathies were not wholly on the side of Tractarianism. To the accusation the Bishop's reply is this—"I have always held the great Evangelical truths as the life of my soul. I always opposed real Tractarianism, *i. e.* the putting tradition into the place which Holy Scripture alone can occupy, ceremony in the place of substance, giving to the sacraments the character belonging only to our Lord, craving after confession and absolution, etc., as sacramentals." To the suggestion the answer was already given. A month before Dr. Dallas' letter, Bishop Wilberforce had requested Dr. Pusey not to preach in his diocese except at Pusey. These proceedings in the matter of Dr. Pusey were by no means acceptable to the High Church party, and tended to

[1] *Charge* 1869, p. 31.

draw upon the Bishop of Oxford disapproval from those whose support he had had in some of his previous difficulties in his diocese. Circumstances were gradually leading up to what was almost the greatest trouble of Bishop Wilberforce's life, the secession of his brother, Archdeacon Wilberforce, to Rome. Letters make it plain that, in the matter of Dr. Pusey, the two brothers were not agreed, and there is a presage of the dreaded outcome of it all in words relating to some passages in the Archdeacon's charge for 1851. The Bishop of Oxford writes to him—"I am very glad that you have got comfortably through your charge, though sorry that you think there is anything in it as to which we should not agree. Oh, may this difference never be widened, I most earnestly pray God!" It was not till 1854 that the decisive step was taken, and so much did the Bishop then feel his brother's decision that he seriously contemplated resigning his Bishopric. The feeling of growing disagreement between them did a great deal, however, to increase the difficulties of the line that, for the sake of the Church and his diocese, the Bishop of Oxford felt bound to take up in the matter of Dr. Pusey and his teaching and influence.

From the very beginning of his episcopacy there had existed in the Bishop's mind a distrust, from his point of view, of the influence Dr. Pusey might exercise in the position of leader of the Tractarian party, which was practically thrust upon him by Newman's secession. Mr. Keble and his friends claimed that Dr. Pusey's influence did really more than anything else to keep in the Church of England many who, but for him, would have gone over to Rome. Thus the following passage occurs in a letter from Mr. Keble to Bishop Wilberforce, written in 1851—" My own conviction is, as I told your Lordship before, that he has been the greatest drag upon those who were rushing towards Rome; that such an abuse being inevitable, under our circumstances, whenever the attention of thoughtful persons should be generally drawn towards the doctrine of the one Catholic and Apostolic Church, Pusey was raised, as it were, for this very purpose, to hinder their defection, as by other ways, so especially by showing them that all their reasonable yearnings are sufficiently provided for in the English system rightly understood." In another letter of the same date, the same writer explains how that by Newman's going, many who were ready to follow Newman were by force of circumstances transferred to Pusey, who kept them back for a time. "He was (as Newman once said of himself) like a hen with a brood of ducklings: no fault of his that they took to the water at last." Now the Bishop of Oxford, while he had a great regard for Dr. Pusey's character, holiness, and learning, and acquitted him of heresy, did think that, however unintentionally, it was his fault that many of those who sought his counsel ended with Rome. In 1850 he writes to his brother, Archdeacon Wilberforce, on the matter, and explains how he has begun to reproach himself with slumbering when he ought to be banishing and driving away strange doctrines from his diocese. It was in this year that Mr. Dodsworth, a London incumbent, called in question the wisdom of Dr. Pusey's course in adapting for English use certain devotional books of Roman origin, specially with reference to the view that they suggested about the sacrament of Holy Communion. Upon this the Bishop of Oxford wrote to Dr. Pusey, calling upon him to give some distinct and public answer to Mr. Dodsworth's charges; and also to satisfy his Bishop, by material changes in the practices he encouraged, and in the tone of his teaching, that he would no longer be likely to lead people to the corruptions, or the Communion, of the See of Rome. The result was that Dr. Pusey acquiesced in a wish of his Bishop's, that he should abstain from preaching in the diocese of Oxford. He was not formally inhibited, and even if he had inhibited him, Bishop Wilberforce makes it clear that he would only have considered himself to be exercising a lesser power vested in him for lesser instances, and by no means to imply that the man thus restrained was a fit subject for a prosecution, or worthy of deprivation. Both Mr. Keble and Mr. Justice Coleridge interceded with the Bishop on Dr. Pusey's behalf, and the latter stated his own belief that nothing could so unsettle the minds of a large number of people, at present quite loyal to the Church, as to see a bishop engaged against Dr. Pusey; he also went on to say, that "though it would not satisfy him with Rome, it would dissatisfy him with the Church of England, did he believe that that Church did not sanction Dr. Pusey's opinions." The Bishop's answer was that he was most anxious not to take further steps, but that he was convinced that Dr. Pusey's adapted books had eminently aided, and were aiding, the Romanizing movement; that there were elements in his private ministry tending the same way, and that there were passages in his adapted books actually censurable in a Church Court. In his charge for 1852, the Bishop of Oxford went fully into the question of the dangers of the adapted books, and explained how they were likely to lead men, specially the more uninstructed, into receiving and adopting erroneous views; he also noted all the dangers which he feared from such a ministry as that which Dr. Pusey seemed to him to exercise, although his own views might nevertheless be in accordance with the Church of England standard of doctrine. The fact that he had done this, taken in connection with private assurances from Dr. Pusey of the strength of his convictions, and the earnestness of his labours against Roman doctrine, seemed to make it right for the Bishop, as he remembered the large liberty allowed to our clergy, to set him free to preach once more, which accordingly he did.

Now one of the things, which the Bishop of Oxford specially feared about Dr. Pusey's ministry was, that he was one who encouraged those who came to him to seek private absolution, and to practise regular confession. He also feared that he put to those who thus came to him questions which might have the effect of suggesting evil to otherwise innocent minds, of weakening parental authority, and revealing the lawful and necessary secrets of private family life. As regards all this we find in Dr. Pusey's letters such answers as these—"I never induce or recommend any person to come a second time"; "All habitual confession is of people's own seeking, and I see them very much less frequently than they wish"; "'We do not object to any manner of confession, public or private, saving compulsion,' seems the language of all the authorities in the Church of England." But the question of confession in the Church of England, and its legitimate use, was one of the points that the Bishop of Oxford was compelled most frequently to explain. The Low Church party often accused him of advocating the Roman system; and when, in 1858, the accusation against Mr. West, of Boyne Hill, for improperly trying to extort a confession from a sick woman, was declared by the Bishop to be unsupported by evidence, and was thrown out by his commission, an attack was made on him, headed by the *Times*, as a favourer of the confessional in its worst and most enslaving form.

In the Sisterhoods of his diocese the Bishop had to set his face against it in an un-Anglican form, as the following passage from a letter to Mr. Carter shows—"If Sisterhoods cannot be maintained, except upon a semi-Romanist scheme with its *direction*, with its self-consciousness and morbid religious affection, with its exaltation of the contemplative life, its perpetual confession, and its un-English tone, I am perfectly convinced that we had better have no Sisterhoods." The same difficulty faced him in a lesser degree at Cuddesdon, in the College, and followed him even to Winchester, where, during the last year of his life, he was called upon to make three distinct public utterances on the subject of private confession. His views then were identical with those expressed in 1850 in the letters which he wrote to Dr. Pusey, and others who then corresponded with him about Dr. Pusey and his teaching. The following extracts from letters written in 1851 show us plainly what those views were—"She [the Church of England] discourages such confession as an habitual custom, and gives no authority to her ministers to treat it as the common diet of the soul under the ordinary circumstances of the spiritual life—still less to press, with all the force of spiritual authority, it and its repetition as a duty and means of grace, so that tender consciences are constrained, and feel well-nigh forced to employ it as almost essential to their safety." And once more in a letter to the Rev. C. Marriott—"There is no subject on which the difference of our Church and the Roman Communion seems to me more important than this—no religious practice as to which it is more dangerous for our clergy to trifle with Roman tendencies. The difference, as I apprehend it, lies here. The Romanists altogether in fact, and very largely in theory, supersede conscience by the priest. They believe that none can safely manage their own conscience—that the state, therefore, of religious health is to practise confession to the priest, and receive from him absolution and direction; and I believe that no single part of their debasing system has produced such deadly fruit as this." It was natural then that in his struggle to disentangle, for the use and life of the Church in his diocese, what was genuine and really Catholic from what was the product of Roman error and corruption, Bishop Wilberforce should find, as he did, peculiar difficulties and misunderstandings in the prejudices and mistakes that gathered round the question of the right use of confession in the Church of England.

One great result of the Church revival, which had for its cause the first phases of the Tractarian movement, was that Churchmen became alive to the necessity of providing some more special and systematic training for candidates for Holy Orders. To this day the Church of England is lamentably defective in this respect, and enforces much too little preparation on those who are called in her to the work of the ministry. Three lines of thought, born of three sorts of error, have all contributed to this result: first, the idea borrowed from Rome, that it requires but little learning to administer the sacraments; secondly, the notion that the call at once makes the instrument fit; and thirdly, the natural sympathy that has too often been supposed to exist between the family living and the family fool. It has moreover been increasingly felt that the Universities, specially since they have been open to men of all denominations, supply no more than a good and wide basis for a later special training. Hence has come the multiplication and foundation of theological colleges; and one of the very first things that Bishop Wilberforce planned for the working of his diocese was a College at Cuddesdon, where graduates might go and spend some time in preparing for their Ordination. His idea was that during their residence these men should receive a threefold training in—(1) Devotion, (2) Parochial Work, (3) Theological Reading. In his charge for 1860 the Bishop expresses thus his opinion of the use and function of these colleges—" All the influences of a well-managed theological college are in favour of its inmates. The experience and personal piety of the principal and his assistant clergy are brought to bear, with a marked individuality of application, upon each one within its walls. The student has everything to invite him to, and to assist him in, theological study; he is taught, to the infinite saving of time and labour, what to notice, what to learn, and what to pass more lightly over. He becomes accustomed to regular hours of prayer, religious reading, and meditation. The unity of object and preparation which pervades the whole body of students—though injurious in its effect upon the mind before general studies and mixture with men of different purposes of life and different habits of thought have given to it elasticity and breadth—is a most wholesome influence after the course of an English school and an English university on one preparing for an office of such difficulty and importance, and which demands so absolutely, for its due fulfilment, the whole devotion of the whole man to its duties."

Round this College at Cuddesdon, and its work, centred the last phase of the almost systematic opposition which, in the period after the Hampden difficulty, the Low Church party felt it their duty to offer to Bishop Wilberforce's efforts at Church extension, revival, and reform in his diocese. There was evidently a distrust existing in their minds of the Bishop's dealings with the younger clergy, an evidence of which is found in a formal complaint, which the Bishop amply and sufficiently answered, one part of which alleged that he had refused a licence, on account of the curate-designate not agreeing with the Bishop's views on baptismal regeneration. Thus the Low Churchmen almost instinctively shrank from Cuddesdon College, and its training, as a place where the younger clergy received a stamp that, in their eyes, was as dangerous in its tendencies, as the Bishop himself considered Dr. Pusey's teaching. Moreover, the life at Cuddesdon, with its quiet order and rule and its devotional character, was strange in those days; and with men who by tradition and training had an unreasonable dread of Rome, it did seem, in its possible suggestions of monasticism, a part of the supposed conspiracy to unprotestantize the Church of England. Men's minds had not learnt to see how much vitality and force was to be found in Catholic practices and doctrines, which, being dangerous perhaps in the ideas that were common at the time of the Reformation, could, as it has been proved, be safely and profitably revived in later times. It is certainly a little difficult now for us to imagine the *Times* maintaining that two bishops of the Church of England would, if they were conscientious men, resign their preferments, because they advocated their clergy preaching in the surplice. We have lived to see that much, which was regarded in the Cuddesdon system as harmful, was, and is, really helpful; though we can also see that the old opposition was, if narrow and illiberal, at any rate conscientious.

In the *Quarterly Review* for January 1858, the writer of an article on "Church Extension" made somewhat severe strictures on Cuddesdon College, which had then been in existence some three years and a half. Before these could be answered, a circular letter was addressed to the clergy and laity of the Oxford diocese, which practically recapitulated the charges made in the *Quarterly*, and made distinct charges against the ritual of the College. The letter was written by the Rev. C. P. Golightly, who had convinced himself that the tendency of the College teaching was "to sow broadcast the seeds of Romish perversion in the counties of Oxford, Berks, and Bucks." He had already had a correspondence with the Bishop in the preceding autumn, and appears, in the face of the many perversions to Rome which had followed from the last phases of the Tractarian movement, to have viewed the College at Cuddesdon and the training that it offered with alarm, and specially the teaching and influence of the Vice-Principal, the Rev. H. P. Liddon. The Bishop's reply was as follows—"You must let me have a full talk with you on the whole matter, for it is too long for a letter. You are quite right in saying that I abhor Romish doctrine, but you are mistaken in thinking that I like Romish rites and ceremonies. Everything Romish stinks in my nostrils. I cannot allow the truth of your remark about Cuddesdon College. Men have come there with strong Roman leanings and left it cured, but I do not believe any one has there acquired any Romish tastes. There are, it is true, little things that I should wish otherwise, but men must work by instruments of the greatest possible excellence in fundamentals; it would, in my judgment, be clearly wrong to cast them away for non-essentials. I think my Vice-Principal eminently endued with the power of leading men to earnest, devoted piety, but with such a man I do not think I ought to interfere, except as to anything substantially important."[1] This does not, however, seem to have satisfied the Bishop's correspondent; it still seemed to him that Bishop Wilberforce's talents and zeal were being misdirected to the support of views and doctrines which were, and ought to be, wholly alien to the mind of the English people at large. A further letter drew from the Bishop a declaration that, in his opinion, Mr. Golightly, and those with him, started from a principle which did not really represent the true spirit and standpoint of the Church of England as the Catholic and Apostolic Church, and that the College might be trusted to turn out then, and in the future, a succession of hearty Church of England men. His own feeling was that the views which were perhaps just then unpopular, and from which the mind of the nation was inclined to

[1] *Life*, ii. pp. 358—367.

alienate itself, were really essential if the Church of England was to be the Church. The attitude which he felt it right to assume in the matter is well explained in a passage from a letter to Mr. Golightly, which runs thus—" If I believe, as in the main I do, that the aversion of the nation is to the declaration of the spiritual presence of Christ, and the personal presence of God the Holy Ghost with the Church, and the consequent truths of God's teaching through sacraments, etc., I could not honestly obtain the sympathy my soul naturally longs for, by in any measure clouding the truth."

All this, however, did not satisfy the party and school represented by Mr. Golightly; they thought that Cuddesdon must unprotestantize the clergy as far as its influence could reach. They could not rest, and therefore, rightly enough, made the article in the *Quarterly* a ground for again pressing their point. The Bishop then appointed a commission to inquire into the charges made against the College, which in its report, to quote the Bishop's words in the letter in which he enclosed it to the Principal, " completely negatived every charge." At the same time the archdeacons, who drew it up, suggested certain alterations in the service-book, and in what they considered the too great ornament displayed in the chapel. Bishop Wilberforce urged attention to these, as touching points which were liable to create serious alarm and misunderstanding in the state of feeling that then prevailed. At the annual gathering of the year 1858, the rural deans carried, by a large majority, a resolution to the effect that they wished to express their thanks to the Principal of the College for the statement which he had made, in answer to a question put to him at their meeting, showing how readily he had complied with the recommendation of the Commissioners. They also assured him of their full confidence in his desire to conduct the College in true allegiance to the Church of England. Thus the agitation ended; though it seemed to some not to be without its effect in the resignations during the following year of the Principal and Vice-Principal of the College at Cuddesdon. The connection, however, between the agitation and these events, if it existed at all, was certainly a remote one, as the Rev. A. Pott, the Principal of the College, found it necessary from ill-health to accept a country living; and the resignation of the Vice-Principal, the Rev. H. P. Liddon, illustrates another phase of the attitude that Bishop Wilberforce felt it right to adopt toward the religious questions of the day.

The after-history of the Rev. H. P. Liddon has shown abundantly his greatness, his ability, and his force of character. It is not wonderful that he should have exercised a remarkable and dominant influence over the Cuddesdon students. Bishop Wilberforce did not think that he differed doctrinally from his able Vice-Principal, but he has thus expressed his own idea of the way in which their theological standing-place was not identical—" On the great doctrine of the Eucharist we should use somewhat different language, and our Ritualistic tendencies would be all coloured by this. On confession, and its expedient limits, we should also, I think, differ." Again in a letter to the Rev. W. J. Butler, of Wantage, he writes thus—" Now I do *not* think the abstract doctrinal difference between us (*e. g.* on Eucharistic adoration) THE point. It seems to me that between all who hold the objective presence, with its consequences, there can be no fundamental difference here. I could quarrel with no man who honestly denied Transubstantiation, as to Eucharistic adoration. It is not therefore exactly Liddon's doctrinal views taken alone, as to which I feel the importance of the difference. It is as much or more a *moral* question." From the Bishop's point of view, the Vice-Principal of Cuddesdon, out of the greatness of his personality, and the force of his own earnest and deep convictions, stamped his best men at Cuddesdon with a peculiar mark. He seemed to feel himself obliged to go beyond the Bishop, where his views were in advance of his; and the result was that there went out of the College men whose views were, to use a now common expression, more sacerdotal than those of his chief. The Bishop of Oxford's close connection with his theological college caused it to be, as he himself puts it, that he was judged of in his secret intention for the diocese by the *exact* shade imparted by it to the men it sent out. His no-party policy in the diocese passed for mere temporizing, and the Cuddesdon man came to be known from the non-Cuddesdon man, not only by his loving more, working more, and praying more, but by other "peculiarities." The Bishop feared that all this might hinder the work he most desired to perform, and so it was that, with a heavy heart, and much regret for what he was losing, he acquiesced in the necessity that caused him to accept the resignation of his Vice-Principal.

He had still to face more fierce outcries against his Romanizing proclivities after the Boyne Hill case; and there are also found letters in which at this period of his career he took the *Record* to task for its persistent calumniations. Then by 1860 came a period of comparative calm; his troubled diocese, for a variety of causes, grew peaceful and harmonious. The Oxford clergy had come to understand their Bishop, and to appreciate his character and work. Further attacks of the same nature on the Romanizing tendency of his episcopate called forth expressions of confidence, both publicly and privately; it began to be freely acknowledged that, as a letter to the *Guardian* expressed it, it would be hard to find in any one, on or off the episcopal bench, the like amount of ministerial exertion. A pamphlet proceeding from the same source as the objections that had been urged against Cuddesdon, and called " Facts and Documents, Showing the Alarming State of the Oxford Diocese, by a Senior Clergyman of the Diocese," was circulated in 1859. But the diocese in general took this rather as an attack on itself; it felt that its Bishop did, as he expressed it, "fully sympathize with all that was positive in the views of his Evangelical brethren, and knew their favourite truths, as the life of his own soul." Clergy and laity, in large numbers, came forward to assure him that they recognized that he had endeavoured to administer his diocese, "so as to maintain and set forward that Evangelical truth and that Apostolical order which, through God's mercy, is the precious inheritance of our own Church of England."

These last are once more the Bishop's own words, contained in his reply to an address of confidence signed by more than five hundred clergy, and sent by one of the oldest clergymen in the diocese, who had, in fact, ministered under six successive Bishops of Oxford.

The detraction and unpopularity of this long period of struggle; the difficulties of the Hampden case; family sorrows, in secessions of some of his dearest relatives to Rome, and in the death of his eldest son—all these things, as his more private letters and writings show, worked together to make him more fit to render important services to the Church, which he loved so well, and whose real character and position he so thoroughly understood. Under them he grew wiser, more appreciative, and more skilful; so that he could better bring the Church away from extremes to a more healthy and free place, and allay panic, while much good was reviving in her, which had, not long since, been almost dead.

CHAPTER VI.

THE REVIVAL OF CONVOCATION.

In the *Quarterly Review* for October 1863, an article by Bishop Wilberforce reviews the episcopates of Bishop Blomfield, Bishop Stanley, and Bishop Wilson. The writer explains that he has chosen to discuss these three "indicative lives," because he believes them to contain in an eminent degree the materials from which the religious character and prospects of his own time may be gathered. In his opinion the history of our Church traced through these lives is "a record of progress—of real and important progress; perhaps, even of progress in every direction"; and he summarizes this in the following words:—"The Church has far more completely than heretofore learned to realize her own principles and position, and this in great measure by the curative and healthful processes of honest and laborious action. Many mists have been swept away; many questions solved; a far higher sense of duty become general; the idea of worship has revived; preaching instead of being undervalued has risen in general estimation (witness the nave services in our cathedrals, and the leading articles of our newspapers), and yet it has taken far more its true second place in our ideas of worship, not because it has sunk, but because prayer has risen in our ordinary estimation. With far less tendency to the corruptions of Rome, we have put forth more abundantly at home the blessed shoots of a loving charity. Our churches have been restored, in some dioceses even marvellously; larger provision has been made for works of charity; Sisterhoods have been founded and matured, in which the quick energies of Christian women, wedded to a life of devotion, can be combined and regulated; associations have risen on every side for increasing church accommodation, the ministry of the Word and sacraments, and the education of all orders and degrees amongst us. Coeval with these signs of life, there may be traced on all sides more unity, diminished suspicion, amongst those who have not yet learned to feel aright the degradations of party designations within the Church Catholic; and this with no repression of the open avowal of legitimate differences; with the laity taking more share than they ever did before in all Church matters; with Convocation sitting regularly, and discussing freely every Church question, and daily more and more referred to, both in and out of Parliament, as the proper exponent of the views of the clergy of England." Under these circumstances, to borrow a telling expression from the same article, it had become clear to far-sighted politicians that the time was passed, "when the Church could be esteemed as a poor relation, whom it was not reputable to disavow, nor possible to acknowledge without certain loss."

Now the change in the position of Convocation, that took place between the years 1847 and 1863, had contributed immensely to the quickening of the vitality of the Church, and its consequent strengthening as an establishment, to which reference is made above. It was both a cause and an effect in this; for, in the first place, it was the increasing power and influence of the Church that made her desire once again to find her long silenced voice; and, in the second place, it was the finding of that voice that gave her a power of protest in times of danger and oppression, and enabled her to claim her true position, and make new demands. Our concern is with the part that Bishop Wilberforce played in this revival, and it is not too much to say at once that, without him, it could not have been as successfully accomplished as it has been. It was not that the idea originated with him, or that he was the first, or only one, to perceive that, by making the meetings of Convocation a reality, the Church of England might find relief from many embarrassments and perplexities. It was rather that his energy, his public and private influence, and his great personal gifts, made him able, beyond all his contemporaries, to carry through the delicate and difficult negotiations, whereby, in the face of much mistrust and dislike, Convocation was allowed to wake up in some measure from its long sleep.

Its suppression, some 140 years before, may be said to have been the outcome of an idea which had long been growing, that the bishops of our Established Church had interests different from those of the Church at large. Their actions and their appointments were governed too much by political and secular considerations; they were willing to think that their seats in the House of Lords gave their Church a sufficient representation in the councils of the nation, and that they, without any thought of, or consultation with, the clergy at large, were in effect the Church of England by themselves. Under Queen Anne there had broken out a violent and unseemly contention between the Upper and Lower Houses of Convocation. The Lower House, even when they had right on their side, grew accustomed to assert themselves in a way that was not creditable or seemly. All this helped to foster the idea which was made the very most of by opponents at the time of the revival of synodal action in the Church; it was repeatedly urged that to call Convocation together for business would only be to initiate strife. But at the time of the actual suppression of the Convocations of the Church of England in the reign of George I., the spirit of the two Houses was better; they had grown more peaceful in a fuller appreciation of the great and serious importance of their common work. It seems clear that the Upper House would have supported the representations of the Lower House against Bishop Hoadley and his heresies, if the Government of the day, fearing their unanimity in the matter, had not brought it about that they were suddenly and summarily prorogued by order of the King. From that time till 1851 Convocation existed indeed, but only to vote an address to the Crown at the opening of a Session of Parliament. So the Church of England suffered a great disability from its connection with the State. It could not, as other religious bodies in the Kingdom, regulate and discuss its own affairs; it could not ventilate its grievances; it could not adapt its organizations and arrangements to the exigencies of the times. And all the while the bench of bishops, as a whole, was well content to have it so; for the State

THE REVIVAL OF CONVOCATION.

generally came first with them, and their duties to the Government which promoted them had the paramount claim. They did not, moreover, recognize that the clergy at large had, or ought to have, a voice in the affairs of the Church; it was altogether convenient to them that meetings of Convocation should be a mere form. It is almost strange, under the circumstances, that Convocation continued to exist at all, and that, when the time came that bishops and Churchmen began to desire a means of making the Church heard, they had not, in starting something new, a task more difficult even than the reviving of the old. As late as 1832 Bishop Blomfield wrote to the Archbishop of Canterbury, "We do not wish for a Convocation," and in 1833 to a clergyman, "I am much inclined to doubt whether it be expedient to revive the ancient functions of Convocation as at present constituted." It is to be noticed also, that Bishop Wilberforce himself, in spite of his later ardent advocacy of the revival, had an open and growing mind in the matter, and was himself once as clear as Bishop Blomfield as to the inexpediency of an operative Convocation. The following passage from a letter to the Rev. W. F. Hook, then Vicar of Coventry, written in 1836, illustrates this—"Some recent meetings, I see, have proceeded to petition for a restoration of Convocation. It is a painful admission; but I am persuaded that we could not risk a Convocation. The examples commonly alleged fail, I think, of agreement with our case. The Kirk Establishment of Scotland, the Methodist Conference, etc., proceed upon generally admitted and maintained general principles; but the great bulk of our clergy are still so ignorant of Church principles, that we have no sufficient bond of union to resist the necessary divisions which must always spring from the shades of individual opinions, and we should fight in the presence of our enemies." The circumstances under which Convocation had been suppressed, made even friends afraid that a revival of its powers, amidst the misunderstandings and oppositions of the two great sections of the Church, might lead to harm and trouble. When, in 1840, Archdeacon S. Wilberforce preached the Latin Sermon before the Convocation of Canterbury, it is plain that he sees its revived activity to be yet nearer and more desirable than when he expressed his opinion in 1836. At the same time he clearly feels that the only real hastening towards the desired end involves making haste very slowly and cautiously indeed. All this is shown in the following extract from a letter written after his sermon to his brother Robert—" My sermon has gone off very well. People seemed pleased. All is stirring here. There is a great talk of amending the Archbishop's address, by putting in a general request for a *soon* Convocation—not that *this* may now sit for despatch of business, which is thought, by most, premature." His final view on the matter is well expressed in his article in the *Quarterly Review* on "The Church of England and her Bishops"; and the passage in question will lead on naturally to a short explanation of the methods by which Bishop Wilberforce laboured to give his ideas effect. It runs thus—" Far-sighted men had, with more or less clearness, foreseen for years that under the changed aspect of the times, the restoration of synodal action was essential to the welfare of the Church. They saw that the absence of free discussion between clergymen, under the restraints of that sense of responsibility which

THE REVIVAL OF CONVOCATION. 115

is ever bred by the consciousness of being met in a 'lawful assembly,' had already led to the prevalence of far more unrestrained discussions, under no authority, where the absence of all duly recognized chiefs gave to those, who could fill it with least advantage to the Church, the actual position of the guides of thought and action amongst their brethren. Further, they saw that the time was come when, whether to resist injurious changes, the imposition of which might be attempted from without, or so to mould from within existing institutions as to make them equal to the new requirements of an expanding body, the clergy must be allowed to exercise their undoubted right of forming and expressing their opinion by full and free debate upon all suggested changes and all needful improvements in the system of their Church."

Now, before this only method of making constitutional changes in the national Church could be once more brought into play, there were a great number of prejudices to be overcome. There existed in the minds of many a profound distrust of the synodal action of the Church. The call for it seemed, to the nation generally, to be an outcome of the much-dreaded Romanizing tendency, which ordinary Englishmen discerned in the return to more Catholic principles and methods, that began in the Church of England with the Oxford movement. For this and other reasons many of the members of Convocation itself were inclined to resist, as a matter of conscience, the efforts that were made to make its meetings no longer a mere formality. In the Upper House the Archbishops and many of the bishops were, at first, much more disposed to hinder than to help all that was being done, and were ready to find reasons against the undertaking. Their order had become quite unaccustomed in the past to co-operate with the other clergy; and, with an ignorance of the real facts, there had grown up an impression that the silencing of Convocation had freed them from a great deal of harassing and unpleasing opposition, which they could only suppose would begin again when the Church again found her proper voice. Besides this, the political aspect of the movement was not regarded favourably. It was not considered by the Ministry and Government that, after all, allowing Convocation to proceed again to business was but a matter of justice, according only a liberty to the Church which was freely at this time given to other religious bodies in the land. The aspect of the matter which was most regarded was that it gave to the Established Church a position of independence, as against the State, which the traditions of the past were supposed to prove to be of necessity dangerous. In this way it was thought and urged in high places that the proposed revival of Convocation was likely to interfere with the royal supremacy, so that the whole movement was regarded with marked disfavour at Court. Here, as elsewhere, confidence had to be won, and prejudice removed, by the wise and cautious use of the slowly increased opportunities, charily meted out to Convocation by authorities that, while they half scorned it and its proceedings, wholly mistrusted both.

By 1850 the circumstances of the Gorham judgment, the course taken by the Church authorities in the ritual difficulties with Mr. Bennett, and the course taken by some of the Ministers in the matters connected with the papal aggressions, brought matters for the Church to a crisis. It was clear that if a great schism was to be avoided, and the Anglican Church to remain as inclusive as her constitution means her to be, some regular and lawful control over her own affairs must be given to her. The Church Unions already made some of those irresponsible bodies eager to promote discussions, which are, as Bishop Wilberforce points out in a passage quoted above, so dangerous from their irresponsibility. At the same time, there had now actually come into existence a Society for the Revival of Convocation, which consisted both of clergy and laity, and gave the impetus to the action which Bishop Wilberforce, with his talents and wide influence, was conspicuous in bringing to a successful issue. As early as 1847 *something* had been done in Convocation. Several amendments to the usual Address to the Crown had been brought forward and discussed in the Lower House; and one, containing an " earnest prayer" that her Majesty would require the advice of the synod, was accepted by the Upper House, and inserted in the Address.[1] This was indeed the *parvula radix* from which, in Bishop Wilberforce's able hands, much was to grow.

His first important action in the matter was in a debate in the House of Lords on July 11th, 1851. At the instance of the Society for the Revival of Convocation, a petition had been presented to the Convocation of Canterbury from the clergy and laity of the province, praying its members to consider the question of the revival of their activity. A motion of Lord Redesdale's, asking for a copy of this petition, brought on a debate on Convocation. Lord Redesdale urged that, if Convocation became a reality, it would do a great deal to save the Church from the danger she was in, owing

[1] Perry's *English Church History*, iii. p. 296.

to the strife of parties. The course of the debate showed two things—firstly, that the Primate feared meetings of Convocation for business; and secondly, that the Government, as represented by Lord Lansdowne, was unfavourable. The Bishop of Oxford replied to Lord Lansdowne's argument, and showed that the dangers feared were unreal, and claimed for the Church that she should be considered to have a divine character, and be freely allowed to exercise her ancient rights. This debate did much to further the cause of Convocation, and to remove prejudicial misunderstanding in the country at large.

In the autumn of the same year a long correspondence took place between Bishop Wilberforce and Mr. Gladstone, and ended in an interview between them at Cuddesdon. It was this that determined the Bishop to a more vigorous effort still to get a fuller liberty for Convocation. Mr. Gladstone, as a layman who was a strong Churchman, thought that late events had shown the bench of bishops to be very much divided, and had also shown that, while they could not unite to defend an endangered doctrine of the Church, they could unite to check certain revivals of ceremonial, which were known to tend as a whole to bring our worship a step nearer to that of the Eastern as well as to that of the Roman Church. He said that it appeared to him that "both the particular question of Baptism and the claim of the Church, as against the civil power, to decide or interpret all doctrine, are, in the views of the episcopate as a body, open questions properly so called." On the whole it seemed to him that, though isolated individuals amongst the English bishops did stand firm to the Church's teaching, yet the great majority, including the Archbishop, seemed utterly indifferent to upholding any dogmatic teaching in the Church. The Bishop of Oxford had his answer in the political considerations that govern appointments to the episcopate; the too great readiness of men at large to accept as true without inquiry charges against the bishops; and the unreadiness of Churchmen in the House of Commons to give explanations on their behalf. At the same time his subsequent activity in the matter of Convocation shows plainly what was in his opinion the true and best remedy.

When Convocation met, on February 4th, 1852, the Bishop of Oxford, acting on the lines of the action of 1847, proceeded to make a fresh effort to waken Convocation into life. The opposition offered by Sir John Dodson, the Queen's Advocate, and the Archbishop's legal adviser, marks out the next stage in the struggle. It now occurred to some Churchmen, and notably to Bishop Wilberforce, that, after all, the legal difficulties in the way of the activity of Convocation might not be so great and insurmountable as was supposed; it was seen to be quite possible that ideas, as to the length it could, or could not, go without royal license and Government permission, might well have grown up, and been acquiesced in, without having any real foundation but custom. The Archbishop had prorogued Convocation till August 12th, but before that time the fall of the Government caused a fresh election of proctors, and rumours, without foundation, went about that Lord Derby and his colleagues, who had just come into power, meant to advise the Queen to let Convocation, when it met at the beginning of 1852, actually sit for the despatch of business. Now the legal opinion, which had been sought and given, had already made it clear that Lord Derby's intervention was not required, and no further license from the Crown either, beyond what was contained in the ordinary writs, which issued as a matter of routine. It was the lawyers' opinion, that in a duly summoned and convened Convocation no royal license was necessary, except to promulge canons; and they also considered it almost certain that the Archbishop could not prorogue *proprio motu*, and without the consent of his suffragans.[1]

Fortified with these opinions, the Bishop of Oxford set himself to do all he could to make the next meetings of Convocation a real step in advance. In the then state of feeling on the subject, it was above all things necessary that all should be harmonious; and there were several points in which collision between conflicting and opposing interests was to be feared. In the first place, it was likely that the choice of a prolocutor by the members of the Lower House might involve a difficulty with the Archbishop, if they should select one unacceptable to him, or he should insist on naming one unacceptable to them. This was arranged satisfactorily by the Bishop of Oxford using his influence on both sides, and the following short letter from the Archbishop to Bishop Wilberforce indicates the result—"My dear Lord—Among the instructions concerning Convocation which I received, it was said that the Archbishop names a prolocutor. After advising with the Bishops of London and Winchester, I have obtained the consent of the Dean of Ely to be so named. But I have no idea of disputing the question, if the Lower House claim the privilege of appointing without reference to the

[1] Perry's *English Church History*, iii. p. 303.

Archbishop. I am faithfully and affectionately yours,
J. B. CANTUAR."

Again, the nature of the business on which the houses should first engage had to be judiciously settled, and Mr. Gladstone was consulted on this matter. He pointed out the inexpediency of asking in any way from the Government for anything that the Convocation might after all be quite competent to arrange for itself; and suggested that a joint committee of the two houses was a better way than a royal commission for rearranging the constitution of Convocation. There were, moreover, symptoms of dangerous questions, such as that of education, being introduced; and there was a fear that the Archbishop's power, or claim of power, of proroguing, might prove a fatal bar to courses that might otherwise have been safe and wise. All these difficulties were, however, overcome, largely by Bishop Wilberforce's intervention, who, to quote from the second volume of his *Life*, "by arguments and by persuasion, induced the Archbishop to declare that no petitions should be presented that did not bear on Convocation itself." How critical was the moment, and how much might be lost by a false step, may be gathered from the fact that a meeting held at this time at Fishmongers' Hall, presided over by Lord Shaftesbury, denounced all attempts to revive Convocation, and once more maintained that it was quite impossible for it to meet and be at all peaceable.

On November 5th, 1852, the Convocation met at St. Paul's, and was then prorogued till November 12th. When it met again the Bishop of Oxford took a prominent part in the proceedings. He expressed his opinion that, in days like those in which discussion could not be stopped, it was better to do that regularly which would otherwise be done irregularly—it was better to call up the proper conciliar action of the Church, than to permit mere popular agitation. He then proposed an amendment to the draft of the Address to the Crown proposed by the President, but withdrew this in favour of an amendment, moved by the Bishop of Salisbury, which set forth that the resumption of active functions by the legislative assemblies of the Church, if granted by her Majesty at no distant date, would be productive of much advantage. On the motion of the Bishop of Oxford, there was also added to the address a protest against the late fresh aggression of the See of Rome, which amounted to a denial of the existence of that branch of the Catholic Church which had been so long established in England. He also moved for the appointment of a Committee to consider the subject of clergy discipline, which was agreed to; and members of the Lower House were added to serve on it conjointly with the Bishops, and instructions given to the committee to draft a petition.[1] After three sessions had been held, the Archbishop prorogued Convocation to February 16th, 1853, though a protest was made against this, as done without the consent of his suffragans, by the Bishops of Oxford, Salisbury, Chichester, and St. David's. Thus the action of Convocation was, in a great measure, restored after some hundred and forty years, during which, owing largely to the ignorance and indifference of the clergy, it had done nothing, and been practically dead. Government was as yet, however, not inclined to sanction its revival as a Church Parliament. The idea prevailed that the Church and its affairs could, and should, be

[1] Perry, *English Church History*, iii. p. 305.

managed by the Parliament of the country, and it was not recognized how unjust and undesirable this had become, in the changes that had of late years rightly given Nonconformists their proper place in the legislative assemblies of England. After the so far successful efforts of 1852, there was danger that much might have been lost by the premature jubilations of injudicious friends; and Bishop Wilberforce did good service by keeping such from proclaiming their triumph in the newspapers. In a letter to his brother, the Bishop explains how the marvellous silence of *John Bull*, the *Guardian*, and the *Morning Chronicle* was due to him, and was intended " to keep all asleep as long as they could act."

At the end of 1852 Lord Aberdeen came into power. He had a great admiration for Bishop Wilberforce, and once said of him that he ought not to have been a Bishop, but Chancellor in his administration. This, and the fact that the Bishop of Oxford's voice and influence in the House of Lords were of importance to the Government, gave him new and larger opportunities for pressing the revival of Convocation, which was then so vital to the interests of the Church. The Bishop's letters show that he accepted the political situation as a real opportunity for improving greatly the position in matters ecclesiastical, as those well-disposed to the Church were in power,—" the popishly inclined Puseyite-Presbyterian," as the *Record* called Lord Aberdeen, being head. At the same time the path of progress was difficult. The Low Church dread of Convocation showed itself in many ways, and, under the pressure of it, Lord Aberdeen's first views about Convocation were, as the Bishop of Oxford expresses it, "utterly dispiriting."

He had said to his son, "I can't allow them to sit"; and had added, as his utmost possible concession— "Very well; they may talk till midnight on the 16th, if they like, and pass the Address if they can, but they must not adjourn again. As it is, already, I have had great difficulty in keeping down a clerical opposition, and have only succeeded by saying that Convocation would be content with one more meeting."

In the course of January 1853, the Bishop of Oxford had an interview with the Prime Minister, from which it became clear that, though he himself meant well and fairly, he was much hampered by his Cabinet. Lord Aberdeen's ideas were in favour of doing if possible as had been done for the past hundred and fifty years. Bills, he said, might be brought in in the House of Lords by bishops, and if they thought the assent of the clergy requisite, they might be far better represented than in Convocation by an informal meeting of delegates. To him it seemed a mistake to stir up quiet waters; he did not understand, as the Bishop of Oxford did, that the waters were not quiet, and that, in the growth of Church feeling, the bishops, in their somewhat divided councils, and want of sympathy in many cases with the reviving Church spirit, had not the power to calm them and keep them still. Knowing that any arbitrary prorogation now, or unconstitutional repression, would cause a disruption in the Church, the Bishop wisely set himself to do all he could to secure the adoption of Lord Aberdeen's other suggestion, that nothing should be done, even by prolonging the Session over one day, to hinder the step already made being brought to a safe and prosperous conclusion. He had been warned that there was a great hankering for a Crown prorogation, if not *dissolution*, even before the 16th, and under the circumstances, wrote to the Archbishop to get him to call together the Committee of Bishops, at the earliest possible day, to meet the Committee of the Lower House, and try to arrange heads of a Bill, which might (according to a suggestion of Lord Aberdeen) be brought into Parliament on the subjects referred to Committees at the last Session of Convocation. On January 19th he was at Windsor, and tried to secure with the highest authorities a more favourable view of the whole question, as the Convocation movement was much misunderstood and misrepresented at Court. His diary for January 19th runs as follows—" Long talk with the Prince in his room on Convocation. Tried to set plainly before him our needs, and internal action our only remedy. He spoke as always, kindly and plainly, and paid great attention to my view." It is clear, however, that it was not accepted at present by the Crown that meetings of Convocation could do anything else but disturb the peace of the Church. Mr. Gordon's account of a discussion of the matter at Windsor is given in the second volume of *Bishop Wilberforce's Life;*[1] and it was suggested that the movement might be made to die a natural death if the most active advocates of it were permanently excluded from preferment. The history of the past shows disastrous results from attempts to govern the Church by patronage; and it is matter for thankfulness that, in the present reign, men of all views and parties have been equally placed in the highest positions. Thus has been secured that balancing and moderating force which, even in the obtaining of such an undoubted

---

[1] *Life,* ii. pp. 168-9.

advantage as a real and not merely formal Convocation, needs to be considered.

Meanwhile there was some talk of Lord Aberdeen's Government issuing a commission to inquire into the working and constitution of Convocation, and to suggest improvements. This commission was, however, never appointed, but Bishop Wilberforce's exertions before, and at the time, secured that no attempt was made to extend the meeting of Convocation beyond the one day on which it assembled, February 16th, 1853. It was then prorogued till August 16th, after voting the Address and, amongst other things, receiving a report on Church Discipline from the committee of the Upper House appointed in the previous session. At the time of prorogation the Lower House was in the middle of a debate as to what was best to be done in the matter of a committee on the Representation of Grievances, which had been appointed, but had been hindered from completing its work. The abrupt ending of the session brought next day a letter to the Archbishop from Archdeacon Denison, which contained the following passage—"I venture to implore your Grace, humbly, respectfully, most earnestly, not to permit for the time to come that the Convocation of the province of Canterbury may be convened for a few hours only of a single day, lest its very assembling at all degenerate once more into that which it has presented to the world for nearly one hundred and fifty years—into an idle and empty parade and form, to the great discredit of the Church, the gradual undermining of her efficiency, and the impairing of her life."

In April 1853 Lord Aberdeen asked Bishop Wilberforce to say what definite objects ought, in his opinion,

THE REVIVAL OF CONVOCATION.

to engage the attention of the proposed Commission on Convocation, if it met. His answer indicates clearly his exact views on the matter at this time. There was, he felt, a widespread belief that the Church at that time required the power of internal action in order to adapt her machinery and organization to the wants and circumstances of the time. There was also a widespread belief that the Church was, "quite competent, as to prudence, knowledge, and other qualifications, to discuss these subjects with every reasonable expectation of reaching conclusions which would heal hearts, unite separated parties, and strengthen what remains." An inquiry by a fairly constituted commission would, he said, clear, or tend to clear, the following questions : (*a*) Are there matters which for the quiet and strength of the Church need its own internal action ? (*b*) Is the present constitution of the Church's synod such as to make it really fit for dealing with them ? (*c*) If not, could its constitution be so altered as to make it fit ? (*d*) What changes should be recommended for its consideration and adoption ?[1] The Bishop had intended to make an effort to proceed to business when the prorogued Convocation met again in August; but the Archbishop was set against it, and plainly told him that Convocation would continue to be one of the subjects on which their views did not coincide, as long as Bishop Wilberforce desired its revival, and he opposed it. On an explanation that the Archbishop did not mean by this that he would necessarily resist the wishes of his suffragans in this matter for the future, the Bishop of Oxford, in deference to his wishes, decided to keep silence, and not, on this occasion, to oppose or hinder the prorogation.

[1] *Life*, ii. p. 183.

Perhaps the fret and worry of all these small negotiations, and the unpopularity and annoyance they involved, were more trying than a more open and public struggle, and due account must assuredly be taken of them in considering Bishop Wilberforce's greatest service to the Church. He was really almost the only person who could have carried them on, from his acquaintance with all the leading personages of the day; and his perseverance in them certainly spoiled the pleasure and confidence of many intimacies which he valued very highly.

The circumstances connected with the Bishop's efforts to make Convocation in 1854 even a greater reality were very trying, and he writes of himself—"Much cast down in view of Convocation difficulties." The Low Church party were more alarmed than ever, and felt it their duty, through Lord J. Russell, Lord Shaftesbury, and Dean Elliott, to do all they could with Lord Aberdeen and the Archbishop to prevent any more successful advances. At one time the Archbishop was nearly persuaded to prorogue, not by his own authority, but by a prepared form of royal exoneration. But at last all went well, and the settlement that the Bishop of Oxford made with Lord Aberdeen on January 4th was acted upon. The Bishop's diary records the somewhat amusing circumstance that, while he was actually in Lord Aberdeen's house on this occasion, a note arrived from the Primate, "fishing for a Government interruption," and that he and Lord Aberdeen together settled the answer to it. It was also agreed between them that there would be "no hindrance to one day's business, or, if need be, to a second." The diary for February 1st records the success of this meeting, with expressions of thankfulness—"To Convocation, where nearly all day, and D. G. most marvellously succeeded, the Bishops, who heretofore had been our chief opposers, moving and seconding our motions. God be praised, whose work I believe it is." An important part of these proceedings was the appointment of a first committee of both Houses, to consider what steps ought to be taken for the improvement of the constitution of Convocation. The Bishop of Oxford, supporting the motion for this committee, explained how the enemies of Convocation found an argument against it in the fact that, from its peculiar constitution, it could not be taken in any way to represent the mind of the Church. The same circumstance was also unsatisfactory to its friends; and as the increase of population, and alteration of the laws and phases of society, made some internal action of the Church needful, a more perfect representation of the Church in Convocation was desirable, "though," said the Bishop, "they did not desire the Crown to send its licence for any other reform than the reform of Convocation." Bishop Wilberforce's diary for February 2nd records that Lord Aberdeen expressed to him very strongly his content with the doings in Convocation on this occasion. From the same source we learn shortly what was the result of the next meeting on July 20th—"To Convocation; all passed most amicably. The Archbishop's opposition appears to be very greatly modified, but his extreme gentleness makes it difficult to be sure of his inner feelings." At this session the report on Convocation reform was presented, and suggestions for making it more representative of all the clergy were made. The question as to how effect should be given to these recommendations was found a very difficult

K

one. The Bishop of Oxford, as we have seen, thought that a Royal Commission might be helpful in the matter. Others thought that Convocation had best proceed to its own reform, and Sir Richard Bethell and Dr. Phillimore, on being consulted, gave it as their opinion that it would be competent for Convocation, having obtained the licence of the Crown, to discuss the question of the alteration of their representative body, and to make a canon enlarging it, on which they could act, after obtaining the approbation of the canon by the Crown. At present the matter rests here.

In 1855 Convocation entered as it were upon quite a new lease of life. The Archbishop spontaneously asked Lord Aberdeen in January for prolonged sittings, and urged that there were many things, as for instance the division of services, to which the clergy would pay more general attention if recommended by Convocation than if recommended by the bishops. Lord Aberdeen secured a letter from the Archbishop to this effect, a step which the Bishop of Oxford urged as important lest he should change. In his diary he records his great relief at such an unexpected turn of events—"I feel as if the stone we had so hardly rolled up the hill were beginning to roll over. May God direct it aright."

The prolocutor of the Lower House, at the request of Bishop Blomfield and Bishop Wilberforce, also wrote to Lord Aberdeen, requesting two or three days for discussion, adding an assurance that he would have the support of a large majority of the house in excluding topics of an obnoxious and personal character. Before Convocation met Lord Aberdeen's Government had fallen, and the Bishop's view of the situation is a gloomy one. He writes thus—"For Church matters

THE REVIVAL OF CONVOCATION. 131

how dark a prospect! The only Government which could, or was minded to, be fair to the Church overthrown, because six miles of road not made from Balaklava to Sebastopol!" Lord Aberdeen's statement as to the views of his successor, Lord Palmerston, on the Convocation question was—"He will do whatever is popular. He has no feelings of his own on the subject."

When Convocation met on Feb. 8th, the three days were more than filled up by discussions on the committee's reports. A debate took place in the Upper House on the alteration of Church services, and the Bishop of Oxford carried a motion that the rubrics might properly be altered, and changes made in the Lectionary. A new departure on this occasion was made by referring resolutions of the Upper House to the Lower House for consideration, and its opinion was found to be unfavourable to altering rubrics, or changing the Lectionary. The proceedings in the Lower House were attended with some difficulty and confusion, many maintaining that, till they were reformed, they were not competent to discuss matters sent down to them. As regards the question of reform, the Bishop of Oxford had moved that it was not expedient at present to attempt any change in the constitution of Convocation. He had been induced, partly by Mr. Gladstone's representations, to look unfavourably, after all, on a Royal Commission, as likely to put the whole question into the hands of Parliament, whereas Convocation had a status independent of Parliament.

When the Houses of Convocation met again on June 28th, fortified by legal opinions, they agreed to take the very important step of asking the Crown for licence to consider changes in their constitution, which might be referred again for the royal approval and consent. This was refused, and Bishop Wilberforce used his influence, both in Convocation itself and outside it, to induce the members of the two Houses to do what they could, with their existing powers, and in their unreformed condition. The following note of a conversation with the Archbishop in Oct. 1855, shows what was the Bishop of Oxford's idea as to the right and best line for Convocation under the circumstances—"He (the Archbishop) assents to my view that, having done what we can to get our instrument perfected, we must use the present, and that time for full discussion is *the* requisite." At the same time the Archbishop agreed to the Lower House of Convocation sitting, unless disturbed by Government, as long as was needed for the discussion of the adaptation of the Church to present wants. Before the Session of Feb. 1856, the Bishop had some further correspondence with Mr. Gladstone, who advised not more than a three days' sitting, lest Government should interfere, and any of the Church of England's slender chances be jeopardized by misuse. As a matter of fact business on this occasion lasted but a single day, though many notices of motion promised no lack of business for the Session to be held in April of the same year. On this occasion the synod of the Southern Province was allowed to proceed in its work unchecked, and the proceedings of both Houses were now fully reported in the *Journal of Convocation*. In his charge for 1857 the Bishop of Oxford speaks thus of the work that had been, so far, successfully accomplished, and steered by his wisdom and courage through many difficulties into comparative safety—"The

THE REVIVAL OF CONVOCATION. 133

two Houses of Convocation of the province have, as you are aware, continued their sittings with regularity, and their consultations with increasing interest, during these three years; and I cannot but recommend you to make yourselves familiar with the published journal of their proceedings, and especially with the reports of their committees, some of which have dealt, with no little wisdom, with most important practical questions."

Thus the Convocation of the Southern Province, and by degrees also the Convocation of the Northern Province, woke up gradually into life. Bishop Wilberforce continued as he had begun, and watched and guided anxiously all the early steps of the Convocation of the Southern Province. One of the means that he used most successfully was what he called his "Convocation breakfasts," which aimed at directing to order, wisdom, and amity the discussions of the Lower House. The following account of them is taken from the second volume of his *Life*. On the mornings when Convocation was in Session the Bishop gathered to his house for breakfast the leading men of the Lower House. Breakfast over, the Bishop would bring forward the subject that was for discussion in the Lower House that day, and call upon one of those present to give his views; others followed, and the discussion ended by the Bishop summing up. By this means, questions which in the early days of Convocation might have created very serious divisions were toned down.

In 1860 licence was asked for, and obtained from, the Crown to alter the 29th canon, which had prohibited parents from becoming sponsors for their children. The Bishop of Oxford on this occasion expatiated on the harm that was done to the now living and active

Church by the present condition of the canons; and the licence obtained on this occasion opened up quite a new field of helpfulness for the Church through her Convocations. The Bishop, in a letter to Mr. Gladstone, explains the movement in these words—" We have agreed *unanimously* to an Address to the Queen praying for her licence to make this canon, which will then be submitted for her assent. That is all a canon needs. There is no going to Parliament. . . . The Lower House of Convocation has unanimously agreed to our Address. Now to refuse this would be really unconstitutional in the highest degree. The clergy submitted to this limiting of their previous right to free discussions in the reign of Henry VIII. on the implied condition that they should receive this licence when they prayed for it." In the same way in 1865 the canons relating to subscription were altered in accordance with the recommendations made by the Royal Commission on Clerical Subscription.

In this, and in many other ways—sometimes by suggestions and discussions, sometimes by initiating desirable changes, and sometimes by giving an authoritative declaration to Churchmen on matters of faith—has Convocation, though, even to this day, unreformed in constitution, done great service to the Church. Many laboured to secure this end, but it was given to the Bishop of Oxford in an eminent degree to be the instrument whereby these labours were brought on to success. His tact and influence guided Convocation through the many dangers of its new beginning; his wisdom and eloquence gave weight and dignity to its debates. It was he who, with patient persistency, procured the synodical condemnation of *Essays and*

Reviews; it was he who defended the action of the bishops and clergy on this occasion, when it was questioned by Lord Houghton in the House of Lords, and even sneered at by the Lord Chancellor; it was he who explained to that august assembly how that voice of condemnation had quieted men's minds, and sent them back to their ordinary duties, "without being stirred up by the feeling that their Church was resting under an imputation of having allowed to pass uncontradicted false doctrine promulgated by her teachers." Here then, as in many matters, Bishop Wilberforce had prevailed to secure that peace for the Church, without which she cannot justify her existence by the due performance of her work.

So much space has been given here to the stages by which Convocation awoke after its "long hybernation," as Bishop Wilberforce, out of his love for natural history, was led to call it, because his share in them was the centre of his episcopal work. The revived Convocation has been since a safety-valve, by whose operation many threatening dangers to the Anglican Church have passed away without hindering or damaging the right working of the organization, which belongs to the Church from primitive and apostolic times. There are still many imperfections, it is true, in its constitution; there is still much for it to gain in authority, and perhaps liberty, as against the State. But meanwhile it is really a voice of the Church, and Churchmen are content that it should speak to, and for, them. So it has helped not a little to find a *modus vivendi* for differences of view and opinion, which, when Bishop Wilberforce's episcopate began, were not at all inclined to dwell together in the Established Church of England, but rather felt it a sacred duty to cast one another out by a rigidly enforced uniformity fashioned on the model of each party's own peculiar point of view.

In connection with the subject just discussed, it is natural to say a few words on Bishop Wilberforce's attitude to another difficulty that caused much dissatisfaction to Churchmen at the time that the agitation for a real Convocation first began. While, after the Reform Bill of 1832, changes were being made in the constitution of the country which gradually removed disabilities under which many had hitherto lain, either from their creed or their class, the bearing of these changes on the liberties of the Established Church, and its members, was not sufficiently realized or regarded. The relations that the Church of England had entered into with the State were such that difficulties arose at once, when men entered Parliament and held the highest offices in the land, who rightly enough in many cases felt conscientiously bound to oppose the Church, and who could in no case have a real sympathy with her views and aims, and must necessarily regard as at least indifferent that which she regarded as vital and essential. To them the Church was, as she had consented of late to be, and desired to be, a department of the State, and they could have little or no understanding of her unwillingness to subject herself in spiritual things, as a matter of course, to the ordinary tribunals, and to State control.

While Convocation was silent, and the Church asleep, cases of burning interest involving questions of doctrine did not come up for decision before the Courts that had jurisdiction in ecclesiastical matters. Churchmen were content to leave things alone, and laxity of doctrine, as laxity of life, and carelessness in duty, were allowed to exist among the clergy, unquestioned and unrebuked. With the reassertion of the Catholic character of the Church of England, which followed the Oxford movement, it was only right that those, who saw in that which was put forward nothing but an attempt to deprotestantize the Church, should put in motion every force available to check what they considered so highly dangerous to all they held most dear. Thus prosecutions in the Church courts became common, and questions were raised before them, that in the years since the Reformation no one had ever thought of agitating. The Gorham judgment made the members of the High Church party realize how very unsatisfactory the composition of the Judicial Committee of the Privy Council was, as giving a final decision on Church questions which came before it. It illustrates the extent to which it was thought unlikely that any vital Church questions could come before it, that we have it on Lord Brougham's authority that, in the steps that transferred the appeal in ecclesiastical causes from the old Court of Delegates to the Judicial Committee of the Privy Council, it was not realized that such causes were likely to be heard in it.[1] What was then done caused a civil court, entirely devoid of any spiritual jurisdiction, to be appointed to try ecclesiastical causes. It was quite possible that all who sat on this committee might be Dissenters, and it was almost impossible that some, or even the majority, should not be. Bishop Wilberforce gave much thought and labour to obviating the difficulties that *must* arise, and the disruption in the

---

[1] *The Church in England from William III. to Victoria*, Hore, ii. pp. 344-5.

Church that *might* arise, from this state of things. It had a great deal to do with some of those secessions to Rome in his own family which caused him so much pain; and it was a subject anxiously discussed with Mr. Gladstone.

Though a Royal Commission has since met and reported on this important matter, nothing has as yet been done; and Bishop Wilberforce had in his time, as in the matter of Convocation, to do all he could to minimize the evils that might arise from the unsatisfactory condition of things. He was first of all anxious to prevent questions that might involve doctrines from getting into the Courts. As in the case of Mr. Allies he was ready, as a last resort, to prosecute, but he aimed at getting men to accept, if they would, the bishop's authority and decision, and to maintain the peace of the Church, as in his dealings with Dr. Pusey, and his conduct of the case of Ditcher against Denison. This policy of his was very successful in his own diocese, more particularly in troubles about Ritualism; it caused him to sign the Declaration of the Bishops, when the difficulties with Mr. Bennett first arose, and it made it possible for him to write as follows in his charge for 1866—"No diocese, perhaps, from various causes, has risen more than that of Oxford with the general rise of Church devotion; none has been more free from these peculiar excesses."

Again, Bishop Wilberforce was very strong in insisting on the real force for Churchmen of the decisions of the Court of Appeal. In matters of ritual he was ready to defer to them, as being herein concerned with that which was expedient rather than that which was essential. In his charges he urged the observance of these decisions on his clergy, and altered his own practice into conformity with them.[1] When, as in the Gorham case, the judgments of the Court seemed to involve questions of doctrines, he was careful to explain that they were but legal decisions interpreting the exact words of formularies in reference to the special circumstances of an individual case, and were in no sense authoritative utterances of the Church. He has set this out very fully in his review in the *Quarterly* of "Aids to Faith," where he shows how Dr. Lushington's judgment in the matter of *Essays and Reviews* did not condemn the errors or the evils of the document, which had been brought before him, but simply its transgression of the law; and that he was maintaining, not truth, but the declaration of truth contained in the articles and formularies of the Established Church. In the matter of *Essays and Reviews*, the thing for Churchmen to rest upon was the synodal condemnation of the book by Convocation; and in his efforts for the revival of that assembly the Bishop was seeking amongst other things a solution of some of the difficulties that grew up out of the thorny question of Church courts.

Lastly, Bishop Wilberforce did not rest from attempting a reform of the Court of Appeal, so as to make it more satisfactory to Churchmen. In 1850 he supported Bishop Blomfield's Bill, which provided that all cases that affected doctrine in ecclesiastical causes should be removed from the Judicial Committee to the Upper House of Convocation. "Purely spiritual questions ought," he said, "to be left to purely spiritual persons." This Bill was lost, and in 1852 he, at Mr. Gladstone's instigation, tried to revive it, but in vain. His further

[1] *Charge*, 1857, pp. 50, 51.

efforts were directed to getting the Archbishops and the Bishop of London removed from the Judicial Committee altogether, as their presence there made a really secular court seemingly spiritual. On this question he expresses himself thus, in his *Quarterly* article on "Aids to Faith"—"The mixture of the spiritual element with the temporal in that Court gives to it an unfortunate appearance of undertaking to decide what is the true doctrine, instead of merely giving a legal exposition to the language in which the true doctrine is already defined." In his charge for 1866 the Bishop writes—"The grave question of the reconstitution of the Court of Final Appeal in matters of doctrine remains unsettled. It is one, the issues of which are so important that, provided only it is not let to fall asleep, I would rather see it wait the gradual clearing away of difficulties, than risk the dangers of a too hasty settlement." Perhaps the wisdom of the Bishop's advice is exemplified by the somewhat disastrous history of the Public Worship Regulation Act, passed soon after his death. Certainly his policy in his lifetime in this matter shows how much he felt that the Church of England must, and may, in spite of drawbacks in her constitution, and in her present relation to the State, go on doing sound and solid work, the performance of which gives to her her best title-deeds.

CHAPTER VII.

THE BISHOP AND THE BROAD CHURCH PARTY.

IN laying out, in the preface to the first volume of the *Life of Bishop Wilberforce,* the lines on which the work in his judgment ought to proceed, Canon Ashwell calls attention to the way in which the Bishop gradually became the "representative man of the English episcopate, and in great measure the representative man of the English Church." The seeds of distrust of him in high places, sown in the Hampden difficulty, and the unhappy and ill-timed secessions from his family to Rome, prevented his ever being Primate or Archbishop; and his succession to Winchester was described by Mr. Gladstone as "a tardy and insufficient acknowledgment of long services to the Church." But for all this, he was by 1867 the "foremost man in the Anglican Communion throughout the world," and very much what Dr. Hook, Dean of Chichester, humorously called him, "the great Lord Bishop of England." It was on, and through, the waves of great controversies that he floated into this position; and it was also from the midst of like waves, that he showed himself the almost generally acknowledged leader of the bench of bishops, and in his leadership helped to win a new confidence for the

Anglican episcopate, to give it a new tradition, and stamp it with a new character.

In the discussions and controversies connected with the publication of *Essays and Reviews*, the Bishop of Oxford's growing ascendancy first became apparent. He drew up the letter in 1861 which was issued by the bishops in answer to addresses asking them what steps they as bishops intended to take in the matter, in which letter they stated that they could not understand how any clergyman could have published such opinions as those concerning which they had been addressed, since they were plainly inconsistent with an honest subscription to the formularies of the Church. He also, in 1864, when Mr. Williams and Mr. Wilson, though condemned in the Court of Arches, had been acquitted on their appeal to the Judicial Committee, obtained the synodical condemnation of the book in Convocation, and as spokesman of the bishops, defended their action against Lord Westbury and Lord Houghton, in the House of Lords. Bishop Wilberforce's defence of the faith on this occasion, and some remarks of his on inspiration, made at Oxford, very much modified the hostility with which the Low Church party had hitherto felt bound to regard him. Dr. McNeile said of him—"In our conflict with infidelity, he is our invaluable champion"; and the *Record* writes—"We are often painfully compelled to differ from his Lordship, but our confidence has not been disappointed, that in a matter so essentially affecting the foundations of Christianity, the Bishop would be found true to the faith." The necessity of combining against a common danger, brought much more closely together the two parties in the Church which had been most opposed; and the fact that Bishop Wilberforce was found, under the circumstances of their union, an efficient and staunch leader, did a great deal to secure for him that dominant position among the English bishops to which reference has been made.

It is clear from charges, sermons, and public utterances, that Bishop Wilberforce regarded the publication of *Essays and Reviews* as an outcome of a rationalizing temper and tendency, which threatened, as he thought, to rob the Church and religion in England of the comfort and support of some of the most vital and important of truths. As regards the book itself, he is careful to explain, in his review of it in the *Quarterly*, that he, at any rate, does not rank its literary merits high. "There is," he writes, "nothing in this volume which is really new, and little which, having been said before, is said here with any new power, or with any great additions, either by way of amplification, illustration, or research." And again he says—" Here then we leave the critical argument, merely suggesting this as the probable cause why no general refutation of the Essays has yet appeared—that they are in fact but a stringing somewhat loosely together of the current, already abundantly repelled objections and fallacies of German rationalism." The popularity and danger of the book seemed to him to lie, like the peculiar piquancy of Sydney Smith's jokes, not so much in what was said, as in the recollection of who it was that said it. The fact that the writers were clergymen, and most of them in prominent positions as teachers, made their utterances of doctrines and sentiments, "which seemed at least to be altogether incompatible with the Bible, and the Christian faith as the Church of England had hitherto received it, to some

delightful, and to others shocking." The Bishop, who has written abundantly on this subject in two articles in the *Quarterly*, expresses very strongly his sense, that some at least of the writers in *Essays and Reviews* ought, if they were honest men, to resign their positions in the Church of England, as it was " impossible honestly to combine the maintenance of their system with the ministry of that Church." One of the Essay writers had dealt with this question from his point of view. He finds a liberty for himself in the matter, which is thus criticized by the Bishop, and thus explained—
" Mr. Wilson proceeds accordingly to consider how far a liberty of opinion is conceded by our existing laws, civil and ecclesiastical. The result of his consideration is as follows :—That as no one can be questioned as to his opinions, the teacher may think what he pleases, provided only he teaches as is prescribed; 'as far,' are his own words, 'as opinion privately entertained, is concerned, the liberty of the English clergyman appears already to be complete.' With most men educated, not in the schools of Jesuitism, but in the sound and honest moral training of an English education, the mere entering on the record such a plea as this must destroy the whole case. If the position of the religious instructor is to be maintained only by his holding one thing as true, and teaching another thing as to be received in the name of the God of truth, either let all teaching cease, or let the fraudulent instructor abdicate willingly his office, before the moral indignation of an as yet uncorrupted people thrust him ignominiously from his abused seat." Mr. Wilson was one of the four tutors who, when Tract 90 was published, raised a charge of dishonesty against

the principles of subscription therein advocated. The Bishop of Oxford points out the irony of circumstances, which made what was a justifiable and not unnatural action then, a condemnation of the protester's own somewhat similar evasion and subtlety at a later time.[1] The question of subscription was one much agitated in Bishop Wilberforce's day; he sat on the Royal Commission appointed to consider it, and wrote an article in the *Quarterly Review* on the subject. The old stringent forms of subscription were, as he showed, the results, not of clerical, but of lay, panic, fearing, in a time of liberty, a return to spiritual tyrannies from which an escape had been found. He advocated, and helped to obtain, a relaxation in the stringency of the terms of subscription, and also a limitation in the number of those, who, not being clergy, ought to be called on to make it; but he had no sympathy with the temper that, having undertaken to discharge certain duties, for certain considerations, on certain conditions, was not prepared to give up position and emoluments on finding it impossible to fulfil its voluntary engagements.

An attempt was made to assert that the speculations on religious questions, which had become common at the time when *Essays and Reviews* were published, and which were "characterized by a repugnance to all fixed belief in dogmas as having been directly communicated by God to man," were the result and issue entirely of a reaction against the Church revival that succeeded the Oxford movement. In his preface to the volume of *Replies to Essays and Reviews*, Bishop Wilberforce very clearly states his view on this matter in the

[1] *Quarterly* Article, *Essays and Reviews*. Bishop Wilberforce's *Essays*, ii. pp. 146-8.

following words—"It is not other than a very narrow philosophy, which would conceive of them as a mere reaction from recently renewed assertions of the preeminent importance of dogmatic truth and primitive Christian practice, or even from the excesses and evils which have, as they always do, attended on and disfigured the revival of the truth. No; this movement of the human mind has been far too wide-spread, and connects itself with far too general conditions, to be capable of so narrow a solution. Much more true is the explanation which sees in it the first stealing over the sky of the lurid lights, which shall be shed profusely around the great Anti-christ. For these difficulties gather their strength from a spirit of lawless rejection of all authority, from a daring claim for the unassisted human intellect to be able to discover, measure, and explain all things."

In Mr. Baden Powell's Essay *On the Study of the Evidences of Christianity,* he speaks of "a work which had then appeared . . . which must soon bring about an entire revolution of opinion in favour of the grand principle of the *self-evolving powers of nature.*" The Bishop of Oxford's criticism on this statement runs thus—"These words, 'the self-evolving powers of nature,' convey no meaning to our mind if they do not intentionally resolve the notion of a Personal Creator into the misty hieroglyphics of the Atheist." The work referred to was Mr. C. Darwin's *Origin of Species,* a more wholesome product of the intellectual activity of the time at which it was published, than the religious speculations that were put forward just then, and which were inclined, as the above extract shows, to make capital out of its conclusions. The Bishop of

Oxford wrote a review of Mr. Darwin's book in the *Quarterly*, and also spoke against the theory he advanced when the British Association met at Oxford in 1860. As regards his qualifications for these undertakings, it is to be remembered that the Bishop, amongst his many other pursuits and duties, was an ardent naturalist. He had written appreciative reviews of the books of Mr. Knox, in articles entitled *The Naturalist in Sussex,* and *The Naturalist on the Spey.* His quick eye for a new plant or a rare bird was always remarked by those who rode with him; and stories are told of his watching from the library at Cuddesdon the species of tit that came to feed on fat placed in a wire cage to attract them; and changing his wrath against a boy caught breaking down the Cuddesdon hedges to a gift of half-a-crown, when the offender assured him that he had kept a rare bird for him. Thus he did not undertake his attack on the soundness of the new views without some fitness for the task; and there was more in his argument than mere *odium theologicum* and natural eloquence, as some of the scientific men gathered at Oxford were disposed to think. Mr. Darwin himself says of the article on which his speech was based—"I have just read the *Quarterly*. It is uncommonly clever; it picks out with skill all the most conjectural parts, and brings forward all the difficulties."[1] But the Bishop did write what he wrote and say what he said, because to him it seemed then that, while the theory put forward was not in accordance with scientific fact, it also tended to views which were not in accord with the teachings of revelation as to man's real state, nature, and

[1] *Life of Darwin,* ii. p. 325.

position. He feared it, and perhaps feared it more because of the dangerous atmosphere of thought and temper in religious matters into which it was, in his opinion, brought. However, therefore, the true bearings of the theory may be seen and understood now, it is to be remembered, in considering Bishop Wilberforce's first attitude to it, that it was for him involved indirectly in the struggle, that he was making at the time of its publication, for questioned and threatened truth. It rejoiced him to feel that he could write thus concerning Mr. Darwin's book—"We think it difficult to find a theory fuller of assumptions—and of assumptions not grounded upon alleged facts in nature, but which are absolutely opposed to all the facts we have been able to observe."[1] His feeling was that the conclusions reached in the *Origin of Species* did in effect banish God from nature, and so it was that he penned the following passage—"And so Mr. Darwin not only finds in it (*i.e.* nature) those bungling contrivances which his own greater skill could amend, but he stands aghast before its mightier phenomena. The presence of death and famine seems to him inconceivable on the ordinary idea of creation; and he looks almost aghast at them until reconciled to their presence by his own theory that 'a ratio of increase so high as to lead to a struggle for life and, as a consequence, to natural selection, entailing divergence of character and the extinction of less improved forms, is decidedly followed by the most exalted object which we are capable of conceiving, namely, the production of the higher animals.' But we can give him a simpler solution still for the presence of these strange forms of

[1] *Essays*, Bishop Wilberforce, ii. p. 97.

imperfection and suffering amongst the works of God. We can tell him of the strong shudder which ran through all this world when its head and ruler fell."[1] In the matter then of his unfavourable criticism of Mr. Darwin's first great book, Bishop Wilberforce spoke because he believed, and was influenced by, the issues involved in the controversy with what has been called the Broad Church party in the Church, in which, in common with the members of the High and Low Church party, he was then engaged.

His wide sympathy with all that was real and earnest in thought and action had made him find friends in all schools of thought. It bears on his fitness to guide the assertion of the truth in the Church of England, which he felt necessary at the *Essays and Reviews* period, to remember that he knew and understood those whom he then opposed. In his early days men had found fault with him for his connection with the Sterling Club, and his meeting there with some who held broad and free opinions on religious matters. He had used his influence, unsuccessfully, to prevent Professor Maurice from being called upon to resign his professorship at King's College because of the unsoundness of his views, holding that explanation might solve the difficulty. He had also had an intimacy with Baron Bunsen, and had entered into his ideas that the Jerusalem Bishopric Bill might be a means of restoring episcopacy in Prussia. Dean Burgon laments his "seeming allowance (sometimes in conversation) of German authors whose writings the Church deservedly holds in abhorrence." This all goes to make it clear that conviction, not narrowness, governed his utterances, and guided his

[1] *Essays*, Bishop Wilberforce, ii. p. 97.

actions, when he felt himself compelled to oppose the movement which, in 1860 and the years that followed, seemed to threaten the right maintaining of vital truths, and to call on him to assist in "banishing and driving away strange doctrines from his diocese," and from the Church.

The Bishop in his charge for 1860 summarizes some of the dangers that seemed to him to threaten from Rationalism. He writes thus—"Surely this is not a time when any of us would do anything which, by ever so remote a consequence, might tend to weaken our Church's hold, or obscure its statement, of fundamental truth. Are there not rather, brethren, signs enough abroad amongst us of special danger from this side to make us drop all lesser differences, and combine together as one man in striving earnestly for the faith once delivered to the saints; when from within our own encampment are heard voices declaring that our old belief in the atonement wrought out for us by the sacrifice of the Cross is nothing better than an ignorant misconception, injurious to the character of God; that the miracles and prophecies of Scripture are parts of 'an irrational supernaturalism,' {which it is the duty of a 'remorseless criticism' to expose."

In the Bishop of Oxford's view the central point in the religious controversies of the time in which *Essays and Reviews* were published was the question of the inspiration of Scripture. The *Essay* writers made much of the necessity of assuming in ourselves a "verifying faculty," in dealing with Scripture. This, and the notion that Holy Scripture is to be treated as any other book, were, as the Bishop thought, THE idea of the whole volume; and he understands by the "verifying faculty" the power that was supposed to be in each man of deciding what is, and what is not, true in the inspired record.[1] It seemed to him, as he explains at the end of his *Quarterly* article on *Essays and Reviews* that it was being asked that a definition of inspiration should be given, exact far beyond what it is possible to have. His words on the subject are—"We maintain that this craving for 'a theory of inspiration' is itself a part of the disease we have to treat. In this sense of the word, Holy Scripture has never laid down any theory of inspiration; the Church has never propounded one; and there are plain and, we think, sufficient reasons for this reticence. On this same subject he expressed himself several times at this crisis; and in a letter to the *Guardian*, written to clear up misinterpretations of some remarks of his made at a large conference held at Oxford in 1864, he explains briefly *his* belief to be that "the whole Bible comes to us as the Word of God under the sanction of God the Holy Ghost; that we cannot pick and choose amidst its contents; that all is God's Word to us. Still the Holy Ghost speaks to men in it in divers manners, sometimes making a merely mechanical use of the human instrument to convey God's message, and sometimes possessing the human instrument with a complete knowledge of what he had to speak, leaving him to express it under His guardianship according to the natural use of the human faculties." It seemed to the Bishop that, if this was grasped, the difficulties which beset the orthodox view, owing to what was called the theory of "verbal inspiration," would be overcome; and that men would realize what was the essential differ-

---

[1] *Essays*, Bishop Wilberforce, ii. p. 114.

ence between Holy Scripture and other books, namely, that "as all truth comes from God, 'other books' may in a sense be said to be inspired because they are true, but Holy Scripture alone can be affirmed to be true because it is inspired."[1] Such were Bishop Wilberforce's views about this central point; it remains to see briefly how he steered the Church of England in other ways through the time of difficulty which was characterized by a tendency to think lightly of creeds and dogmas, and to trust in religious questions too entirely to reason.

The Bishop has a word of warning, first of all, for those who hoped that a high morality could be maintained without the support and sanction of definite teaching as to God—"The articles of the Christian creed," he says, "are in truth as much the basis of Christian morals as of Christian faith."[2] And again, "Remove the theology, and you take away the morality."[3] In two University sermons published with the title of "The Revelation of God the Probation of Man," he protests against the tendency shown to suggest doubts to the young, and to treat them, not as a disease, but a state to be encouraged, and "a sacred agony of man's nature in its noblest and most typical embodiments."[4] Against this he urges as a principle that "doubts about revelation are to be met like any other temptations to evil thoughts." Not, however, that doubt, in itself, is to be regarded as sinful, but the allowance and encouragement of doubting; for it is, as he explains, a peculiar form of temptation, and ought therefore to be resisted as a temptation. He has also a word to say against those who urged that the putting aside of

[1] *Life*, iii. p. 149. [2] *Essays*, Bishop Wilberforce, ii. p. 160.
[3] *Ibid.* p. 161. [4] *Ibid.* p. 210.

differences, which he advocated in the face of a common danger, was too much an attempt to unite, by a community of present hatred, those who had before represented really different sides of the common truth. His answer is, that it is "the agreement rather of men, who have inherited jointly some vast treasure, and who in times of security have differed, it may be, something in their several estimates of the value of its various parts, to defend in a moment of danger the priceless deposit against the common robber." Thus their bond of union was not hatred of the assailant, but love for that which he assails.

In the whole matter there were three things at which Bishop Wilberforce aimed, so as to get the truth established and maintained. Firstly, at direct assault on the assailants in defence of the threatened doctrines. Secondly, at the calm, comprehensive, and scholarlike declaration of positive truth upon all the matters in dispute. Lastly, at "the distinct, solemn, and if need were, severe decision of authority, that assertions of the character found in *Essays and Reviews* could not be put forward as possibly true, or even advanced as admitting of question by honest men, who were bound by voluntary obligations to teach the Christian revelation as the truth of God." It was to this end that he moved Convocation to do as it had not been able to do for a hundred and fifty years, and censure and condemn the book that caused the offence, and so, by implication, the phase of thought to which it belonged. And the result has been here, as so often in the long and chequered history of Christ's Church, that the attempts of teachers of error have been overruled, and have led, as in the case of Arius, to a more complete assertion, understanding, and triumph of the impugned truth.

There are yet one or two other actions of Bishop Wilberforce which should be mentioned here, as belonging to his defence and maintenance of the authority of Scripture, and the creeds of the Church. The temper of the times towards this authority led him to resist the attempts to alter the Prayer-Book, so as to make the Church of England more comprehensive, that there might be included in the Established Church, as it was urged, a "Livingstone or a Havelock." He would have no such sacrifices of truth as were thus proposed, and, knowing the danger of even more sweeping demands and comprehensions, advised to let the quiet waters remain still and leave the Prayer-Book alone. We can trace his reverence for Scripture in his dealings with the Divorce Bill in 1856, when he fought against provisions such as that allowing the re-marriage of divorced persons during the lifetime of the divorced husband or wife, as being in opposition to the Word of God which is embodied in the law of our Church. Again in 1872 he resisted proposals that would have led to the practical shelving of the Athanasian Creed. The time was a critical one, as the Broad Church party were urgent for a change in the use of the Creed to the extent, at least, of making it always alternative with the Apostles' Creed. The High Churchmen, on their side, threatened a serious defection from the Church of England if the Creed were touched. The situation was further complicated by the fact that the Letter of Business sent to Convocation, when it met at that time, gave it a new liberty in allowing its members to debate, consult, and agree upon points, matters, and things contained in the fourth and final report of the Ritual Commissioners. This involved the consideration of the use of the Athanasian Creed in the Church Services; and it was mainly by the Bishop's tact that the matter was left in a condition that at any rate saved a disruption. Witness Dr. Pusey's words in a letter to him—"Thanks be to God. I bless Him for your Lordship's interposition."

It remains to say a few words about the counsels suggested by Bishop Wilberforce in the difficulties with Bishop Colenso. On this occasion, as in the matter of *Essays and Reviews*—where the two writers who were prosecuted, though condemned in the Court of Arches, were acquitted on appeal—it became plain that, when men were called on to answer charges involving false doctrine, their position in the eye of the law was likely to seem different from what it would appear in the eye of the Church. Their offences were criminal under the existing institutions, and thus they got the benefit of every doubt, and were very properly tried by the *letter* of the formularies. Bishop Wilberforce would have liked Convocation, or a body of episcopal referees, to have expounded first, in all these cases, what the real doctrines involved in them were, and then that the Courts should have decided under the guidance thus given. Failing this, decisions given in the Courts involving doctrines were often eminently unsatisfactory to Churchmen, and seemed to bring very perilously near a secession from the Church. It was to allay the alarms of men like these, that Convocation was brought to condemn *Essays and Reviews*, and that it was moved also to give opinions on Bishop Colenso's position after the publication of his books, and especially after his excommunication by the Bishop of Capetown. Once again, in all this, Bishop Wilberforce took a prominent part, and worked to bring about such a position of affairs as would give Churchmen a ground for being satisfied, and cause the Anglican Communion in England, and beyond it, to seem to speak with one voice. In the Colenso trouble the situation was much complicated by the divisions of opinion amongst the English bishops themselves, not indeed as to the errors contained in Bishop Colenso's books on the Epistle to the Romans and the Pentateuch, but as to the possibility, the expediency, and even the justice of accomplishing anything real against him.

In 1862, after the publication of the first book, and a letter from Bishop Gray to Bishop Wilberforce asking that he would consult the Archbishop and the other bishops on his behalf, Bishop Wilberforce tried to get a common agreement of the bishops. His idea was that they should say to Bishop Colenso, on his arrival in England, "that he came under a sort of question as to his soundness by his metropolitan; that *they* had read the book, and without adjudging whether it was heretical or not, were persuaded that its language was, to say the least, such that it *must* suggest to the reader the most unsound views; that they therefore invited its suppression; and, failing that, agreed to request him not to officiate in their dioceses until the matter had been legally examined."[1] Common action proved impracticable, but individual bishops meant to proceed on the above lines. For the peace of the Church, Bishop Wilberforce, who had a friendship with Bishop Colenso, and by his addresses in Cornwall had first roused in him the missionary spirit, tried privately to induce him, while in England, to do nothing to compel the bishops, either individually or collectively, to notice his publication.

[1] *Life*, iii. p. 115, etc.

This was in vain, and the bold statements in *The Pentateuch Critically Examined*, published soon after, forced on some action. At a meeting of bishops, Bishop Wilberforce tried to pass a resolution, "that the bishops agreed, under a great scandal, without passing judgment as to heresy, to inhibit." Stormy scenes and divided counsels characterized this "painful meeting," and at the end a committee was appointed, of which Bishop Wilberforce was a member, to draw up a letter to Bishop Colenso, which was signed by forty-one bishops. The essence of this letter is contained in the following passage—"It cannot have escaped you, that the inconsistency between the office you hold and the opinions you avow is causing great pain and grievous scandal to the Church. And we solemnly ask you to consider once more, with the most serious attention, whether you can, without harm to your own conscience, retain your position, when you can no longer discharge its duties, or use the formularies to which you have subscribed."

This was all of no effect, as was also the desire of the Lower House of Convocation that the book on the Pentateuch should be synodically condemned. The Upper House would take no action then, as they believed the book was to be submitted to the judgment of an ecclesiastical court. It had already been ruled, in the case of Long *v.* Bishop of Capetown, that the letters patent, constituting the Bishop of Capetown metropolitan and giving him jurisdiction, were invalid. The Bishop of Capetown therefore claimed a consensual jurisdiction, as the Bishop of Natal had accepted his metropolitical authority; and the only appeal from himself, that *he* would acknowledge, was to the Archbishop of Canterbury as Patriarch. On his return to Capetown, the metropolitan tried and condemned Bishop Colenso and deposed him from his See, and was prepared to excommunicate him if contumacious. Bishop Colenso then presented a petition to the Crown, which was referred to the Judicial Committee, not appealing against the sentence of his metropolitan, for he ignored it, but asking that all the proceedings should be declared null and void, and that he should be entitled to hold his See until the letters patent granted to him should have been cancelled by due process of law.

At this juncture, Bishop Wilberforce was anxious, first of all, to keep the Bishop of Capetown from taking any further steps till the members of the Judicial Committee had given their decision; and was disposed to think that, after the judgment in the case of Archdeacon Long, they would refuse to hear the case at all. His influence brought it about that, when the suit was heard, the Bishop of Capetown did appear by counsel under protest; and, though this was beyond his instructions from the Bishop of Capetown at the time, the latter afterwards acquiesced in the arrangement as wisest and most respectful to the Queen. When the judgment given by Lord Westbury decided that Bishop Gray's letters patent did not give him supreme control over the Church in South Africa, and that *in law* his deposition of Bishop Colenso was null and void, the Bishop of Oxford tried to persuade him not to excommunicate. His opinion was that, while the deposition, though canonically and spiritually valid, was not legally so, to excommunicate would only be to increase difficulties; he knew that bishops at home would not be got, as a body, to ratify a sentence of excommunication; and he felt that an opinion sorrowfully expressed by Mr. Keble at the time was a right one, viz., "that nobody then—at least no Anglican—with very few exceptions, really believed in excommunication," and so it would be disregarded and a world-wide scandal. His advice was that Bishop Gray should at once consecrate a new bishop for Natal. In a letter to him in 1865 he accordingly writes thus—"I should advise you to get the laity and clergy to meet and elect a bishop. . . I would then have a trust deed carefully drawn, which he and those who would should sign, declaring himself bishop of the South African Church in full communion with us. I would have him take office on condition of being able to carry out all the resolutions, canons, etc., diocesan and provincial, of your own body; and one of them should be to submit himself to your judgment, etc., when need was, *in camera*, as completely and in the same degree as he would be bound to do if you had legal jurisdiction as metropolitan." This was at last done; but, by the time the new bishop was consecrated, Bishop Colenso had returned to Natal, having also obtained a decision that forced the Colonial Bishoprics Fund still to pay him his salary on the ground that his letters patent still held good. The account of the struggle between the Church in South Africa and Bishop Colenso does not belong to the matters we are discussing. In May 1865, Bishop Wilberforce moved an address to the Bishop of Capetown, which was carried, commending his courage, and thanking the Church in South Africa for its "noble stand against heretical and false doctrine." This address passed no opinion on any of the real points of difficulty, and was really a well-meant effort to end the matter decently and quietly.

In November 1865, Bishop Gray did excommunicate Bishop Colenso; and though the Church at home was quite ready to declare that it recognized and held communion with the new Bishop of Natal, it was found very difficult to get a formal recognition of the excommunication. In 1868 the Lower House of Convocation was prepared to give this, but the Upper House was not; and the matter ended by the adoption of two suggestions of a committee appointed by the Upper House, setting forth that "substantial justice had been done to the accused, and that though the Bishop of Capetown's sentence could claim no legal effect, yet the Church, as a spiritual body, could rightly accept its validity." The whole case illustrates the way in which the Established Church was hampered by its legal position, and the timidity with which its leaders faced new situations born from developments in Church life, which, though healthy and wholesome, were to them strange. The Bishop of Oxford used his great influence to hinder disruptions, which were threatened under such circumstances, and to secure opportunities for the Church to justify herself in the eyes of men by her work.

In 1867, the first meeting of what is now known as the Pan-Anglican synod was held at Lambeth. It was a natural outcome of the great growth in organized Church life, which had taken place as the American, colonial, and missionary episcopates increased and extended. It was undertaken at the suggestion of the Canadian and colonial bishops, and was regarded with some suspicion at first by authorities in England, as an undue and dangerous advancement of ecclesiastical claims, and as implying a sort of insubordination against legitimate State control. Thus it was that Dean Stanley felt himself obliged to refuse the use of Westminster Abbey to the seventy-eight bishops, who wished to communicate together there, before they began their deliberations at Lambeth. The fact that Bishop Gray desired to obtain on this occasion a condemnation of Bishop Colenso, while the Archbishop had practically pledged himself to some of his suffragans that this matter should not be brought up, threatened troubles that might well have made the first meeting of the Pan-Anglican synod its last. Once again the Bishop of Oxford, as he expresses it, "gentled" the Bishop of Capetown, and the question of the validity of the excommunication was not brought formally forward, though fifty-six of the bishops signed a declaration pronouncing it a "spiritually valid sentence." The following passage from a letter to Bishop Milman shows us what Bishop Wilberforce really thought and felt in this "very anxious matter of the Pan-Anglican synod." "We cannot," he writes, "act synodically; and yet to meet and not to act has a damaging air of weakness. The great practical difficulty is Colenso. Passing him over *is* a practical recognition of the excommunication, which is of no small value; and yet being silent when the Church, if she could, certainly ought to speak, is no small evil, and must be a scandal."[1] The result of his work and efforts is indicated in the following passage in his diary for September 27, 1867— "Carried, against London, Winchester and St. David's, our acquiescence in the advice tendered by Convocation to Natal." This was in effect to declare the See vacant; and the committee appointed to consider the Natal

[1] *Life*, iii. p. 229.

scandal reported to the same effect, and urged the Church in South Africa to consecrate another bishop. At the same time a committee was also appointed to report on the best means of maintaining unity in faith and discipline among the several branches of the Anglican Communion, which recommended the organization of a synodal order. Its reports were received and published, though not formally adopted by the conference; and it illustrates the position that the Bishop of Oxford held amongst the bishops of his communion to note that the Encyclical Letter was drawn up by him; and a letter to him from the Rev. Sir H. Thompson describes it "as a very creditable document, of which the vast body of the clergy would greatly approve, owing to the calm, dignified and affectionate spirit that it breathed throughout." A further extract from a letter to Mr. Gordon, written by the Bishop in November, shows how much he thought that the Pan-Anglican synod, with its suggestions, might be a means of settling many difficulties in a manner satisfactory to Churchmen. His words are—
"The Lambeth gathering was a very great success. Its strongly anti-Erastian tone . . . . strengthening those who hope to maintain the Establishment by maintaining, instead of by surrendering, the dogmatic character of the Church, was quite remarkable. We are now sitting in committee trying to complete our work, by agreeing to a court of highest doctrinal appeal for the free colonies of America. If we can carry this out, we shall have erected a barrier of immense moral strength against the Privy Council Latitudinarianism. My view is that God gives us the opportunity, as at home Latitudinarianism must spread, of encircling the home

Church with a band of far more dogmatic truth-holding communions, who will act most strongly in favour of truth here."

This last idea of Bishop Wilberforce's, that the English Church in foreign lands might, from her greater liberty and perhaps reality, re-act favourably and usefully on the Church at home, is altogether a most important one to dwell upon in considering his work and services. It was very necessary that the Church, in face of panics, and jealousies, and Erastian notions about her position that prevailed at home, should have a field where she could be seen working as a spiritual organization, and not so much as a State machine. We are told that Bishop Wilberforce's diaries and letter-books show that he came at last to be consulted in matters of doubt and difficulty, by bishops and others belonging to the Anglican Communion in all parts of the world. Certainly he had a very great part and share in the development of all the daughter churches, which now send their bishops to attend the Pan-Anglican synods at Lambeth. He was an unwearied and enthusiastic supporter of Bishop Blomfield's great movement for increasing the colonial episcopate, and he laboured unceasingly to establish for the colonial missionary dioceses their right and true position of freedom from legal trammels, that are part of the burden that the Church of England bears, in England itself, from its establishment.

We have already seen how strongly Bishop Wilberforce pressed the necessity, in efforts made for spreading Christianity over the whole world, of missions and colonial churches being headed by bishops, if the Christianity taught was to be a sound and real one based upon a distinct dogma of the faith, and connected with the distinct discipline of the English Church. Now there was long a deep-rooted prejudice, in the minds of many Churchmen and men in authority in England, against this sending out of bishops for foreign Anglican churches; it was thought that they might well be put under the control of bishops at home. Thus in 1829, when the Duke of Wellington felt that the rapidly increasing Australian colonies must have a Church, it seemed to him sufficient to send out *one archdeacon*. Bishop Wilberforce was unceasing in his efforts to destroy the evil effects of this fallacy, and in maintaining the principle that it was essential that a Church in a new country should have a bishop, if it was to grow and develope, and that the appointment of a bishop should come first, and not last, in its organization. Some thought that, in the matter of missionary churches especially, the only safe thing was to have them under central control. It was this feeling that led the Church Missionary Society to hinder in 1853 the passing of the Church Missionary Bishops' Bill, to enable English prelates to consecrate British subjects to act as bishops in a foreign or heathen country. Bishop Wilberforce was active in obtaining its passage through the House of Lords, and getting support for it in the Commons, where it was lost. In the second volume of his *Life*, there is a correspondence with Sir James Stephen, whom the Bishop takes to task for misrepresenting the bishops and their aims and objects in passing this Bill. The Bishop complains there, that it was the fear that was felt by the Church Missionary Society of missionary bishops superseding Church Missionary committees, which really hindered the bishops from being allowed to head a mission of their Church in Borneo with one of their own order.

But most difficult of all was the question as to the colonial and missionary bishops and the royal supremacy, and their relations to the See of Canterbury. Gradually it has become clear how apparently conflicting interests and principles may be reconciled in this matter; and so a position and understanding fairly satisfactory to the Churches of the Anglican Communion has been reached. Ministers have come to see that the appointment of bishops in colonies and lands beyond the jurisdiction of the Crown are not rightly dependent on a royal license, and that an Anglican Church's free and voluntary action in choosing a bishop is no violation of royal supremacy, or subversive of any vital principle governing the right relations of Church and State in the British constitution. Those who once thought that there could be no episcopacy without prelacy, and that an Anglican bishop must always be, in his appointment and legal position, just as a bishop of the Established Church in England, have learnt to see their error in this respect, and to acknowledge that such a theory was calculated rather to hinder than aid that Church life and expansion which they themselves most desired to advance. Many laboured to secure what the Church needed in this matter, and to show that for them, as Bishop Blomfield put it, "an episcopal Church without a bishop is a contradiction in terms." Many also laboured to bring it about, that Anglican bishops might be seen to be something different from that which Lord Westbury described Bishop Gray and Bishop Colenso to be, in the preamble of his judgment on the Colenso case, where he speaks of them as "ecclesiastical persons who have been created bishops by the Queen, in the exercise of her authority as sovereign of this realm, and head of the Established Church." On all occasions, however, where these points and questions were under discussion, and some new step was to be made, Bishop Wilberforce took a prominent part, vindicating now the right of English bishops to consecrate men for the new work abroad; now the necessity of these new leaders taking the oath of canonical obedience to their own metropolitans; and now, as in the Colenso case, the importance to the Church and Churchmen of decisions that had a spiritual rather than a merely legal character. So it was that he, and others of like mind, found in Lord Westbury's Colenso judgment, "bristling as it was with Erastian insults," the charter of freedom for the colonial Church. In declaring that the Crown had no power to grant authority by letters patent to one bishop as metropolitan in a colony which had secured a constitution, it had decided that the Church in South Africa was only capable of holding jurisdiction when it was given by the State *there*. This was what Bishop Wilberforce had always wished to secure, and his desire for it may explain, in some measure, his much criticized action in 1853, when he supported the measure for giving to the Canadian Legislature the power and right to deal with the lands belonging to the Church in Canada called the "Clergy Reserves." Unexpectedly, Lord Westbury's judgment was seen to be after all "of good omen for the Church." It seemed to set the colonial Church free from being hampered, from home, with State restrictions. "The Churches might now be at liberty to uphold discipline by consensual arrangements, and the domination of the Privy Council was at an end."[1]

So it was again that, in 1867, Bishop Wilberforce was able to deliver himself of the following opinion as to the true position of colonial Churches, with some confidence that his ideas were at least in a fair way to be realized. He explained that the Church of England was a purely voluntary body in the colonies, and had no connection with the Crown, save that its members were subjects of the Queen. He showed that it was a mistake to suppose, therefore, that the Church in the colonies had the same power of appeal to the Privy Council as the Church at home. Lastly, he said that "the connection between the colonial Church and the Church in England was to be maintained by allowing the Church in the colonies to develope for itself the true Church of England temper, profession of faith, doctrine, and internal government, thus giving it the help they could give it to stand up among free men there, itself there a free Church, among free religionists a free religion." A zeal for missionary enterprise and Church extension is an essential part of the work of a living Christian Church; it follows necessarily from a right recognition by the Church of its real responsibilities and privileges. Bishop Wilberforce's efforts to direct the awakening zeal in this respect that characterized the Church movements of his day, and his unwearied labour and care for the right development of the Anglican episcopate abroad, did almost more than anything else to raise and improve the general standard of episcopal life and work amongst the members of the bench of bishops at home.

[1] Perry's *English Church History*, iii. p. 379.

CHAPTER VIII.

RITUALISM AND DISESTABLISHMENT.

THESE pages have traced thus far Bishop Wilberforce's part, sometimes by way of sympathy and sometimes by way of restraint, in the onward and developing movement in the Church of England, which belonged to the time of his episcopate. He had a firm belief in his Church as divinely instituted and commissioned, and felt sure that, if only she had scope, time, and opportunity, she would amply justify herself to the world. Above all things he tried to secure for her this necessary liberty, and was ever conspicuous in his efforts to obtain for the Church her right position as against the State, and to free her from disabilities, in this direction, which past mistakes and errors, partly in action, partly in acquiescence, had laid upon her. The fact that, at different times, he incurred obloquy from all parties and schools of thought in the Church, shows that at any rate, in his endeavours, he did achieve his own expressed ambition of not being the Bishop of a party; and more than any one else he did over and over again manage to secure a *modus vivendi*, at times when a disruption seemed inevitable.

Now, at no time, and under no circumstances, was

this more conspicuously shown than in Bishop Wilberforce's guidance of the Church of England, through all the troubles which arose, in the Church revival of his times, from what we know as Ritualism. To this hour, long after the grave has closed over the great Bishop of Oxford and Winchester, those troubles still exist. Some have seen in the steps taken since his death, and the exasperations consequent upon them, a greater witness than in anything else to the influence that he exercised in putting forward wise and moderate counsels, and restraining ill-advised attempts at repression. There is a story told of a visit paid by Dean Stanley to St. Alban's, Holborn, after which he was asked by the Bishop of London what he had seen. "I saw," he said, "three men in green, and your Lordship will have great difficulty in putting them down." We have now to consider what Bishop Wilberforce did in the two directions of preventing ill-considered and ill-devised measures for putting Ritualists down, and hindering men inclined to Ritualism from setting up, at their own pleasure and inclination, rites and ceremonies long in abeyance.

From the first, in his diocese, and in the Church at large, Bishop Wilberforce had a sympathy with the movement, out of which ritual excesses and extravagances at last sprang. He quite saw that the standard of ritual in the Church of England had fallen below what decency and order required, and that it needed to be brought up to it. All efforts in this direction had his fullest sympathy and support, and he evidently felt that, for the time at any rate, progressive, as distinct from merely repressive, zeal in the Church of England was found most in those who were disposed to work for this end. Men were learning to beautify their houses in a time of considerable material prosperity; he quite thought that it was only right to make the "houses of God in the land" beautiful too. Better modes of teaching were being used everywhere, and, more particularly in the education of the poor, there was a general desire and tendency to make instruction more interesting. Bishop Wilberforce quite felt that the Catholic Church had, as part of her lawful heritage, a resource of long-neglected ceremony and ritual, which might well be drawn upon to make worship more instructive and interesting too. Lastly, truer and fuller views on Eucharistic doctrine had come to prevail in the Church of England; and Bishop Wilberforce knew that there were lawful ceremonies, connected with the great sacrament of the Church, which would, if used, help to inspire a greater reverence, and bring out true doctrine rather than suggest, as many feared they would, that which was false. With ritual excess and extravagance, however, he had no sympathy, and is found to speak and work against it quite as strongly as he spoke and worked against the errors of the Church of Rome.

Events had shown that there was, in the Established Church of England, a greater liberty and elasticity, in matters of doctrine, than many had supposed, or desired to suppose. The Ritualistic difficulties brought out the fact that a like greater elasticity in ritual was also not only allowable, but desirable. This was a point on which Bishop Wilberforce was disposed most clearly and pointedly to insist, as the following passage from his Charge in 1866 shows:—"Such a moderate and sober development of its ceremonial seems to me to belong necessarily to the Church as a living body; nor, if it be at all in its normal condition, can its Ritual be healthily congealed into absolutely unalterable forms. Life implies, of necessity, change . . . . Death only secures immutability. No less certainly must the outward expression of the life spiritual change with the changes of its inner currents. Again, in any normal condition of the Church, the spiritual necessities of the body necessitate changes. Every varying phase through which it is passing renders some change expedient, perhaps essential to life. The bark-bound tree, the hide-bound animal, must suffer, and too often die. The rigid clasp of an unalterable ritual may fatally repress zeal, generate formality, or nourish superstition. In the normal condition, therefore, of the Church, ritual must be, and ought to be, elastic and subject to variations." [1]

In the development, and in the application of this requisite liberty, Bishop Wilberforce held that it was not desirable to apply for legal decisions to the Church Courts, and also that it was too long and hazardous to "wait for the tedious issues of actual legislation." His idea was that peace was largely attainable, if men would leave matters in their bishop's hands, as the following passage shows—" How often, alas, in our own and in every other Church has the ebbing tide of the spiritual life, by its mere listlessness, reduced to its own new level its nominally unaltered ritual! How often, thank God! has renewed love and renewed earnestness in devotion filled the old limbs with a flood of life which has transfigured forms which it retained! And it is the special duty of the Church's governors to understand such symptoms, and to minister to their relief whatever powers of relaxation or control have

[1] *Charge* 1866, pp. 52-3.

been left to them, without incurring the hazard or waiting for the tedious issues of actual legislation. Many such powers our own Church has lodged in its living governors. It is their charge to interpret ambiguous rubrics, to reduce to unity matters diversely taken, to acquiesce in or disallow changes which by minute accretions the living body has silently developed. Great, no doubt, is the judgment, the courage, the knowledge, and, above all, perhaps, the impartiality which is needful to enable them to discharge aright these delicate and often momentous duties. But they cannot leave these duties undone without grievous danger to the polity over which they are appointed overseers; and, however difficult be the task, there is a strength for its discharge which they who seek it faithfully will find. Such difficulties are the sure accompaniments of times of earnestness and growth; when the full amount of the inner life must, by reason of its strength, cast itself forth into some new development. Dull and lazy governors marvel at and hate such things; and there is a mixture enough of evil in all such movements to make such a feeling plausible at least, if not natural." Thus it was that he and the other bishops in 1867, on receiving the report of the Lower House of Convocation on Ritualism, sent down a resolution based on the rubric concerning the service of the Church in the Book of Common Prayer, in which the Lower House concurred, to the effect that "no alterations from long sanctioned and usual ritual ought to be made in Churches until the sanction of the bishop of the diocese had been obtained thereto." So it is again that many letters of Bishop Wilberforce are extant in which, while on the one side, to quote his words, he tries to restrain the "parish Diotrephes seeking to dictate merely to those who are set over him in the Lord," on the other he rebukes the zeal, indiscretion, or perversity which suddenly started changes in the externals of worship, without due regard for the feelings or prejudices of the body of worshippers on whom they were imposed.

Bishop Wilberforce was always strong in insisting that in all ritual changes, however slight, as they had to do with accessories and not with essentials, the thing to be first regarded was the welfare and, to some considerable extent, the wish of the people. "I do *not*," he writes in 1866, "call on you to preach in the surplice, if you in your discretion think it not for the peace of the Church to do so." In the whole question he held that allowance ought to be made for the "differing conformations of men's minds." A speech of his in Convocation contains the following words on this point—"The conformation of my mind leads me to be satisfied with the simplest form as being the most productive of devotion; but it is not so with others, and I have no right to make what suits me the law for everybody else."

A ritual revival under the then existing circumstances of the Church, and temper of the times, seemed to Bishop Wilberforce natural enough. It was the right reaction against a too great dread of lawful ritual as superstitious, and belonged to a needed effort to bring the standard of the celebration of the Holy Eucharist in the Church of England up to that set by the Reformers.[1] At the same time the Bishop seemed to see everywhere, not only in our own Communion, but in the more earnest

---

[1] *Charge* 1866, p. 50.

of the religious sects around it, "a craving for a more expressive symbolism in worship, which was probably a reaction against the chillness in which Puritanism had long been dying out, and against the utter vagueness of modern doubts."[1] In his Charge for 1866, however, the Bishop makes it clear that the healthy tendency had to his mind more than begun to pass into an unhealthy extreme. He says plainly that he considers "actual ritual developments so hastily adopted, in their novelty, multiplication, and amount, as rash, unadvisable, and dangerous." He deplores what seems to him "the unquestionable fact that in some instances there had been a studied introduction of names and usages, which seemed to him to have nothing else to commend them than their distinctively Roman character."[2] Under the circumstances, and in face of the difficulties and excesses of the time, the Bishop in his Charge lays down four conditions under which ritual progress is allowable. It must not, he urges, be contrary to the law; it must not tend to promote any false doctrine or corrupt practice; it must be at the least not condemned by living authority; it must be the gradual expression in outer things of the advancement of the Church's inward life.

In his own diocese the Bishop of Oxford proceeded successfully on the lines that we have considered. He advocated advance by "insensible gradation rather than a studied display of large and rapid change." He tried to induce all who were making ritual changes to "lay their case before their Bishop, and act absolutely on his direction." He urged the necessity of considering congregations and their wants, tempers, and capa-

[1] *Charge* 1866, p. 55.   [2] *Ibid.* p. 45.

bilities, and impressed the error of trying to maintain "frozen uniformity" in any direction. The following passage from his Charge shows the result—" It is carefully to be noted, that where the Church movement itself has been the deepest, there Ritualistic extravagances have the least appeared. No diocese, perhaps, from various causes, has risen more than that of Oxford, with the general rise of Church devotion; none has been more free from these peculiar excesses."

A brief account of Bishop Wilberforce's more public labours in the matter of Ritualism will best show how he aimed at serving and strengthening the Church, by retaining for her the good in the movement, and rejecting what seemed to him the evil in it. In 1851 Mr. Bennett's proceedings in the London diocese first raised the question as to the limits of ritual in the Church of England. He put forward, amongst other things, the plea that omission in the rubrics of the Prayer-book was not prohibition; and claimed to revive a great deal of ceremony that had long been in abeyance, on the ground that it was inherited from the primitive Church, and was not really connected with Roman error, though cast aside in the reactionary panic of the Reformation. At the time Bishop Wilberforce expresses himself on these points to the Hon. R. Cavendish and Mr. Gladstone as follows—"I cannot admit that any individual clergyman has a *right* to restore pre-Reformation observances, merely because they are not *totidem verbis* condemned by our Church." And again—"The ground on which the Bishop of London accepted Mr. Bennett's resignation, I understood to be the principle avowed by Mr. Bennett of *continual progression*, combined with an assertion of his right to introduce any ceremony which had ever been used in the Church, and which was not expressly condemned and forbidden at our Reformation. This principle I also esteem to be faulty, believing that our system was intended to be affirmative and not simply negative, and that it does not therefore become individual clergymen to restore from ante-Reformation times whatever was not *totidem verbis* forbidden."[1] On these grounds Bishop Wilberforce joined in the united pastoral issued by the Bishops in 1851, protesting against Mr. Bennett's point of view, and specially his way of asserting it.

Meanwhile till 1867 the Ritualistic development went on; and was at once restrained and encouraged in the Oxford diocese, where the Bishop recognized that, in such things as choral services, surpliced choirs, Church decorations, using of hymns, things lawful and helpful were being revived. Of course, to the school represented by the *Record*, improvements in the service in the direction of legitimate increases of ritual seemed dangerous, and its adherents felt bound to resist them. The Bishop of Oxford, however, while expressing his utter disapproval of all attempts to introduce "unusual Ritualistic developments," saw that, in many cases, laity and clergy alike were ripe and ready for some ceremonial changes and restorations. This might well be, he maintained, where there was no revival of the obsolete, without the allowance of living authority, and where, in the case of a parish linked by long tradition to a lower but lawful use, "there was no arbitrary alteration for the pastor's pleasure to the wounding of his flock."[2] At the same time in his charges, and by his own practice, he directed obedience

[1] *Life*, ii. pp. 126-7. [2] *Ibid.* iii. p. 197.

to the decisions, on points of ritual, of the highest court of appeal in causes ecclesiastical. Thus we have the following passage in his Charge for 1857—"The peace which God's mercy has given to us in this diocese on these matters (*i.e.* questions of ritual) makes it needful for me to speak but of two points, in the late judgment, as to which my own observations would lead me to think that in our conduct of our public services we are violating, in some of our parishes, what we are now authoritatively reminded is the plain and express law of this Church and realm; and to obey which, now that it is so pointed out, we of the clergy are in conscience bound by our oaths and promises at our ordination, licensing, or institution." In the spirit here indicated Bishop Wilberforce, after the Martin *v.* Mackonochie judgment, changed the position in which he had previously stood; and, during the Consecration Prayer in the office for Holy Communion, stood in front of the Table. When again at a later time the point was otherwise decided, the Bishop, in obedience to the law, reverted to his original position at the north end. The Bishop's action in his own diocese showed a mode by which, if all could have agreed to act on it, without the dangers of legislation and judicial decisions, the worst difficulties occasioned by Ritualistic extravagances might have been obviated and controlled to the great advantage of the Church, and the furthering and advancement of her most important influence and work.

But a general consensus on the matter was by no means easy to obtain. What must be described as the puritanical spirit was strong in England, objecting to the Church's whole system of external rites and ceremonies, and regarding, as Bishop Wilberforce says, "our limited customary rites as an essential part of our protest against Popery." It was a perplexity that some of the bishops themselves were not free from this spirit; and, while there were dioceses in which Churchmen were not at all ready to defer to the "living authority" placed at their head, divided counsels prevailed on the bench of bishops itself. By 1866 it had become plain that, in the opposition and apprehension excited by a not uncommon display of large and rapid changes in ritual of an extreme character, something must be done. There was great danger lest attempts might be made to bind the Church of England down to a rigid minimum in the matter, which might lead to the loss of some of the most earnest of her sons. In his Charge for 1866, Bishop Wilberforce expresses, in the following passage, this difficulty—"We are bound to admit that amongst the clergy and laity (for this has been anything but an exclusively clerical movement), who are conspicuous for the introduction of these novelties, are men inferior to none in self-devotion, in apparent love to Christ, in tenderness towards His poor, in zeal for His truth, or in the fervour of their own devotion. Such men we can ill afford to lose. •I trust that no taunts from without, and no timorousness within, will lead any of the rulers of our Church to aid in driving out any one who can, consistently with truth and faithfulness, be kept amongst us, lest we repeat again our fathers' fault, and lose our brethren, as they lost John Wesley, and his noble fellows." It was this that he strove to prevent. The Lower House of Convocation in 1866 asked the Upper House to take steps, in conjunction with them, for "clearing the doubts and allaying the anxieties that existed on the subject of Ritualism." As a result, a committee was appointed, which reported in the following year, deprecating attempts to establish a uniformity of ritual practice, "incompatible with the power, which had ever existed in the Church, of permitting differences of practice, according to the different circumstances and requirements of different times, places, and congregations." The report further suggested, that differences of ritual practice, within the limits of the law, ought to be regulated by resort to the fatherly counsel of the bishop, and dutiful acquiescence in his suggestions, and also by "discreet and charitable consideration of the circumstances of different places and congregations." This was endorsed by the Upper House, and runs very much on the lines on which Bishop Wilberforce acted in his own diocese, and which he laid down in his charge.

Meanwhile other action was being taken, by way of legislation through Parliament, without any previous consultation of Convocation. Bishop Wilberforce thought any legislation just then dangerous; but that proposed, ignoring, as it did, the Church's voice and opinion, seemed to him absolutely fatal, a surrender of much that had been laboriously gained, and certain to cause a secession from the Church. He did a great service in averting it, and preventing any new departure, even though it was done at the cost of preserving the, not very satisfactory, *status in quo ante*.

In 1865 the Archbishop was stirred up to some action by the Marquis of Westmeath calling attention in the House of Lords to alleged innovations in the Anglican service. He desired to issue an address to the clergy, signed by all the bishops, but by the advice of the Bishop of Oxford, and owing to the difficulty of getting anything signed by all the bishops which was not very general indeed in its character, this was not done. Some of the bishops were for trying a test case; some were for "fatherly counsel"; some for legislation; and the difficulties of the situation were set out in a remark of the Bishop of Exeter—"If you try to enforce the rubric, you will have a rebellion; try to alter it, and you will cause a shipwreck."

At this time, as before, in matters touching the interests of the Church, Bishop Wilberforce consulted much with Mr. Gladstone, following largely his advice, and relying on his political influence for support of wise measures. The great problem was how to prevent legislation, which would fetter the Church, and hopelessly alienate many staunch Churchmen. The gist of Mr. Gladstone's opinion on this matter may be gathered from the following paragraph—"I am against attempts, in present circumstances, to define ritual too much by quantity; it is quality, proportion, relation, which seem to me to have the true claim to regard. I do not think you can define the maximum of true legitimate demand; which, under much of the existing demand, in appearance moderate, may notwithstanding be quite illegitimate." Bishop Wilberforce's own ideas on these matters are expressed fully in his Charge for 1866. In his diocese, and with the Archbishop, his words were generally approved, though a small section sent an address to the Bishop, complaining of "his Lordship's elaborate, but, in their judgment, singularly ambiguous and unsatisfactory charge."[1] His efforts, after this

[1] *Life*, iii. p. 203.

plain expression of his opinions, were directed towards preventing any hasty and unwise legislation. The result has been, largely through his influence, that the matter, as far as legislation goes, has practically been left alone—the only safe course, when desirable changes and interpretations must inevitably have been balanced by most undesirable ones.

An extract from a letter to Mr. Gladstone shows the first difficulty which Bishop Wilberforce had to face and overcome. The letter asks for Mr. Gladstone's intervention with the Archbishop to prevent the evil of the bishops coming with a gagging bill before the House of Commons. The passage in question runs thus—" Last Monday it transpired that Lord Shaftesbury had printed and proposed to read at once a first time a bill, drawn by A. J. Stephens, for making the 58th canon the absolute and sole rule of the Church of England as to ornaments, dresses, etc., throwing over the rights of congregations, the discretion of bishops, and the liberty of the Church for all future expansion. . . . The Archbishop called a meeting of the bishops next day, at which it at once appeared that the whole phalanx of Archbishop and bishops from the north, and all the puritan bishops were hot for it—only three of us opposed it. Worst of all, our own Archbishop, though he did not like it, 'did not see how he could oppose it.' I set before them at length the ignominy of the course, its shameless party spirit, the suicide of the English episcopate being dragged at the tail of Shaftesbury; and I so far succeeded that the bishops in league with Shaftesbury said that, if the Archbishop would undertake to legislate, they would persuade Shaftesbury to wait."[1]

[1] *Life*, iii. p. 206.

The alternative seemed to Bishop Wilberforce bad enough; it was almost worse that the Archbishop should legislate, as it made even more offensive to many "the going to Parliament without Convocation to alter a leading rubric governing all the ornaments and official vesture of the Church of England." After stating his views and apprehensions plainly to the Archbishop, he asked Mr. Gladstone to use his influence to prevent the Archbishop and other bishops proceeding on the lines proposed, either by supporting Lord Shaftesbury, or bringing in another bill. Mr. Gladstone deprecated the raising of the questions in the House of Commons that the bringing in of any such bills would involve, and said that he feared the introduction of them would throw him into a "very anti-episcopal position." His letter also mentions that he had interviewed the two Archbishops and the Bishop of London, and left them in mind "to drop the bill and propose a commission." Lord Shaftesbury did move the second reading of his bill in May 1867, but an amendment, moved by the Archbishop of Canterbury, and supported by Bishop Wilberforce, postponing the second reading till that day two months, was carried by a majority of fifteen, eleven bishops voting in the minority. The bill was not brought on again, and expired with the session; but the entry in the Bishop's diary for the day is significant as to the peril of the moment—"Lord Derby having sent Lord Malmesbury to me to say that the whips reported that he was in a minority, and must give up, I protested. Carried by a good majority of fifteen."

Thus this danger was passed, and a Royal Commission on Ritual appointed in 1867 by Lord Derby's Government. The Bishop of Oxford was desirous that it should be instructed to inquire only into the ornaments rubric, and that something should be said in the Commission as to the results of its labours being submitted afterwards to Convocation. He wrote to Sir C. Anderson in March 1867—"I have no patience with *our* being driven to legislate, to put ourselves in the utterly false position of asking for more power from the House of Commons." His views were not accepted by the Government; it was determined to examine all the rubrics, and also the Lectionary, and no mention was made, in the Commission, of Convocation. It is to be noticed, however, that the two pieces of legislation that followed on this report—the Act of Uniformity Amendment Act of 1872, and the Prayer-Book Act of 1872—allowing the shortening of services, and revising the Lectionary, were approved by Convocation, before coming into Parliament. After the last report of the Ritual Commission, the Crown took the important step of recognizing the several Convocations so far as to issue to them letters of business, authorizing them to consider, and report on, the final recommendations of the Commission. Thus the thing which Bishop Wilberforce stood almost alone in asking for the Church's satisfaction at first was, in effect, granted at last.

Some difficulty arose about Bishop Wilberforce becoming a member of the Commission. Mr. Walpole, in inviting him to serve on it, said that, without him, it would be the drama of *Hamlet* with Hamlet left out; and Lord Shaftesbury said in the House of Lords that, as he himself refused to serve on it as an extreme man, extreme men, like the Bishop of Oxford, ought to keep off it too. The Bishop's reply contained the following words—"It is very easy for the noble Lord to attack me, though he knows I have no extreme views, and though he confesses that he is himself an extreme man. I am not an extreme man. I am one who holds that middle position as to doctrine in the Church that Richard Hooker held." Ultimately he was on the Commission, and took a prominent part in its work, and exercised a large influence over its report. The first report was issued on August 19th, after nineteen sittings, and the draft that was accepted, though nominally the work of Mr. Hubbard, was really the Bishop of Oxford's, as the following extract from his diary for August 19th shows—"Ritual Commission. Long debate on draft report I had drawn up on Tuesday, 13th, and given Hubbard to circulate; substantially adopted." His influence, as Lord Beauchamp testifies, had immensely determined the issue. "I fully recognize," he writes, "the discretion and skill with which you have steered us. How others could have been brought to agree I cannot divine. Our escape has been marvellous." By the Bishop of Oxford's suggestion, the report stated that "it was expedient to *restrain* in the public services of the united Church of England and Ireland, all variation in respect of vesture from that which has long been the established usage of the said United Church." The word used did not make the vestments in themselves illegal; every allusion to doctrine was carefully shut out of the report, and Dr. Pusey's statement, "that it was a complete defeat, and that it would have been better to have had all Shaftesbury's bill and let him do his worst," shows that its elasticity was hardly appreciated on the High Church side. When the second report was issued in 1868, the Bishop of Oxford dissented from a clause in it that recommended that the usage of the Church of England and Ireland for the last *three hundred and sixty years* should be deemed the rule of the Church in respect of vestments, lights, and incense. It was wrong, he thought, to attempt to stereotype by legislation for perpetual observance any use not actually enjoined in matters ceremonial. In the fourth and last report Bishop Wilberforce, then Bishop of Winchester, was one of those who signed with reservation; and many of his fellow commissioners on this occasion dissented from the report on various grounds. His attitude as regards the question raised on the subject of the position of the Athanasian Creed in the services of the Church, has been already discussed. It showed him anxious to prevent secession from the Church on the one hand, and rigid legislation on the other, in accordance with the policy that he had favoured on the ritual question from the time when it was first agitated. On the whole, he obtained such a measure of success, that he once again secured for the Church, during his lifetime, a fair measure of justice and liberty.

As he was in 1851 in this matter so was he in 1866, and so was he in 1873. Dean Burgon quotes from his last address to his rural deans, delivered shortly before his death in 1873, as a clear proof that with Ritualistic teaching he had no sympathy. He tells us in the following passage some of the Bishop's feelings in this matter—"Sometimes he would express his secret personal dislike to the very environments of the party with a grotesque fervour which was irresistible. 'I suspect,' I once said to him, 'you *like* embroidered stoles, surplices cut short at the waist, Gregorian chants, and so on?' '*I* like Gregorian music!' he exclaimed, with a look of mingled terror and annoyance. 'I assure you I never hear a Gregorian without feeling a wish to lie down on my stomach and howl.'"[1]

The address referred to speaks plainly of the teaching that habitual confession is almost necessary for the leading of the higher Christian life, as dangerous to the penitent, to the peace and confidence of family life, and to the confessor's own purity of thought.[2] It condemns the new doctrine of fasting Communion, and the growing practice of non-communicating attendance as leading to the great abuse "of coming to the sacrament to be spectators instead of partakers." "Thus," says the Bishop, "the Roman theory is creeping in. The sacrificing priest stands between your soul and your God and makes atonement for you." A strong passage, quoted also by Dean Burgon, from this same last utterance, may fitly close this brief account of Bishop Wilberforce's dealings with the Ritualistic movement. It runs thus—"There is a growing feeling, which I can only describe as an 'ashamedness' of the Anglican Church, as if our grand old Anglican Communion contrasted unfavourably with the Church of Rome. The habitual language held by many men sounds as if they were *ashamed* of our Church and its position; it is a sort of apology for the Church of England, as compared with the Church of Rome. Why I WOULD AS SOON THINK OF APOLOGIZING FOR THE VIRTUE OF MY MOTHER TO A HARLOT! I have no sympathy in the world with such a feeling. I abhor this fidgety desire to make everything un-Anglican. This is not a grand development as some seem to think. It is a decrepitude. It is not

[1] *Lives of Twelve Good Men,* ii. p. 59.   [2] *Ibid.* ii. pp. 55-7.

something very sublime and impressive, but something very feeble and contemptible."[1]

It is to be noticed that, all through the difficulties we have just considered, Bishop Wilberforce felt that unwise and unlawful actions from within the Church, met by sharp repressive measures from the State without, might do much to imperil the Establishment. In the opening of an article on "The Church and her Curates," in the *Quarterly Review* for 1867, he notices how the "electric" temper of the times threatens the testing anew, by searching popular inquiry, of some of the noblest institutions of the country, and that among these the Established Church stood perhaps in the fore-front. In the same article the Bishop writes, half-humorously, the following words—"An electric condition of the air quickens into a very troublesome activity all the lower forms of animal life; and speculators and nostrum-mongers, and men of one idea, are always excited by a thundery state of the political and social atmosphere. Societies for the Revision of the Prayer-Book, and Anti-State Church Societies, and Liberation Societies, and the like, feel that their time is come, and begin buzzing about amidst the larger and more highly animated organizations which they so pertinaciously infest, and stinging or irritating all whom they can reach."[2] The Bishop felt that the position of the Dissenters towards the Established Church was, by force of circumstances, now changed. The time was past when the Dissenters were asking for equal civil rights, and the removal of tests injurious to their conscience. Writing to Mr. Gladstone

[1] *Lives of Twelve Good Men,* ii. pp. 58-9.
[2] *Essays,* ii. pp. 85-6.

in 1863, on the subject of Mr. Hadfield's bill, which proposed to abolish the declaration made by mayors, that they would not use their office against the Established Church, the Bishop explains that he cannot support it, and adds—"They (the Dissenters) are now professedly seeking, not for freedom for themselves, but the abolition of the Establishment; wherever, therefore, they ask for what tends *only* to that, we are bound to refuse."[1] In the same correspondence also he states that he is unable to admit that the bishops of the Church of England could take the ground that "their strength lay in the affection of the people, and not in the legal defences of an Establishment." This would be in effect to admit that they belonged to the strongest *sect*, and not to claim to be, what they were, the national Church. The relation that seemed to him to exist between Church and State was the result of a concordat between the Catholic Church and the Realm. Changes, then, which affected the national Church, were only to be made constitutionally, after consultation with the clergy, through Convocation, since her existing system is the result of the joint assents of the clergy, the laity, and the Crown of England. The following passage from a speech made at Hastings in 1864 puts clearly the Bishop of Oxford's ideas as to the charge, duties, and position, that he conceived the nation to have intrusted to the Church of England in its establishment. "By the providence of God this much is certain, and must be admitted by every one, that the Church of England, as treated at present by the State and the nation, is the religious teacher of the people. Mark you that this is so. There has been

[1] *Life*, iii. p. 80.

given, and I think very properly given, perfect liberty to all other religious bodies, and I for one would not see that liberty infringed by prerogative or other legislation in the least degree. But that is not in the least degree giving up the claim that the Church of England is the teacher of the people. . . . If you ask me how I can say that the Church of England is the only Apostolic Church in the land, I say that she only possesses the two qualifications, perfectness of organization in a transmitted line of authorized teachers from the Apostles, as apostles from the Lord, combining with that the true transmission of the primitive doctrine. The Church of Rome, as I maintain, failed on both sides. . ."[1]

In his Charge for 1866, he refers to the mischievous fallacy that made many think that, because our Church was a national Church, the nation was entitled to settle its doctrine. The compact between the Church and State was not, in the Bishop's view, that the Church shall be the State's instrument for teaching what the State shall from time to time approve, but the teacher for the State of that which she has already convinced the State is—"the Truth." Accordingly, if any new forms of error ever made new definitions of the faith needful, not to change, but to secure the continued sameness of the Church's teaching, it was necessary that both parties to the contract must agree to such an alteration before it could justly be enforced. The Church must propose these definitions in her Convocations, and the State assent to them in her Parliaments. Church questions, then, coming up in the law courts of the realm, look to have it settled what the law in the matter under consideration is, and not what it ought to be. What is to be decided

[1] *Life*, iii. p. 150.

there is whether, for instance, a teacher, against whose teaching complaint has been made, has or has not taught against that old truth which the Church covenanted to declare, and the State covenanted to receive. There was during Bishop Wilberforce's episcopacy, again and again, ground for fearing that the concordat that bound together Church and State might come to an end. He often expresses his own view that it was quite possible that the evil day for the peace and the religion of the land might come, which should sever from each other the Church and State of England. Writing to Mr. Gladstone in 1853, he expresses his opinion that, if the Irish Church is to remain established, she must needs show that she *is* the Irish Church. The question of her being kept in alliance with the State turns, he sees, on her efficiency most of all, however good her title, however pure her succession, however strong her legal position. So it was that he did all he could to increase the efficiency of the Church in England. In his Charge, delivered in 1863, he notes with satisfaction the encouraging change in the mind of the British Parliament towards the Church. This he attributes to the marks of life and vigour so obviously shown in the Church herself; and it is plain that he always felt very strongly that the best, and really the only, defence for the Church is to be found in her devotion, efficiency, and usefulness. Many changes, such as the Divorce Act, and the Deceased Wife's Sister Bill, and the claims for an undenominational elementary education, brought embarrassment and perplexity in the relations that existed between the Church of England and the State of England. While these difficulties could not, in his opinion, be ignored or compromised, they need not prevent the machinery from working on, and, in working on, finding strength and power and liberty for more work still.

The question of the disestablishment of the Irish Church came on in 1869, and Bishop Wilberforce's proceedings in the matter illustrate to some extent the views that he held on the Establishment question generally. At first he was opposed to it, though apparently accepting Archbishop Trench's opinion that if, after a struggle, the Irish Establishment could not be maintained, and Disraeli's proposal of cutting it down to small dimensions seemed sure to prevail, it would be better to go in for "instant death at the hands of Gladstone, than Disraeli's process of gradual starvation." Thus both in Parliament, and outside in public meetings, he did all he could against it. When, moreover, Mr. Gladstone had carried his resolutions in the House of Commons, he was one of those who opposed the Suspensory Bill which was, though carried in the House of Commons, thrown out in the House of Lords. After this, when Mr. Gladstone had appealed to the country on the question, and been returned to power with a large majority, his opposition died away. He told Archbishop Trench that the time had come to consider "whether any and what compromise was possible."[1] In opposing the Suspensory Bill in the House of Lords, Bishop Wilberforce had argued that, "as a condition precedent to disestablishment, the nation ought to have declared in favour of such a course." This had now been done in a very distinct and emphatic way, and

[1] *Life*, iii. p. 276.

though personally he could have wished it otherwise, he now used his influence to induce the Irish archbishops and bishops so to act that, in the disendowment matter which followed, they might profit by Mr. Gladstone's Churchmanship, and get the most liberal and generous terms possible. In this matter he was disposed to fight to the end that endowments once given to the Church were henceforth Church property, and ought not to be alienated from that Church for any purpose whatever. Ultimately the Bishop did not speak or vote against the second reading of the Irish Church Bill; and in the committee stage explained his action by stating that, in his opinion, that matter had been settled by the answer of the constituencies.

On the subject of this answer he wrote a pamphlet, which however he did not publish, partly because of Mr. Gladstone's advice, and partly because he was told that Archbishop Trench eagerly deprecated his doing so, and would regard it as "an act of most injurious hostility, which would stir up widespread wrath, and probably require *his* answering it in a tone which would make all future negotiations more difficult."[1] In the discussions on the subject, Bishop Wilberforce said that "of one thing he was convinced—that while an Establishment is to a particular Church in many ways a blessing unspeakable, no Church which cannot stand without an Establishment is worth being established."[2] He looked forward, he said, moreover, much as he lamented the present blow, to the Irish Church showing herself in the future "the true Catholic Church in Ireland, rising into greatness, and leavening more than she had yet done the bulk of the population."

[1] *Life*, iii. p. 283.   [2] *Ibid.* iii. p. 290.

His action on this occasion did not escape the severest criticism from Churchmen and his intimate friends. He was even said "to have been influenced" (to quote his own words from a letter of defence written to the Rev. H. Majendie) "by a miserable desire to get the denuded See of Winchester." Perhaps, however, strange as his action seemed, it did but illustrate his theory that the much-to-be-desired concordat between Church and State, called Establishment, could not be rightly maintained, when one of the parties concerned had declared against it; and he attributed the unfavourable verdict of the constituencies on the Irish Church question to the fact that, from a variety of causes, she had not been able to make herself the Church of Ireland. His labour was that the Church of England might not, by a like failure, incur a like disability.

His ideas on the Establishment question also governed his ideas concerning home reunion and the reunion of Christendom. He longed for both, and as in his younger days he had hoped for a reunion with the Church in Prussia, so also he longed for reunion with the great Eastern Church. Some of his aspirations in the matter are to be found in his Charge for 1866. As regards the home separation, he declares that he sees no formal differences of the faith which need hopelessly part Churchmen and Nonconformists; and that time has to a great degree worn away the causes of existing division. As regards the Eastern Church, he writes—"Old ways, old thoughts, old words, seem indeed to hang unchangeable, as in a charmed air, throughout the venerable East; and many of these are diverse from ours. Still the East is bound to no irreversible sequence of developed corruptions of the One

Faith, and with Her it may be that we may again open intercommunion." But he goes on then to add the following words—"Earnestly as we may long and pray for unity, we can make no overtures for it to any whose first principle is the absolute retention of what we hold to be grave error in doctrine and in practice. I see not how to avoid the conclusion that this must make, at present, impossible all such overtures from us to Rome."[1] But with every desire for reunion, and with a capacity, as various occasions in his ministry showed, for living on good terms with men of other denominations, Bishop Wilberforce would neither abate any of the claims of the Church of England to be the authorized religious teacher of the realm, nor favour any of the "comprehension schemes," that, in Prayer-Book revision, and other directions, sought to take into the Church some at least of those who dissented from her doctrinal statements. "Concessions so devised," he writes in his Charge for 1860, "from a conviction of their expediency as measures of comprehension, and not from a belief in their truth, would be fatal to those who made, and most hurtful to those who accepted, them. To strive earnestly for the faith, as they have received it, is the common duty of all religious bodies who would not sink into the Dead Sea of absolute unbelief. Such a sacrifice of truth as has been suggested would ruin us, and it would, I am convinced, be most injurious to the highest interests of the Dissenting bodies themselves to accept of such concessions as the terms of restored communion."[2] In the same way he was urgent in insisting (and a letter from the Rev. Newman Hall endorses his views) that it was no use concealing the fact that real differ-

---

[1] *Charge*, 1866, pp. 62-3.   [2] *Life*, iii. pp. 152-3.

ences existed where they did; more was gained on all sides by a frank and free acknowledgment, that both Nonconformists and Churchmen were what they were on principle, than by feeble attempts to make out that their separation did not involve vital truths. Once again, he felt that the best service he could render to the cause of home reunion was to do all he could to make the Church, in her assertion of Church principles, as thorough as possible, and to secure for her liberty and opportunity for the work which the carrying out of those principles necessarily involved.

CHAPTER IX.

LITERARY INFLUENCE AND PERSONALITY.

These pages have so far aimed at indicating some of the main points and phases of Bishop Wilberforce's career; they have tried to show that, as Canon Ashwell expresses it, "his life was not merely *connected with*, but actually involved, the history of the English, and in great measure of the colonial, Church during his episcopate." Much remains that might be said, but, for limitation of space, must remain unsaid. The present short and concluding chapter has for its object to speak shortly of the great Bishop of Oxford's literary labours; and to call attention to some of the personal traits that enabled him to accomplish so much.

The Bishop was once twitted with the ease and dignity that attached necessarily to his position. The occasion was a gathering of working-men, where some, at any rate, of those present had learned only from past traditions of episcopal non-residence and diocesan neglect, and where the audience was inclined to think that labour was a thing unknown, save in the class to which they belonged. "I am," said the Bishop, "as much a labouring man as any one here, and I work longer and harder every day." Dean Burgon has also remarked that he "habitually *forced* the work of eighteen, if not of twenty-four, hours" into the twelve hours in which man ought to work. It was but natural that, in such "a continuously active life," little time should have been found for the reading and study which must necessarily lie behind any great book. Bishop Wilberforce's pen was as ready as his tongue, but he has not, from force of circumstances, left behind any great literary monument of himself. His collected essays from the *Quarterly Review*, his charges, his sermons, his works, written in the more abundant leisure of Checkendon and Brighstone days, show us what he was capable of doing, and suggest that he might have succeeded here, as in almost any other department of life upon which he might have entered. In that which he has written there is shown a wonderful command of language, a great power of illustration and a singular clearness of thought; he can so well appreciate the ideas of other men, detect at once the key to some new intellectual position, expose a fallacy, or explain the strength or weakness of an argument. At one time he thought of delivering a course of Bampton lectures; he had even begun his reading for them, and advanced in it to some length, but the death of his wife brought this work to an untimely end. Again he was asked to undertake the *Lives of the Archbishops of Canterbury*, but he found it, on experiment, too great a task for his busy life, and it fell into the able hands of Dean Hook. Either of these works might have given him a wide influence and fame as a man of letters, greater than that which his more ephemeral, though nevertheless distinguished and remarkable, labours in that direction have secured for him. But, having said this much of him as a writer, a word must be added about his character as a reader and learner. His "readiness" in later life was the result of much careful and systematic reading in his earlier days. The temper of his times and the general tone of his countrymen demanded, as he often said, not merely an earnest and active, but a learned, clergy. He studied to understand the spirit of his Church and the spirit of the age to which he had to present it; and, to this end, used his times of comparative leisure, and his odd moments, to gather information on all subjects. At the end of a long day, he would take away with him to his bedroom a volume of one of the Fathers which he wished to consult; a visitor at Cuddesdon observed in his library a "pile of the newest sceptical books and reviews upon his table, with each salient passage in their arguments underlined and commented upon in their margin"; he could rise at six to master twenty pages of *Pusey on Daniel*, which he was reading through; his letters show that he mastered strange subjects of interest, as he gave his opinion on such matters as mesmerism and table-turning. All these things indicate the cost to him of that "readiness," and wideness of view and interest, for which he was famed. They show us how he was able to write all those manifold and various essays, in such a first-rate periodical as the *Quarterly*, to many of which reference has been made in these pages, as a good index of his own mind in many a crisis, and an evidence of the importance men attached to his utterances, and the help they found in them. The five or six editions asked for of the number containing his review of *Essays and Reviews* are a proof that he had not "shut himself up at Cuddesdon for a fortnight, to write it," in vain.

But, more even than from books, did Bishop Wilberforce learn from men. Frank and free intercourse with great men of all sorts had very much to do with his marvellous understanding of great questions, and his insight into great affairs. He had the advantage of being able to learn from rulers how to rule; and he was by nature fitted to profit by, and gather stores of lasting knowledge from, intercourse with famous men. He could hold his own with them; and the quickness of observation which made him an interested and successful student of natural history, made him also an observer of men's characters, and ready to gather and retain the suggestions made to him by their information and their knowledge. He was fond of social intercourse, and almost unrivalled in his day as a conversationalist; while he talked his best himself he had the power of making his audience talk their best too. He loved to surround himself with interesting people, and to get them to bring out, for his own benefit, and that of his guests, his friends, or his company, the treasures of knowledge or talent that made them interesting. Many stories are told of the silence of breathless attention that would fall on social gatherings, in order to hear sometimes Bishop Wilberforce's story, or some passage of his talk. His old butler recounts the good-tempered dismay with which his faithful and attached servants (for Bishop Wilberforce was ever kind to his servants, and frankly apologized to them for any hasty and impatient word of his) greeted his sudden return to his home after a three months' absence, with almost more than a houseful of guests. Lord Carlisle writes in his diary:—"I admire and envy the Bishop's fearless hospitality, not minding who know each other, and how they will suit." Men have laughed at, or spoken with something of horror and alarm, of some of the Bishop of Oxford's friendships and intimacies; they have urged that he should have consorted more with the rigidly orthodox, and somewhat less with the great. But he had a marvellous faculty for mixing the apparently incongruous, for getting out of all their best, for turning the dangerous into the safe. He was always striving to learn of men and from men, and in this way amassed stores of knowledge, which the incessant activity and occupation of his life forbade him to gather (even if it could so have been gathered) from books.

Rather, then, as a speaker and preacher, than as a writer of books, has Bishop Wilberforce influenced the thoughts of his countrymen and others. We have already said a few words about his powers as a speaker; and in the House of Lords, and on platforms, at congresses, at conferences, and in social and other public gatherings, a speech from him came to be looked for, and listened to, with eager longing, and earnest attention. Many was the good cause that his eloquence carried forward, and lifted into popularity; not seldom, in the days of his difficulties, did he win a hearing from a hostile meeting, till those who came to hiss and oppose remained to listen and applaud. So was it at Bradford, in 1858, when he went to address a meeting where many came "to resist in a voice of thunder the Tractarian confessionals." He gained a hearing by addressing the turbulent mob as "Brother Yorkshiremen"; having gained it he kept it, and, to use the words of his biographer, "turned the angry crowd into an orderly and enthusiastic meeting." So again in the House of Lords, he could, and did, hold his own, and proved himself a match for Lord Westbury and Lord Derby in speaking and in debate. He was a power there indeed, and well sustained, and even advanced, the reputation in the matter of oratory which had come back to his order since the day when Bishop Blomfield caused one, whose delight it had been to bait the bishops in the House of Lords, to exclaim to a friend, "There is a devil of a bishop up at last!" As a chairman, Bishop Wilberforce was inimitable; quick to guide or check meeting or speaker; skilful at bringing all, through many risks and dangers, to a right issue. It was his wisdom and adroitness that saved many troubles, in the infant days of Church congresses, by convincing those who met under his presidency at Oxford of the entire inexpediency of passing resolutions at those gatherings. "At public meetings," writes a clergyman of the Oxford diocese, "as well as in smaller meetings of committee, the decision (as has been often noticed) seemed almost invariably on the side which the Bishop advocated. As an opponent in argument he was always most formidable; scarcely any one seemed able to grapple with him. However fortified his adversary might be in facts, he found himself unable to resist the influence of the Bishop, and probably a laugh would be raised by some joke at his expense."

As a preacher, the Bishop was perhaps even more remarkable still among his contemporaries. We have many of his sermons; and their clearness, their variety, their wealth of illustration, their appeals, carrying conviction to the mind and head, and rousing enthusiasm through the affections and the heart, cannot fail to strike those who read them; though they cannot lie under the spell of the "irresistible voice," that added a vastly greater force and power to these "winged words." Bishop Wilberforce did much by his preaching to raise the standard of the Church of England in this matter. He felt, as he himself says, that the inquiring tone of the times, and the general activity of the day, called for thoughtful, earnest, careful sermons, full of reality, free from affectation, breaking through worldliness by the stirring up of the spiritual affections. The utterances of the pulpit were, and had been, in his opinion, "dull, monotonous, and droning"—mere essays, and not rousing appeals. There was a tendency in the better understanding of the Church's sacramental teaching, and the growing care for worship, to disparage preaching, "so that one of the very chiefest instruments which God has provided for the saving of souls was likely through carelessness and neglect to lose its efficiency."[1] It is plain too from many of the Bishop of Oxford's charges, that he felt strongly that the growing idea that unwritten sermons ought to be preached, even by those who had no gift for such preaching, was leading to weakness, to vapid utterances, which were but words, and "the mere pouring off of the first frothy surface of the mind." For himself he tells us that, with all his natural readiness and eloquence, it was quite fifteen years before he allowed himself to preach without writing. He served a long and laborious apprenticeship, and his power and facility in the pulpit was, after all, made, rather than born in him. Canon Ashwell tells us how for months together, in his early days at Brighstone, the course of preparation of each sermon is specified and recorded in his diary, together with memoranda as to its efficiency when delivered.

[1] *Charge*, 1857, p. 19.

Often, and often, as his diary records, he rose early in the morning to write his sermon; and, says Dean Burgon, "even to the last he stuck to the practice of at least endeavouring to commit to paper—at the Athenæum probably, or in the train,—what he proposed to deliver from the pulpit."[1] And again, to quote from the same source,—"There is no describing how exquisite was his oratory. Such a delightful voice and persuasive mode of address; such a happy admixture of argumentative power with rhetorical skill; such wealth of striking imagery and unrivalled beauty of diction; and all this, recommended by the most consummate grace and a truly mellifluous utterance, made him *facile princeps*, beyond a doubt the greatest living master of his art." He understood well his audience—their capacities, their difficulties, and their wants. To undergraduates in the University church, to a London congregation in a West-End church, to the labourers on his Lavington estate, he was alike acceptable; he could fathom their wants and difficulties; he could find words to bring home great truths and realities to all. A working-man once waylaid him, as he left the pulpit in a crowded church, and explained how his fellows had deputed him to ask the Bishop to come and speak to them about religion. They trusted him, of all men, to make them feel and understand; and the sequel tells us that the Bishop went.[2] So again, there exists a humorous correspondence in verse between the Bishop and Dr. Monsell, wherein the latter's importunity gets a promise from the Bishop that he will come and preach for him at Egham. The Bishop proposes substitutes, but in vain.

[1] *Lives of Twelve Good Men*, ii. p. 40.   [2] *Life*, iii. p. 33.

But though Bishop Wilberforce, as much as he could, wrote and prepared those many great sermons, the delivering of which, with an almost prodigal activity and readiness to be spent in his work, made him well-known throughout England; it was at last most common for him to preach extempore. His diaries often record how, after preparing a written sermon, on entering the church where it was to be preached, he would perceive that what he intended to say would be unsuitable, and then and there change his subject. Partly, as he said, because he was nervous, and partly for the sake of weaker brethren who were too ready to discard the MS. which they needed, where he did not, he liked to take something with him into the pulpit, if only a bundle of blank paper. But, even if he had a written discourse, he often did not use it at all, or left it to enlarge on some point suggested by it, that struck him as likely to be useful at the time. There is a well-known story which tells how, when Bishop Claughton asked him once to let him read again a striking passage, in which he had just spoken, in a sermon, of religious perplexity, the preacher handed him a paper on which was written the single word "fog." Sometimes he would exclaim in the vestry before service, to the friend with whom he was, if suddenly called upon to preach—"Tell me what to say." A few moments of concentrated thought would then suffice; and, when the time came, he would set forth in a most telling and attractive way the idea suggested. Stories of his wonderful readiness in this way are many. Once he had undertaken to give at Cuddesdon an address on a particular subject; on his arrival, the Vice-Principal was horrified to find that he had entirely forgotten that he had promised to speak on any special point. On being reminded, however, he discharged with wonderful effect the task originally assigned to him. Again, coming to Ryde, prepared to preach for an infirmary, he learnt in the vestry that his sermon had really been promised for schools, and, when the time came, made a striking appeal on their behalf. It was hard indeed to find him, as a preacher, unready at an emergency or unprepared; but his readiness was nevertheless the result of painful and laborious attention to this part of his work, from the time that he first took Holy Orders, and for long years after that.

The subject of preaching is often discussed by him in his charges, and he has much advice to give concerning it, which has a great and unique value as coming from one who was in his day such a "master." "His strength," says Dean Burgon, "lay, not so much in the exposition of obscure passages of Scripture, or in the eliciting of important ethical teaching from unpromising texts, as in the living power with which he brought home Divine precepts to the heart and conscience of his auditory."[1] All this was his own, and, "in the best sense of the word, original"; but he reached this by diligent study of the famous preachers of the day. When he first resided in London he was wont to go about to hear other men's sermons, and to make careful notes of what he heard; but he was ever a generous critic, quick to note and praise excellencies, tolerant of all that was interesting and well-meant, and had in it anything of thought and meaning; though he could be unsparing in his criticisms and condemnations where carelessness and deadness evidently prevailed. The experience he gained in the matter caused

[1] *Lives of Twelve Good Men*, ii. p. 45.

him to give counsels such as these. He told his clergy that to prepare their sermons they must first prepare themselves, and in his Charge for 1863 expresses himself thus—"It is, I believe, mainly idleness which ruins sermons, which makes them vague, confused, powerless, and dull. We need ever to remember the somewhat caustic words, 'The sermon which has cost little is worth just what it cost.'" And again—"Suffer me to recapitulate in the form of a few direct counsels what, on this great subject, I have gathered from experience or the writings of others. To secure thought and preparation, begin, whenever it is possible, the next Sunday's sermon at least on the preceding Monday. Let prayer for God's help be the beginning. Then select carefully your subject—if possible from the Gospel, Epistle, Lessons or Psalms of the day. Choose it according to your people's need, and your power. Let it be as much as possible resolvable into a single proposition. Having chosen it, meditate upon it as deeply as you can. Consider, first, how to state correctly the theological formula which it involves; then how to arrange its parts so as to convince the hearer's understanding. Think, next, how you can move his affections, and so win his will to accept it. See into what practical conclusions of holy living you can sum it up. Having thus the whole before you, you may proceed to its actual composition. And in doing this, if any thoughts strike you with peculiar power, secure them at once. . . . Until you have preached for many years, I would say, set yourself to write at least one sermon weekly. Study with especial care all statements of doctrine; to be clear, particular, and accurate. . . Having written your sermons, if you *must* deliver them with the manuscript before you, strive to do it as little as if you were reading, and as much as if you were speaking them as possible. Do not be the slave of your manuscript, but make it your servant. If you see that a word is not understood, vary it; that an appeal is reaching some heart, press it home. If you have the gift, after having written your sermon carefully, make short notes of it and preach from these. This will help you greatly to show in your manner that you feel what you say—the first and chiefest rule for making it felt by others."[1] Such are Bishop Wilberforce's words about preaching; and they are worth quoting, and worth studying, for they concern, and more or less contain, the secret of that which was perhaps his most effective weapon for guiding, influencing, and instructing the minds of many different men. Thousands came under the spell of the majestic presence, the marvellous voice, the wonderful eloquence of Bishop Wilberforce, as he preached to them, now in the village church, now in the crowded city, touching all classes and kinds of men alike—learned and ignorant, gentle and simple, rich and poor.

A story is told illustrating his evident appreciation of other men's trials and temptations, when he spoke on these subjects in his sermons and addresses. On the occasion of the re-opening of a restored church, the Bishop was thanking the churchwarden, an old farmer, for his share in the good work. "And I must thank your Lordship for your sermon," was the reply. "But I could not help thinking, as you talked about sin, that your Lordship must have been a little wildish yourself when you were a young man." In their

[1] *Charge*, 1863, p. 83.

knowledge of human nature, in their earnestness, in their clear and full assertion of truth, Bishop Wilberforce's sermons had a great influence indeed on the thought of his time; and, written and unwritten, published and unpublished, must be regarded as a distinct and valuable part of the literary activity of the day, brought home as they were to many by the great gifts and striking personality of the man who delivered them.

A kindly, appreciative, and sympathetic picture of the man, as he was known by those who knew him best, is drawn by Dean Burgon in his *Lives of Twelve Good Men*. 'There was," writes the author of this pleasant sketch, "a rare amount of real sympathy between him and myself in matters of religious thought and opinion;" and some of those who were most closely attached to Bishop Wilberforce testify that the Dean's kindly pen has done a fair measure of justice to his friend's character. To men who were not strongly set against him from principle or prejudice, Samuel Wilberforce was singularly attractive. He had a happy knack of drawing the best out of those who were under him; he showed that he expected earnest effort, and respected it too; he always backed men up who were working, even if they got into scrapes and made mistakes. Gradually there gathered round him, in his Oxford diocese, a band of devoted men ready to do their utmost to carry out their leader's plans. He was wont to call the "inner circle" of these his "body-guard," and it was his delight to gather them around him, and to feel, and show, that with them he could be frank and open, and live in pleasant intercourse, fearless of misunderstanding, and without constraint. He rejoiced unfeignedly in their successes, and appreciated thoroughly their strong points, and was eager to hold up to admiration (as, for instance, in the case of Dr. Woodford's preaching) that which they did well. But the tongue that could praise, where praise was due, could also rebuke terribly sometimes, and was not afraid to speak out. Thus, as Dean Burgon writes, "the men who neglected their parishes, their churches, their work—they hated him with a cordial hatred." Bishop Wilberforce was a wonderful kindler of enthusiasm; and those who knew him and worked under him grow enthusiastic still, as they tell you of his making some new departure or experiment in Church work, or quietly crushing and paralyzing a formidable opposition, or defeating a dogged and obstinate obstruction.

It was natural, indeed necessary, that one who did so much to quicken the devotional and spiritual life of others, should himself have the devotional side of his nature strongly developed and carefully trained. His diaries, and his addresses to his candidates for Orders, let us see that he gave himself, and desired to lead others to give themselves, much to prayer and communings with God. He made a great deal of the more spiritual side of the training given at Cuddesdon College; he shared in its opportunities and privileges when he was at home. A story is told of his remarking, when some were discussing in his presence the obligations of the clergy to say daily the Morning and Evening Prayer, that he had found four o'clock a good time to say the evening office, in a cab. One who often had the opportunity of observing, writes—"His devoutness in communicating must have struck all who were ministering with him. He evidently made it an occasion for prolonged and special prayer—furnishing himself with a manual partly printed, partly written. He always seemed to me *absorbed* in the business of the sanctuary."[1] His work and life were based then on a real and fervent appreciation of the highest things.

Some one has said that Bishop Wilberforce's best testimonial was the affection with which he was plainly regarded by good men of undoubted spirituality. He speaks almost pathetically of his own craving for sympathy and affection, and it is plain that, while he showed it abundantly to others, he rejoiced and desired to have it returned. The bereavements which came to him were terrible blows, never forgotten; his wife's grave, and the resting-place of his "best-beloved son," were sacred spots, and to the last he was accustomed whenever he came home to Lavington, to visit them, and place flowers there. In all his cares and business, he was full of thoughts of his children, anxious to an uncommon degree about their amusements even, and all their interests.

It was this affectionateness of disposition that inspired that sympathy which has been picked out as *the* strong point in his character. Bishop Wilberforce, by nature, by training, by the experience of his life, with its many successes, its great sorrows, and its bitter disappointments, was made to help other men to bear their burdens, and to put himself into their place. He could lend his wonderful powers to enhance the joys of a time of happiness, or to soothe the bitterness of an hour of sorrow. There is quite a marvel of thoughtful, hopeful tenderness in many of the letters of condolence that he

---

[1] *Lives of Twelve Good Men*, ii. p. 60.

wrote; it is good to read of his enjoyment of a Christmas revel with his children at Cuddesdon; it is touching to find him suggesting rest to one of his plainly overworked clergy, and, with much tact and delicacy, sending timely help to one with narrow means. The same power of sympathy, too, would make him do many little kindnesses, showing, for instance, special hospitality to the more friendless of the Cuddesdon students, drawing out the more shy amongst his candidates for Ordination, setting himself at the end of a long and laborious day to read for the entertainment of guests in some house where he was staying. In all these ways he conciliated many, even of those who were inclined to regard him with suspicion, or possibly dislike; and he could disarm prejudice with that happy temper, which Lord Derby once observed and welcomed, when he remarked, "I see the Bishop of Oxford can take a joke." So wide indeed was his sympathy, so all-inclusive, that some who had tasted of it were apt to feel disappointed, and to doubt its reality, when they found with how many their privilege was shared.

The Bishop was remarkable for his power of remembering men and their names, and he increased his capability in this respect by practice. It was not uncommon for clergy and others to be much surprised to find themselves not forgotten by the Bishop, though years perhaps had passed since they had met him. A lady who had once met the Bishop of Oxford after a Confirmation in his diocese, was waiting soon after to cross at the top of Regent Street. She was surprised to hear some one saying to her, "You seem in difficulties, Miss ———; let me help you." It was the Bishop, who piloted her safely to the other side. An amusing story is also told, illustrating how this instinct was sometimes at fault. At a Confirmation, Bishop Wilberforce saw a boy amongst the candidates, whom he felt sure he had confirmed before. He sent a message to him to say so, and received a denial. Still unconvinced, he sent the clergyman who presented the candidate to say that the Bishop was sure he had confirmed him before. "Tell him he is a liar," was the response. His skill in recognitions was, however, no small element in the Bishop of Oxford's influence with people. It was with many a cause of wonder, and so common and remarkable that stories were current to account for it, as that the Bishop kept photographs of his clergy, and carefully studied beforehand those belonging to any district he meant to visit. Again, there is a story of the Bishop, after leaving his diocese, meeting one of his old clergy, and astonishing his chaplain, who was with him, by the wonderful memory that could bring him to ask the stranger after "the old gray horse." The story goes on to say that, on further inquiry being made as to how the Bishop could have thought of it, the answer was, "Did you not see the hair on his coat?"

There was in the Bishop of Oxford, too, in spite of his labours, his sorrows, and his anxieties, a wonderful elasticity of spirits, an almost boyish gaiety, and even boisterousness; often it was but the reaction, it is true, from deep depression, or the light cloak that concealed a world of sorrow. People saw, as his biographer says, a quickness of transition in his moods, according with the mood of those around him, which must have perplexed, and often did perplex, comparative strangers, or persons of less susceptible dispositions.[1] "Often," he

[1] *Life*, i. p. 178.

writes to a friend, "when I seem the gayest, I am indeed the most utterly sad." But, any way, the Bishop had a great facility for leaving his cares; and though, in his later years, illness left him much less able to overcome depression, that facility stood him in good stead in the wear and tear and worry of his laborious life. Dean Burgon's story of the way in which he "took a blessing from him" by playfully pinning him to the wall outside All Souls', and forcing him to say, "God bless you," on his translation to Winchester, illustrates the trait in Bishop Wilberforce's character to which reference is made. So, too, does the story of his ride with the Bishop of London, in which he gave his brother bishop a lead over the hedge by the roadside.

The same playfulness of spirit appeared in the Bishop's conversation, in his jokes, his stories, and his quiet repartees. He became almost proverbial for these; and, though there are many and many that are ascribed to him which he did not say, or use, or make, still, in his lighter moments, there would always be an abundance of good things of this sort going about where he was. Here again Dean Burgon tells how many recollections there are with those who knew him, of incidents "which can only be designated as *laughable*. He was so full of boyish spirits, boyish glee, so versatile moreover, and apt (without *real* levity) to descend from the sublime to the ridiculous in a moment." There were those, of course, who thought all this ill-timed, and out of place; they were inclined to regard it, not as the lawful and happy recreation of a busy and devoted life, but as ill-suited to the high calling of a bishop. One story may be told here which illustrates the Bishop's readiness in answer and defence. Every one knows that, early in his career as Bishop, some person or persons gave him the sobriquet of "Soapy Sam." A lady once asked him why he was called thus. "Because, madam," he answered, "I am always in hot water, and always come out of it with clean hands."

Bishop Wilberforce had, and has, a great reputation for his witty speeches, his good stories, and his jokes. A ruthless literalness has exploded many of them; as, for instance, his reported answer to a lady who asked him who were the two best preachers of the day. "Why, madam, think of a part of your dress,"—meaning *hook-and-eye*. Some he has been heard to deny, as that he capped Lord Palmerston's rallying of him from his carriage, when the Bishop had preferred to walk to church on a wet day. Lord Palmerston is said to have quoted at the Bishop the line, "How blest is he, who ne'er consents by ill advice to walk." The Bishop quoted the next, in playful reference to his host's carriage, "Nor stands in sinners' way, nor sits where men profanely talk." Many of his jokes are too personal to bear repetition in the lifetime of those at whose expense they were, in all good-humour, made. But it is to the point to give from various sources illustrations of a side of Bishop Wilberforce's character which added a great deal to his acceptability with, and influence upon, his contemporaries. Dean Burgon describes him, at his own table, turning round to his neighbour, Archdeacon Clerke, and asking him why an Archdeacon's apron is like unwholesome food? and supplying the answer—"Because *it goes against his stomach.*" He also tells us of his reply to an inquiry whether he had not cancer in his mouth—"Yes, to be sure, *when I'm eating crab.*" The same authority speaks of this readiness of wit, even in the Bishop's early days. Once when his tutor appeared with rod in hand on a scene of disorder, Wilberforce thrust forward a certain Jewish schoolfellow with the plea, "The Jew first, and then the Gentile." Hearing a young man describe how he had the misfortune to slay a deer when permitted to shoot rabbits in the royal park, Bishop Wilberforce expressed a hope that after that the authorities did not give the offender *the cold shoulder*. So again, to a mechanic, thinking to confound him by asking suddenly the way to heaven, the Bishop at once replied, "Turn to the right, and go, my friend, straight on." After the Bishop of Peterborough's great speech in the House of Lords, on the Irish Church, the speaker's hat was inadvertently taken up by Bishop Wilberforce. On being reminded of his mistake the Bishop surrendered it, remarking gracefully, that he wished he had the brains which the hat rightfully covered. So was it given to Bishop Wilberforce to conciliate many by his happy power of saying bright and pleasant things.

Beyond all this, which we have mentioned,—a result perhaps of his wide sympathies, his power of winning men, and his capacity for getting recreation— was Bishop Wilberforce's readiness for hard work. In his Oxford days he did not a little in giving help to other bishops in their diocesan labours; and, on his translation to Winchester, a near relation said, that his larger sphere of work would, at any rate, save him from being "a hack bishop" any longer. Work brought him relief in some of those great troubles that clouded his life. Far from allowing them to keep him, even for a time, inactive, he carried his heavy heart at once to the routine of duty, and found in this way the true solace; though he writes in his diary at one such time of trouble, "Very weary at night, a sad heart so increases fatigue." There is a striking passage, bearing on this habit of his of resuming his wonted occupations when in trouble in a letter from Archdeacon Randall to the Rev. R. C. Trench, written just at the time when the Bishop lost his eldest son. The letter has described his many engagements, which the Bishop was even then fulfilling, and the writer adds—"These details will make you fear, as I do, that all this must be a heavy wear and tear upon the inward man. But what an astonishing creature he is! what is he made of? what is he made *for?* Surely there must be some great purpose for him to fulfil."[1] We find some answer to the Archdeacon's question, in the recollection that Bishop Wilberforce was pre-eminently the man who steered the Church of England some way along the safe course, in a time of crisis, and brought her out at least into a place of greater liberty. He was ready to spend and be spent ungrudgingly in this, which seemed to him *the* want and necessity of his day; and, as is usual with men who give themselves wholly to any work or cause, he was able to get through so much, that men were fairly astonished at all he accomplished. The trouble involved, the opposition that threatened, the novelty of an undertaking, never deterred Bishop Wilberforce from any departure, which his clearness of perception made him see to be desirable, in Church life or Church work. Of course he made some mistakes, and

[1] *Life*, ii. p. 311.

incurred some grievous defeats; but he brought much out to a real success, largely because of his untiring energy, and readiness for laborious work. Not only could he plan, and organize, but details even were not trifles in his eyes—a fortunate circumstance indeed, when the smallest defect might well have given opportunity to prejudice, to timidity, to suspicion, to wreck utterly some of his most important efforts after Church growth and development.

But Dean Burgon has reminded us that there is another side—or at least that there has seemed to many to be another side—to the character of the great Bishop of Oxford. Men have often questioned the motives of some of the Bishop's actions, and accused him of acting from expediency, and being a man of the world. His quick changes from grave to gay have troubled them, and his social successes and reputation have been regarded (specially by men disposed to judge him hardly) as unbecoming a really spiritual and deeply religious man. Dean Burgon speaks from the point of view of one who knew him intimately and well. He has shown abundantly that he had the entire respect, and the full confidence and affection, of the band of true, earnest, and devoted men, who have the best right, from their close intercourse with him, to speak of him as he really was. He was clearly too great to escape detraction, and even envy; and it is only natural, perhaps right, that conscientious men, who dreaded many of his ideas as dangerous to Church and State, should have been glad to hear whispers against him, and above all, to disparage him in high places. Cautious, Bishop Wilberforce was not; he learnt a lesson certainly in this respect, notably from the Hampden case. "Sure of himself, and unsuspicious of others, he was habitually too confiding, too unguarded in his utterances." So writes Dean Burgon, and he adds—" But above all, his besetting fault was that he was a vast deal *too facile*. The consequence might have been foreseen. He was sometimes obliged to 'hark back'—to revoke—to unsay. This occasioned distrust." It was no small matter, and no easy task, for Bishop Wilberforce, with his quick wit and ready tongue, to prevent himself from saying much too often those smart things which leave a sting behind them. He tells us plainly that he had to put a strong restraint upon himself in this matter, specially as a speaker in the House of Lords, and often regrets that he has been betrayed into saying what might seem unkindly. Detraction, calumny, and misrepresentation were very bitter to him, and it hurt his affectionate nature very deeply to have to be out with any man. His own words on this point are—"I have no doubt that the sharp frosts of suspicion and detraction are specially useful to those who, like me, naturally crave for sympathy, and shoot out too readily the tendrils of affection; but certainly, the process of being frostnipped, though useful, is painful enough to the shootbearer, and often makes me long, if my boys were launched, to lie down and die."[1] Several times in his life, the Bishop was obliged to make his defence. But he was able, as in the Hampden difficulty, in the Boyne Hill case, in the controversy with Mr. Golightly, to make it clear that he had a pure and disinterested motive. There may have been unwisdom and want of judgment; but a principle lay behind his action all through, and a real desire to do his duty by the Church.

[1] *Lives of Twelve Good Men*, ii. p. 66.

It cannot be surprising that a character, versatile and mobile as his was, should have puzzled and caused offence to many. Ordinary human nature may well stand excused if it failed to understand how any one could be so many things to so many men, and yet be no actor, but true to his best self all the while. Circumstances were sure to give them many opportunities for having their wonder and astonishment turned into horror, mistrust, and even into absolute want of confidence. Fearless, outspoken, trusting much to his own great powers, and his personal influence, Bishop Wilberforce did sometimes say too much, go too far, and, above all things, give too much freedom to men who needed rather restraint. All these things marred, and hindered, the carrying out of some of the projects with which he identified himself. It was not a small disability, in the temper and tone of the day in which he lived, that so many of his family and friends seceded to Rome. He rather forgot the weakness that this could not fail to cause, and the suspicion it could not fail to arouse. The consciousness of his own integrity; his unfeigned horror of Roman error, and the Roman system; the great powers that he knew were his—all went to blind him to the consequences to himself and his work of these defections. So Bishop Wilberforce never sat in St. Augustine's chair. But he did give to the work and office of a bishop in the Church of England a new meaning; he gave Church life a new enthusiasm and reality; he laboured abundantly amongst those who, in the last fifty years, have done so very much to make the great Anglican Communion able to feel its great mission, and eager to accept its high destiny. Looking back now, and contrasting the Church of England as it is with what it was when Samuel Wilberforce was called, in 1845, to the See of Oxford, one wonders how she has come safely through so many dangers. His life and work are no small part of the answer to such a question. His gifts, his knowledge of men, his appreciation of his Church—all these have done much, very much, to make it possible that that Church should live, and move onward, in very stormy waters, on very troubled seas.

On Saturday afternoon, July 19th, 1873, an accident, while riding on the Surrey Downs, took away from the great work of organizing his still new diocese of Winchester, the man who had laboured at Oxford to show what being a bishop really meant. For himself it was as he would have had it; he desired that thus, if it might be, the night should come to him "in which no man can work." For others there seemed a great blank, a desolation, a power passed from earth. A hand which had pointed men upward, would point them upward no more. Men told each other, as the tidings of his sudden death spread through the country, that another great Englishman was dead, and one who had truly "served his generation," before he fell asleep.

INDEX.

ABERDEEN, Lord, 71, 123, 124-5, 127-8, 130-1
Alderson, Baron, 88
Allies, Mr., 87-8, 138
Alverstoke, 25-6, 46
Anderson, Sir C., 5, 15, 16, 17, 183
Anson, Mr., 67
Apostolic Ministry, 17, 45, 90, 103, 107, 189
Arches, Court of, 80, 142
Ashwell, Canon, 4, 6, 10, 54, 56, 63, 69, 78, 141, 196, 202
Athanasian Creed, 154, 185

BAGOT, Bishop, 41
Beauchamp, Lord, 184
Bennett, Mr., 74, 116, 138, 175-6
Blomfield, Bishop, 109, 113, 130, 139, 165, 175, 201
Board of Education, Diocesan, 60
Boyne Hill Case, 97, 106
Bradford, 68, 200
British Association, 69, 147
Broad Church Party, 149, 154
Brougham, Lord, 127
Bunsen, Baron, 19, 30, 43, 149
Burgon, Dean, 1, 6, 8, 24, 33, 47, 54, 71, 73, 80, 82, 149, 185, 186, 197, 205, 208, 209, 213
Butler, Canon, 66, 85, 105

CALTHORPE, Lord, 18
Cambridge, 63, 69
Canadian Clergy Reserves, 166
Canons, alteration of, 134

Capetown, Bishop of, 69, 155
Carlisle, Lord, 199
Cathedrals, 29
Church Congress, 201
Church Missionary Society, 19, 63, 164
Church Unions, 117
Clapham Sect, 9
Clerical Subscription, 145
Clewer, 65
Colenso, Bishop, 155-161
Coleridge, Mr. Justice, 96
Colonial Bishops, 159, 164-6
Colonial Church, 30, 63
Commission on Ritual, 183-5
Confession, 97, 98, 105
Confirmation, 25, 52-4, 212
Consort, the Prince, 31, 36, 69, 89, 125
Convocation, 31 ; Revival of, 119-136 ; Proposed Commission on, 126-7 ; on Bishop Colenso, 160 ; on Ritualism, 179
Corn Laws, 67
Cuddesdon, 36, 41-2, 51, 58, 59, 60, 100-106, 147, 198, 204, 209, 211
Curates, 61, 64

DARWIN, Mr. C., 146-7
Denison, Archdeacon, 59, 126, 138
Derby, Lord, 120, 182, 201, 211
Diocesan Church Building Society, 61

INDEX.

Diocesan Conferences, 62
Diocesan Synod, 62
Disraeli, 191
Divorce Act, 154, 190
Dodson, Sir John, 119
Dodsworth, Mr., 95
Doubt, 152

Eastern Church, 118, 193
Ecclesiastical Commission, 29
Ecclesiastical Courts, 137-140, 155, 171
Education, 23, 24, 59-60, 69, 190
Elliot, Dean, 128
Essays and Reviews, 139, 142-154
Eucharistic Doctrine, 87, 91-2, 105, 173
Evangelical Party, 71-2, 93, 101-5, 124, 128, 142
Excommunication, 159, 160

Factory Act, 68
Fasting Communion, 186
Free-trade, 38
Fust, Sir H. J., 79

Gladstone, W. E., 40-1, 118-19, 121, 131, 132, 138, 140, 141, 175, 181, 187, 191-2
Golightly, Mr. C. P., 5, 102-105, 218
Gordon, Mr., 162
Gorham Judgment, 78, 84, 90, 116, 137, 139

Hampden, Dr., 17, 75—84, 108, 141, 217
Hawkins, Dr., 81
High Church Party, 93, 154
Hoadley, Bishop, 112
Holy Orders, Training for, 99-100
Hook, Dean, 5, 19, 24, 25, 43, 113, 141, 197
Hooker, Richard, 65, 72, 86, 184
Howley, Archbishop, 76, 81

Inspiration, 142, 150-1
Irish Church, 190-3

Jerusalem Bishopric, 30
Judicial Committee, 74, 137, 138

Keble, J., 94, 96
Knox, Mr., 147

Lavington, 12, 33, 37, 203, 210
Lectionary, New, 131, 183
Lenten Sermons, 56
Liddon, Canon, 102, 105
Long, Archdeacon, 157-8
Lords, House of, 66-7, 111, 117, 123, 135, 142, 180, 191, 200-1
Lushington, Dr., 88, 139

Majendie, Mr. H., 193
Manning, Cardinal, 21
Marriott, Mr. C., 93-99
Maurice, F. D., 19, 149
Milman, Bishop, 161
Missions, Diocesan, 54-6
Monsell, Dr., 203

National Society, 59
Newman, J. H., 5, 15, 16, 39, 40
Noel, Miss L., 38, 47, 67, 78, 87
Non-communicating Attendance, 186
Nonconformists, 56, 123, 187-8, 193-4

Ordinations, 44, 46-9, 55
Oxford Journal, opinion on Bishop Wilberforce's work, 5

Palmerston, Lord, 16, 131
Patronage, Diocesan, 63
Peel, Sir R., 35, 38, 40
Philpott, Bishop, 18, 74, 83
Pott, Archdeacon, 105
Powell, Mr. Baden, 146
Preaching, 206-7
Public Worship Regulation Act, 140
Pusey, Dr., 5, 16, 39, 93-7, 98, 138, 155

Quarterly Review, 109, 114, 139, 140, 144, 145, 147, 151, 187, 197

INDEX.

Queen, the, 31, 36, 38, 78, 84, 117, 120, 134

RANDALL, Archdeacon, 216
Rationalism, 143, 150
Record, The, 28, 83, 123, 142, 176
Redesdale, Lord, 117
Reform Bill, 13, 16, 29, 136
Reformation, the, 86, 176
Retreats, 58
Ritualism, 169-195
Royal Supremacy, 116
Rural Deans, 57
Russell, Lord John, 39, 74, 75-78, 128

SELLON, Miss, 65
Selwyn, Bishop, 30
Sermons, 202
Shaftesbury, Lord, 86, 121, 128, 181, 183
Sisterhoods, 64-6, 98, 110
Smith, Sydney, 143
Society for the Propagation of the Gospel, 17, 19, 31, 63
South London, 22
Spiritual Help Society, 61, 64
Stanley, Dean, 161, 169
Sterling Club, 19, 149
Sumner, Archbishop, 13, 118-9, 121, 122, 129-30, 161, 181
Sumner, Bishop, 13, 19, 21, 161
Sunday Question, the, 32, 88
Synod, Pan-Anglican, 160

THOMPSON, Sir H., 162
Titles Bill, 74, 90
Tractarian Movement, 26-8, 39, 71, 75, 84, 93, 114
Tracts for the Times, 15
Trench, Archbishop, 25, 191-2, 216

VESTMENTS, 184, 185

WANTAGE, 65
Wellington, Duke of, 16, 164
Wesley, John, 178
Westbury, Lord, 135, 142, 165-6, 201
Wilberforce, Bishop, divisions of his life, 6, 7; school days, 10; Oriel, 11; marriage, 12; ordination, 12; first curacy, 12; Brighstone, 13-14; his Toryism, 14; literary work, 15; Rural Dean, 18; Archdeacon, 21-24; Alverstoke, 25-6; speeches, 31, 68; wife's death, 33—35; consecration, 37; Natural History, love of, 147; writings, 197-8; death, 220
Wilberforce, Henry, 9
Wilberforce, Mrs., 12, 33-5
Wilberforce, R. G., 68
Wilberforce, Robert, 9, 32, 94, 114
Wilberforce, William, 9, 10-12, 89
Wilson, Mr., 144
Wiseman, Cardinal, 90
Woodford, Bishop, 49, 209

THE END.

RICHARD CLAY & SONS, LIMITED,
LONDON & BUNGAY.

A SELECTION OF BOOKS PUBLISHED BY METHUEN AND COMPANY LIMITED 36 ESSEX STREET LONDON W.C.

CONTENTS

	PAGE		PAGE
General Literature	1	Little Library	20
Ancient Cities	15	Little Quarto Shakespeare	21
Antiquary's Books	15	Miniature Library	21
Arden Shakespeare	15	New Library of Medicine	21
Classics of Art	16	New Library of Music	22
"Complete" Series	16	Oxford Biographies	22
Connoisseur's Library	16	Romantic History	22
Handbooks of English Church History	17	Handbooks of Theology	22
		Westminster Commentaries	23
Illustrated Pocket Library of Plain and Coloured Books	17		
Leaders of Religion	18		
Library of Devotion	18	Fiction	23
Little Books on Art	19	Books for Boys and Girls	28
Little Galleries	19	Novels of Alexandre Dumas	29
Little Guides	19	Methuen's Sixpenny Books	29

MARCH 1911

Bennett (Joseph). FORTY YEARS OF MUSIC, 1865-1905. Illustrated. *Demy 8vo.* 16s. net.

Bennett (W. H.), M.A. A PRIMER OF THE BIBLE. *Fifth Edition. Cr. 8vo.* 2s. 6d.

Bennett (W. H.) and Adeney, (W. F.). A BIBLICAL INTRODUCTION. With a concise Bibliography. *Sixth Edition. Cr. 8vo.* 7s. 6d.

Benson (Archbishop). GOD'S BOARD. Communion Addresses. *Second Edition. Fcap. 8vo.* 3s. 6d. net.

Benson (R. M.). THE WAY OF HOLINESS. An Exposition of Psalm cxix. Analytical and Devotional. *Cr. 8vo.* 5s.

*Bensusan (Samuel L.). HOME LIFE IN SPAIN. Illustrated. *Demy 8vo.* 10s. 6d. net.

Berry (W. Grinton), M.A. FRANCE SINCE WATERLOO. Illustrated. *Cr. 8vo.* 6s.

Betham-Edwards (Miss). HOME LIFE IN FRANCE. Illustrated. *Fifth Edition. Cr. 8vo.* 6s.

Bindley (T. Herbert), B.D. THE OECUMENICAL DOCUMENTS OF THE FAITH. With Introductions and Notes. *Second Edition. Cr. 8vo.* 6s. net.

Binyon (Laurence). See Blake (William).

Blake (William). ILLUSTRATIONS OF THE BOOK OF JOB. With General Introduction by LAURENCE BINYON. Illustrated. *Quarto.* 21s. net.

Body (George), D.D. THE SOUL'S PILGRIMAGE: Devotional Readings from the Published and Unpublished writings of George Body, D.D. Selected and arranged by J. H. BURN, D.D., F.R.S.E. *Demy 16mo.* 2s. 6d.

Boulting (W.). TASSO AND HIS TIMES. Illustrated. *Demy 8vo.* 10s. 6d. net.

Bovill (W. B. Forster). HUNGARY AND THE HUNGARIANS. Illustrated. *Demy 8vo.* 7s. 6d. net.

Bowden (E. M.). THE IMITATION OF BUDDHA: Being Quotations from Buddhist Literature for each Day in the Year. *Fifth Edition. Cr. 16mo.* 2s. 6d.

Brabant (F. G.), M.A. RAMBLES IN SUSSEX. Illustrated. *Cr. 8vo.* 6s.

Bradley (A. G.). ROUND ABOUT WILTSHIRE. Illustrated. *Second Edition. Cr. 8vo.* 6s.
THE ROMANCE OF NORTHUMBERLAND. Illustrated. *Second Edition. Demy 8vo.* 7s. 6d. net.

Braid (James). Open Champion, 1901, 1905 and 1906. ADVANCED GOLF. Illustrated. *Sixth Edition. Demy 8vo.* 10s. 6d. net.

Braid (James) and Others. GREAT GOLFERS IN THE MAKING. Edited by HENRY LEACH. Illustrated. *Second Edition. Demy 8vo.* 7s. 6d. net.

Brailsford (H. N.). MACEDONIA: ITS RACES AND THEIR FUTURE. Illustrated. *Demy 8vo.* 12s. 6d. net.

Brodrick (Mary) and Morton (A. Anderson). A CONCISE DICTIONARY OF EGYPTIAN ARCHÆOLOGY. A Handbook for Students and Travellers. Illustrated. *Cr. 8vo.* 3s. 6d.

Brown (J. Wood), M.A. THE BUILDERS OF FLORENCE. Illustrated. *Demy 4to.* 18s. net.

Browning (Robert). PARACELSUS. Edited with Introduction, Notes, and Bibliography by MARGARET L. LEE and KATHARINE B. LOCOCK. *Fcap. 8vo.* 3s. 6d. net.

Buckton (A. M.). EAGER HEART: A Mystery Play. *Ninth Edition. Cr. 8vo.* 1s. net.

Budge (E. A. Wallis). THE GODS OF THE EGYPTIANS. Illustrated. *Two Volumes. Royal 8vo.* £3 3s. net.

Bull (Paul), Army Chaplain. GOD AND OUR SOLDIERS. *Second Edition. Cr. 8vo.* 6s.

Bulley (Miss). See Dilke (Lady).

Burns (Robert), THE POEMS. Edited by ANDREW LANG and W. A. CRAIGIE. With Portrait. *Third Edition. Wide Demy 8vo, gilt top.* 6s.

Bussell (F. W.), D.D. CHRISTIAN THEOLOGY AND SOCIAL PROGRESS (The Bampton Lectures of 1905). *Demy 8vo.* 10s. 6d. net.

Butler (Sir William), Lieut.-General, G.C.B. THE LIGHT OF THE WEST. With some other Wayside Thoughts, 1865-1908. *Cr. 8vo.* 5s. net.

Butlin (F. M.). AMONG THE DANES. Illustrated. *Demy 8vo.* 7s. 6d. net.

Cain (Georges), Curator of the Carnavalet Museum, Paris. WALKS IN PARIS. Translated by A. R. ALLINSON, M.A. Illustrated. *Demy 8vo.* 7s. 6d. net.

Cameron (Mary Lovett). OLD ETRURIA AND MODERN TUSCANY. Illustrated. *Second Edition. Cr. 8vo.* 6s. net.

Carden (Robert W.). THE CITY OF GENOA. Illustrated. *Demy 8vo.* 10s. 6d. net.

Carlyle (Thomas). THE FRENCH REVOLUTION. Edited by C. R. L. FLETCHER, Fellow of Magdalen College, Oxford. *Three Volumes. Cr. 8vo. 18s.*
THE LETTERS AND SPEECHES OF OLIVER CROMWELL. With an Introduction by C. H. FIRTH, M.A., and Notes and Appendices by Mrs. S. C. LOMAS. *Three Volumes. Demy 8vo. 18s. net.*

Celano (Brother Thomas of). THE LIVES OF FRANCIS OF ASSISI. Translated by A. G. FERRERS HOWELL. Illustrated. *Cr. 8vo. 5s. net.*

Chambers (Mrs. Lambert). Lawn Tennis for Ladies. Illustrated. *Crown 8vo. 2s. 6d. net.*

Chandler (Arthur), Bishop of Bloemfontein. ARA CŒLI: AN ESSAY IN MYSTICAL THEOLOGY. *Fourth Edition. Cr. 8vo. 3s. 6d. net.*

Chesterfield (Lord). THE LETTERS OF THE EARL OF CHESTERFIELD TO HIS SON. Edited, with an Introduction by C. STRACHEY, with Notes by A. CALTHROP. *Two Volumes. Cr. 8vo. 12s.*

Chesterton (G.K.). CHARLES DICKENS. With two Portraits in Photogravure. *Seventh Edition. Cr. 8vo. 6s.*
ALL THINGS CONSIDERED. *Sixth Edition. Fcap. 8vo. 5s.*
TREMENDOUS TRIFLES. *Fourth Edition. Fcap. 8vo. 5s.*

Clausen (George), A.R.A., R.W.S. SIX LECTURES ON PAINTING. Illustrated. *Third Edition. Large Post. 8vo. 3s. 6d. net.*
AIMS AND IDEALS IN ART. Eight Lectures delivered to the Students of the Royal Academy of Arts. Illustrated. *Second Edition. Large Post 8vo. 5s. net.*

Clutton-Brock (A.) SHELLEY: THE MAN AND THE POET. Illustrated. *Demy 8vo. 7s. 6d. net.*

Cobb (W. F.), M.A. THE BOOK OF PSALMS: with an Introduction and Notes. *Demy 8vo. 10s. 6d. net.*

Cockshott (Winifred), St. Hilda's Hall, Oxford. THE PILGRIM FATHERS, THEIR CHURCH AND COLONY. Illustrated. *Demy 8vo. 7s. 6d. net.*

Collingwood (W. G.), M.A. THE LIFE OF JOHN RUSKIN. With Portrait. *Sixth Edition. Cr. 8vo. 2s. 6d. net.*

Colvill (Helen H.). ST. TERESA OF SPAIN. Illustrated. *Second Edition. Demy 8vo. 7s. 6d. net.*

*****Condamine (Robert de la).** THE UPPER GARDEN. *Fcap. 8vo. 5s. net.*

Conrad (Joseph). THE MIRROR OF THE SEA: Memories and Impressions. *Third Edition. Cr. 8vo. 6s.*

Coolidge (W. A. B.), M.A. THE ALPS. Illustrated. *Demy 8vo. 7s. 6d. net.*

Cooper (C. S.), F.R.H.S. See Westell (W.P.)

Coulton (G. G.). CHAUCER AND HIS ENGLAND. Illustrated. *Second Edition. Demy 8vo. 10s. 6d. net.*

Cowper (William). THE POEMS. Edited with an Introduction and Notes by J. C. BAILEY, M.A. Illustrated. *Demy 8vo. 10s. 6d. net.*

Crane (Walter), R.W.S. AN ARTIST'S REMINISCENCES. Illustrated. *Second Edition. Demy 8vo. 18s. net.*
INDIA IMPRESSIONS. Illustrated. *Second Edition. Demy 8vo. 7s. 6d. net.*

Crispe (T. E.). REMINISCENCES OF A K.C. With 2 Portraits. *Second Edition. Demy 8vo. 10s. 6d. net.*

Crowley (Ralph H.). THE HYGIENE OF SCHOOL LIFE. Illustrated. *Cr. 8vo. 3s. 6d. net.*

Dante (Alighieri). LA COMMEDIA DI DANTE. The Italian Text edited by PAGET TOYNBEE, M.A., D.Litt. *Cr. 8vo. 6s.*

Davey (Richard). THE PAGEANT OF LONDON. Illustrated. *In Two Volumes. Demy 8vo. 15s. net.*

Davis (H. W. C.), M.A., Fellow and Tutor of Balliol College. ENGLAND UNDER THE NORMANS AND ANGEVINS: 1066–1272. Illustrated. *Demy 8vo. 10s. 6d. net.*

Deans (R. Storry). THE TRIALS OF FIVE QUEENS: KATHARINE OF ARAGON, ANNE BOLEYN, MARY QUEEN OF SCOTS, MARIE ANTOINETTE and CAROLINE OF BRUNSWICK. Illustrated. *Second Edition. Demy 8vo. 10s. 6d. net.*

Dearmer (Mabel). A CHILD'S LIFE OF CHRIST. Illustrated. *Large Cr. 8vo. 6s.*

D'Este (Margaret). IN THE CANARIES WITH A CAMERA. Illustrated. *Cr. 8vo. 7s. 6d. net.*

Dickinson (G. L.), M.A., Fellow of King's College, Cambridge. THE GREEK VIEW OF LIFE. *Seventh and Revised Edition. Crown 8vo. 2s. 6d. net.*

Ditchfield (P. H.), M.A., F.S.A. THE PARISH CLERK. Illustrated. *Third Edition. Demy 8vo. 7s. 6d. net.*
THE OLD-TIME PARSON. Illustrated. *Second Edition. Demy 8vo. 7s. 6d. net.*

Douglas (Hugh A.). VENICE ON FOOT. With the Itinerary of the Grand Canal. Illustrated. *Second Edition. Fcap. 8vo. 5s. net.*

Douglas (James). THE MAN IN THE PULPIT. *Cr. 8vo.* 2s. 6d. net.

Dowden (J.), D.D., Late Lord Bishop of Edinburgh. FURTHER STUDIES IN THE PRAYER BOOK. *Cr. 8vo.* 6s.

Driver (S. R.), D.D., D.C.L., Regius Professor of Hebrew in the University of Oxford. SERMONS ON SUBJECTS CONNECTED WITH THE OLD TESTAMENT. *Cr. 8vo.* 6s.

Duff (Nora). MATILDA OF TUSCANY. Illustrated. *Demy 8vo.* 10s. 6d. net.

Dumas (Alexandre). THE CRIMES OF THE BORGIAS AND OTHERS. With an Introduction by R. S. GARNETT. Illustrated. *Cr. 8vo.* 6s.
THE CRIMES OF URBAIN GRANDIER AND OTHERS. Illustrated. *Cr. 8vo.* 6s.
THE CRIMES OF THE MARQUISE DE BRINVILLIERS AND OTHERS. Illustrated. *Cr. 8vo.* 6s.
THE CRIMES OF ALI PACHA AND OTHERS. Illustrated. *Cr. 8vo.* 6s.
MY MEMOIRS. Translated by E. M. WALLER. With an Introduction by ANDREW LANG. With Frontispieces in Photogravure. In six Volumes. *Cr. 8vo.* 6s. *each volume.*
VOL. I. 1802-1821. VOL. IV. 1830-1831.
VOL. II. 1822-1825. VOL. V. 1831-1832.
VOL. III. 1826-1830. VOL. VI. 1832-1833.
MY PETS. Newly translated by A. R. ALLINSON, M.A. Illustrated. *Cr. 8vo.* 6s.

Duncan (David), D.Sc., LL.D. THE LIFE AND LETTERS OF HERBERT SPENCER. Illustrated. *Demy 8vo.* 15s.

Dunn-Pattison (R. P.). NAPOLEON'S MARSHALS. Illustrated. *Demy 8vo. Second Edition.* 12s. 6d. net.
THE BLACK PRINCE. Illustrated. *Second Edition. Demy 8vo.* 7s. 6d. net.

Durham (The Earl of). A REPORT ON CANADA. With an Introductory Note. *Demy 8vo.* 4s. 6d. net.

Dutt (W. A.). THE NORFOLK BROADS. Illustrated. *Second Edition. Cr. 8vo.* 6s.
WILD LIFE IN EAST ANGLIA. Illustrated. *Second Edition. Demy 8vo.* 7s. 6d. net.

Edmonds (Major J. E.), R.E.; D. A. Q.-M. G. See Wood (W. Birkbeck).

Edwardes (Tickner). THE LORE OF THE HONEY BEE. Illustrated. *Cr. 8vo.* 6s.
LIFT-LUCK ON SOUTHERN ROADS. Illustrated. *Cr. 8vo.* 6s.

Egerton (H. E.), M.A. A HISTORY OF BRITISH COLONIAL POLICY. *Third Edition. Demy 8vo.* 7s. 6d. net.

Everett-Green (Mary Anne). ELIZABETH; ELECTRESS PALATINE AND QUEEN OF BOHEMIA. Revised by her Niece S. C. LOMAS. With a Prefatory Note by A. W. WARD, Litt.D. *Demy 8vo.* 10s. 6d. net.

Fairbrother (W. H.), M.A. THE PHILOSOPHY OF T. H. GREEN. *Second Edition. Cr. 8vo.* 3s. 6d.

Fea (Allan). THE FLIGHT OF THE KING. Illustrated. *New and Revised Edition. Demy 8vo.* 7s. 6d. net.
SECRET CHAMBERS AND HIDING-PLACES. Illustrated. *New and Revised Edition. Demy 8vo.* 7s. 6d. net.
JAMES II. AND HIS WIVES. Illustrated. *Demy 8vo.* 10s. 6d. net.

Fell (E. F. B.). THE FOUNDATIONS OF LIBERTY. *Cr. 8vo.* 5s. net.

Firth (C. H.), M.A., Regius Professor of Modern History at Oxford. CROMWELL'S ARMY: A History of the English Soldier during the Civil Wars, the Commonwealth, and the Protectorate. *Cr. 8vo.* 6s.

FitzGerald (Edward). THE RUBÁIYÁT OF OMAR KHAYYÁM. Printed from the Fifth and last Edition. With a Commentary by Mrs. STEPHEN BATSON, and a Biography of Omar by E. D. Ross. *Cr. 8vo.* 6s.

*****Fletcher (B. F. and H. P.).** THE ENGLISH HOME. Illustrated. *Second Edition. Demy 8vo.* 12s. 6d. net.

Fletcher (J. S.). A BOOK OF YORKSHIRE. Illustrated. *Demy 8vo.* 7s. 6d. net.

Flux (A. W.), M.A., William Dow Professor of Political Economy in M'Gill University, Montreal. ECONOMIC PRINCIPLES. *Demy 8vo.* 7s. 6d. net.

Foot (Constance M.). INSECT WONDERLAND. Illustrated. *Second Edition. Cr. 8vo.* 3s. 6d. net.

Forel (A.). THE SENSES OF INSECTS. Translated by MACLEOD YEARSLEY. Illustrated. *Demy 8vo.* 10s. 6d. net.

Fouqué (La Motte). SINTRAM AND HIS COMPANIONS. Translated by A. C. FARQUHARSON. Illustrated. *Demy 8vo.* 7s. 6d. net. *Half White Vellum,* 10s. 6d. net.

Fraser (J. F.). ROUND THE WORLD ON A WHEEL. Illustrated. *Fifth Edition. Cr. 8vo.* 6s.

General Literature

Galton (Sir Francis), F.R.S.; D.C.L., Oxf.; Hon. Sc.D., Camb.; Hon. Fellow Trinity College, Cambridge. MEMORIES OF MY LIFE. Illustrated. *Third Edition.* Demy 8vo. 10s. 6d. net.

Garnett (Lucy M. J.). THE TURKISH PEOPLE: THEIR SOCIAL LIFE, RELIGIOUS BELIEFS AND INSTITUTIONS, AND DOMESTIC LIFE. Illustrated. *Demy 8vo.* 10s. 6d. net.

Gibbins (H. de B.), Litt.D., M.A. INDUSTRY IN ENGLAND: HISTORICAL OUTLINES. With 5 Maps. *Fifth Edition.* Demy 8vo. 10s. 6d.
THE INDUSTRIAL HISTORY OF ENGLAND. Illustrated. *Sixteenth Edition.* Cr. 8vo. 3s.
ENGLISH SOCIAL REFORMERS. *Second Edition.* Cr. 8vo. 2s. 6d.
See also Hadfield, R.A.

Gibbon (Edward). MEMOIRS OF THE LIFE OF EDWARD GIBBON. Edited by G. BIRKBECK HILL, LL.D. *Cr. 8vo.* 6s.
*THE DECLINE AND FALL OF THE ROMAN EMPIRE. Edited, with Notes, Appendices, and Maps, by J. B. BURY, M.A., Litt.D., Regius Professor of Modern History at Cambridge. Illustrated. *In Seven Volumes.* Demy 8vo. Gilt Top. Each 10s. 6d. net.

Gibbs (Philip.) THE ROMANCE OF GEORGE VILLIERS: FIRST DUKE OF BUCKINGHAM, AND SOME MEN AND WOMEN OF THE STUART COURT. Illustrated. *Second Edition.* Demy 8vo. 15s. net.

Gloag (M. R.) and Wyatt (Kate M.). A BOOK OF ENGLISH GARDENS. Illustrated. *Demy 8vo.* 10s. 6d. net.

Glover (T. R.), M.A., Fellow and Classical Lecturer of St. John's College, Cambridge. THE CONFLICT OF RELIGIONS IN THE EARLY ROMAN EMPIRE. *Fourth Edition.* Demy 8vo. 7s. 6d. net.

Godfrey (Elizabeth). A BOOK OF REMEMBRANCE. Being Lyrical Selections for every day in the Year. Arranged by E. Godfrey. *Second Edition.* Fcap. 8vo. 2s. 6d. net.
ENGLISH CHILDREN IN THE OLDEN TIME. Illustrated. *Second Edition.* Demy 8vo. 7s. 6d. net.

Godley (A. D.), M.A., Fellow of Magdalen College, Oxford. OXFORD IN THE EIGHTEENTH CENTURY. Illustrated. *Second Edition.* Demy 8vo. 7s. 6d. net.
LYRA FRIVOLA. *Fourth Edition.* Fcap. 8vo. 2s. 6d.
VERSES TO ORDER. *Second Edition.* Fcap. 8vo. 2s. 6d.
SECOND STRINGS. *Fcap. 8vo.* 2s. 6d.

Goll (August). CRIMINAL TYPES IN SHAKESPEARE. Authorised Translation from the Danish by Mrs. CHARLES WEEKES. *Cr. 8vo.* 5s. net.

Gordon (Lina Duff) (Mrs. Aubrey Waterfield). HOME LIFE IN ITALY: LETTERS FROM THE APENNINES. Illustrated. *Second Edition.* Demy 8vo. 10s. 6d. net.

Gostling (Frances M.). THE BRETONS AT HOME. Illustrated. *Second Edition.* Demy 8vo. 10s. 6d. net.

Graham (Harry). A GROUP OF SCOTTISH WOMEN. Illustrated. *Second Edition.* Demy 8vo. 10s. 6d. net.

Grahame (Kenneth). THE WIND IN THE WILLOWS. Illustrated. *Fifth Edition.* Cr. 8vo. 6s.

Gwynn (Stephen), M.P. A HOLIDAY IN CONNEMARA. Illustrated. *Demy 8vo.* 10s 6d. net.

Hall (Cyril). THE YOUNG CARPENTER. Illustrated. *Cr. 8vo.* 5s.

Hall (Hammond). THE YOUNG ENGINEER: or MODERN ENGINES AND THEIR MODELS. Illustrated. *Second Edition.* Cr. 8vo. 5s.

Hall (Mary). A WOMAN'S TREK FROM THE CAPE TO CAIRO. Illustrated. *Second Edition.* Demy 8vo. 16s. net.

Hannay (D.). A SHORT HISTORY OF THE ROYAL NAVY. Vol. I., 1217-1688. Vol. II., 1689-1815. *Demy 8vo.* Each 7s. 6d. net.

Hannay (James O.), M.A. THE SPIRIT AND ORIGIN OF CHRISTIAN MONASTICISM. *Cr. 8vo.* 6s.
THE WISDOM OF THE DESERT. *Fcap. 8vo.* 3s. 6d. net.

Harper (Charles G.). THE AUTOCAR ROAD-BOOK. Four Volumes with Maps. *Cr. 8vo.* Each 7s. 6d. net.
Vol. I.—SOUTH OF THE THAMES.
Vol. II.—NORTH AND SOUTH WALES AND WEST MIDLANDS.

Headley (F. W.). DARWINISM AND MODERN SOCIALISM. *Second Edition.* Cr. 8vo. 5s. net.

Henderson (B. W.), Fellow of Exeter, College, Oxford. THE LIFE AND PRINCIPATE OF THE EMPEROR NERO. Illustrated. *New and cheaper issue.* Demy 8vo. 7s. 6d. net.

Henderson (M. Sturge). GEORGE MEREDITH; NOVELIST, POET, REFORMER. Illustrated. *Second Edition.* Cr. 8vo. 6s.

Henderson (T. F.) and Watt (Francis). SCOTLAND OF TO-DAY. Illustrated. *Second Edition. Cr. 8vo. 6s.*

Henley (W. E.). ENGLISH LYRICS, CHAUCER TO POE, 1340-1849. *Second Edition. Cr. 8vo. 2s. 6d. net.*

Heywood (W.). A HISTORY OF PERUGIA. Illustrated. *Demy 8vo. 12s. 6d. net.*

Hill (George Francis). ONE HUNDRED MASTERPIECES OF SCULPTURE. Illustrated. *Demy 8vo. 10s. 6d. net.*

Hind (C. Lewis). DAYS IN CORNWALL. Illustrated. *Second Edition. Cr. 8vo. 6s.*

Hobhouse (L. T.), late Fellow of C.C.C., Oxford. THE THEORY OF KNOWLEDGE. *Demy 8vo. 10s. 6d. net.*

Hodgetts (E. A. Brayley). THE COURT OF RUSSIA IN THE NINETEENTH CENTURY. Illustrated. *Two volumes. Demy 8vo. 24s. net.*

Hodgson (Mrs. W.). HOW TO IDENTIFY OLD CHINESE PORCELAIN. Illustrated. *Second Edition. Post 8vo. 6s.*

Holdich (Sir T. H.), K.C.I.E., C.B., F.S.A. THE INDIAN BORDERLAND, 1880-1900. Illustrated. *Second Edition. Demy 8vo. 10s. 6d. net.*

Holdsworth (W. S.), D.C.L. A HISTORY OF ENGLISH LAW. *In Four Volumes. Vols. I., II., III. Demy 8vo. Each 10s. 6d. net.*

Holland (Clive). TYROL AND ITS PEOPLE. Illustrated. *Demy 8vo. 10s. 6d. net.*

Horsburgh (E. L. S.), M.A. LORENZO THE MAGNIFICENT; AND FLORENCE IN HER GOLDEN AGE. Illustrated. *Second Edition. Demy 8vo. 15s. net.*
WATERLOO: with Plans. *Second Edition. Cr. 8vo. 5s.*

Hosie (Alexander). MANCHURIA. Illustrated. *Second Edition. Demy 8vo. 7s. 6d. net.*

Hulton (Samuel F.). THE CLERK OF OXFORD IN FICTION. Illustrated. *Demy 8vo. 10s. 6d. net.*

*****Humphreys (John H.).** PROPORTIONAL REPRESENTATION. *Cr. 8vo. 3s. 6d. net.*

Hutchinson (Horace G.). THE NEW FOREST. Illustrated. *Fourth Edition. Cr. 8vo. 6s.*

Hutton (Edward). THE CITIES OF UMBRIA. Illustrated. *Fourth Edition. Cr. 8vo. 6s.*
THE CITIES OF SPAIN. Illustrated. *Third Edition. Cr. 8vo. 6s.*
FLORENCE AND THE CITIES OF NORTHERN TUSCANY, WITH GENOA. Illustrated. *Second Edition. Crown 8vo. 6s.*
ENGLISH LOVE POEMS. Edited with an Introduction. *Fcap. 8vo. 3s. 6d. net.*
COUNTRY WALKS ABOUT FLORENCE. Illustrated. *Fcap. 8vo. 5s. net.*
IN UNKNOWN TUSCANY With an Appendix by WILLIAM HEYWOOD. Illustrated. *Second Edition. Demy 8vo. 7s. 6d. net.*
ROME. Illustrated. *Second Edition. Cr. 8vo. 6s.*

Hyett (F. A.) FLORENCE: HER HISTORY AND ART TO THE FALL OF THE REPUBLIC. *Demy 8vo. 7s. 6d. net.*

Ibsen (Henrik). BRAND. A Drama. Translated by WILLIAM WILSON. *Fourth Edition. Cr. 8vo. 3s. 6d.*

Inge (W. R.), M.A., Fellow and Tutor of Hertford College, Oxford. CHRISTIAN MYSTICISM. (The Bampton Lectures of 1899.) *Demy 8vo. 12s. 6d. net.*

Innes (A. D.), M.A. A HISTORY OF THE BRITISH IN INDIA. With Maps and Plans. *Cr. 8vo. 6s.*
ENGLAND UNDER THE TUDORS. With Maps. *Third Edition. Demy 8vo. 10s. 6d. net.*

Innes (Mary). SCHOOLS OF PAINTING. Illustrated. *Cr. 8vo. 5s. net.*

James (Norman G. B.). THE CHARM OF SWITZERLAND. *Cr. 8vo. 5s. net.*

Jeffery (Reginald W.), M.A. THE HISTORY OF THE THIRTEEN COLONIES OF NORTH AMERICA, 1497-1763. Illustrated. *Demy 8vo. 7s. 6d. net.*

Jenks (E.), M.A., B.C.L. AN OUTLINE OF ENGLISH LOCAL GOVERNMENT. *Second Edition.* Revised by R. C. K. ENSOR, M.A. *Cr. 8vo. 2s. 6d.*

Jerningham (Charles Edward). THE MAXIMS OF MARMADUKE. *Second Edition. Cr. 8vo. 5s.*

Johnston (Sir H. H.), K.C.B. BRITISH CENTRAL AFRICA. Illustrated. *Third Edition. Cr. 4to. 18s. net.*

*THE NEGRO IN THE NEW WORLD. Illustrated. *Demy 8vo*. 16s. net.

Jones (R. Crompton), M.A. POEMS OF THE INNER LIFE. Selected by R. C. JONES. *Thirteenth Edition. Fcap 8vo*. 2s. 6d. net.

Julian (Lady) of Norwich. REVELATIONS OF DIVINE LOVE. Edited by GRACE WARRACK. *Fourth Edition. Cr. 8vo*. 3s. 6d.

'Kappa.' LET YOUTH BUT KNOW: A Plea for Reason in Education. *Second Edition. Cr. 8vo*. 3s. 6d. net.

Keats (John). THE POEMS. Edited with Introduction and Notes by E. de SÉLINCOURT, M.A. With a Frontispiece in Photogravure. *Second Edition Revised. Demy 8vo*. 7s. 6d. net.

Keble (John). THE CHRISTIAN YEAR. With an Introduction and Notes by W. LOCK, D.D., Warden of Keble College. Illustrated. *Third Edition. Fcap. 8vo*. 3s. 6d.; *padded morocco*. 5s.

Kempis (Thomas à). THE IMITATION OF CHRIST. With an Introduction by DEAN FARRAR. Illustrated. *Third Edition. Fcap. 8vo*. 3s. 6d.; *padded morocco*, 5s.
Also translated by C. BIGG, D.D. *Cr. 8vo*. 3s. 6d.

Kerr (S. Parnell). GEORGE SELWYN AND THE WITS. Illustrated. *Demy 8vo*. 12s. 6d. net.

Kipling (Rudyard). BARRACK-ROOM BALLADS. 96th Thousand. *Twenty-eighth Edition. Cr. 8vo*. 6s. Also *Fcap. 8vo, Leather*. 5s. net.
THE SEVEN SEAS. 83rd Thousand. *Seventeenth Edition. Cr. 8vo*. 6s. Also *Fcap. 8vo, Leather*. 5s. net.
THE FIVE NATIONS. 69th Thousand. *Seventh Edition. Cr. 8vo*. 6s. Also *Fcap. 8vo, Leather*. 5s. net.
DEPARTMENTAL DITTIES. *Nineteenth Edition. Cr. 8vo*. 6s. Also *Fcap. 8vo, Leather*. 5s. net.

Knox (Winifred F.). THE COURT OF A SAINT. Illustrated. *Demy 8vo*. 10s. 6d. net.

Lamb (Charles and Mary), THE WORKS. Edited by E. V. LUCAS. Illustrated. *In Seven Volumes. Demy 8vo*. 7s. 6d. each.

Lane-Poole (Stanley). A HISTORY OF EGYPT IN THE MIDDLE AGES. Illustrated. *Cr. 8vo*. 6s.

Lankester (Sir Ray), K.C.B., F.R.S. SCIENCE FROM AN EASY CHAIR. Illustrated. *Fifth Edition. Cr. 8vo*. 6s.

Leach (Henry). THE SPIRIT OF THE LINKS. *Cr. 8vo*. 6s.

Le Braz (Anatole). THE LAND OF PARDONS. Translated by FRANCES M. GOSTLING. Illustrated. *Third Edition. Cr. 8vo*. 6s.

Lees (Frederick). A SUMMER IN TOURAINE. Illustrated. *Second Edition. Demy 8vo*. 10s. 6d. net.

Lindsay (Lady Mabel). ANNI DOMINI: A GOSPEL STUDY. With Maps. *Two Volumes. Super Royal 8vo*. 10s. net.

Llewellyn (Owen) and Raven-Hill (L.). THE SOUTH-BOUND CAR. Illustrated. *Cr. 8vo*. 6s.

Lock (Walter), D.D., Warden of Keble College. ST. PAUL, THE MASTER-BUILDER. *Third Edition. Cr. 8vo*. 3s. 6d.
THE BIBLE AND CHRISTIAN LIFE. *Cr. 8vo*. 6s.

Lodge (Sir Oliver), F.R.S. THE SUBSTANCE OF FAITH, ALLIED WITH SCIENCE: A Catechism for Parents and Teachers. *Tenth Edition. Cr. 8vo*. 2s. net.
MAN AND THE UNIVERSE: A STUDY OF THE INFLUENCE OF THE ADVANCE IN SCIENTIFIC KNOWLEDGE UPON OUR UNDERSTANDING OF CHRISTIANITY. *Ninth Edition. Demy 8vo*. 5s. net.
THE SURVIVAL OF MAN. A STUDY IN UNRECOGNISED HUMAN FACULTY. *Fourth and Cheaper Edition. Demy 8vo*. 5s. net.

Lofthouse (W. F.), M.A. ETHICS AND ATONEMENT. With a Frontispiece. *Demy 8vo*. 5s. net.

Lorimer (George Horace). LETTERS FROM A SELF-MADE MERCHANT TO HIS SON. Illustrated. *Eighteenth Edition. Cr. 8vo*. 3s. 6d.
OLD GORGON GRAHAM. Illustrated. *Second Edition. Cr. 8vo*. 6s.

Lorimer (Norma). BY THE WATERS OF EGYPT. Illustrated. *Demy 8vo*. 16s. net.

Lucas (E. V.). THE LIFE OF CHARLES LAMB. Illustrated. *Fifth and Revised Edition in One Volume. Demy 8vo*. 7s. 6d. net.
A WANDERER IN HOLLAND. Illustrated. *Twelfth Edition. Cr. 8vo*. 6s.
A WANDERER IN LONDON. Illustrated. *Tenth Edition. Cr. 8vo*. 6s.
A WANDERER IN PARIS. Illustrated. *Sixth Edition. Cr. 8vo*. 6s.

THE OPEN ROAD: A Little Book for Wayfarers. *Seventeenth Edition*. Fcp. 8vo. 5s.; *India Paper*, 7s. 6d.

THE FRIENDLY TOWN: a Little Book for the Urbane. *Sixth Edition*. Fcap. 8vo. 5s.; *India Paper*, 7s. 6d.

FIRESIDE AND SUNSHINE. *Sixth Edition*. Fcap. 8vo. 5s.

CHARACTER AND COMEDY. *Sixth Edition*. Fcap. 8vo. 5s.

THE GENTLEST ART. A Choice of Letters by Entertaining Hands. *Sixth Edition*. Fcap 8vo. 5s.

A SWAN AND HER FRIENDS. Illustrated. *Demy 8vo*. 12s. 6d. net.

HER INFINITE VARIETY: A FEMININE PORTRAIT GALLERY. *Fifth Edition*. Fcap. 8vo. 5s.

LISTENER'S LURE: AN OBLIQUE NARRATION. *Eighth Edition*. Fcap. 8vo. 5s.

GOOD COMPANY: A RALLY OF MEN. *Second Edition*. Fcap. 8vo. 5s.

ONE DAY AND ANOTHER. *Fourth Edition*. Fcap. 8vo. 5s.

OVER BEMERTON'S: AN EASY-GOING CHRONICLE. *Ninth Edition*. Fcap. 8vo. 5s.

M. (R.). THE THOUGHTS OF LUCIA HALLIDAY. With some of her Letters. Edited by R. M. *Fcap. 8vo*. 2s. 6d. net.

Macaulay (Lord). CRITICAL AND HISTORICAL ESSAYS. Edited by F. C. MONTAGUE. M.A. *Three Volumes*. Cr. 8vo. 18s.

McCabe (Joseph) (formerly Very Rev. F. ANTONY, O.S.F.). THE DECAY OF THE CHURCH OF ROME. *Second Edition*. Demy 8vo. 7s. 6d. net.

McCullagh (Francis). The Fall of Abd-ul-Hamid. Illustrated. *Demy 8vo*. 10s. 6d. net.

MacCunn (Florence A.). MARY STUART. Illustrated. *New and Cheaper Edition*. Large Cr. 8vo. 6s.

McDougall (William), M.A. (Oxon., M.B. (Cantab.). AN INTRODUCTION TO SOCIAL PSYCHOLOGY. *Third Edition*. Cr. 8vo. 5s. net.

'Mdlle. Mori' (Author of). ST. CATHERINE OF SIENA AND HER TIMES. Illustrated. *Second Edition*. Demy 8vo. 7s. 6d. net.

Maeterlinck (Maurice). THE BLUE BIRD: A FAIRY PLAY IN SIX ACTS. Translated by ALEXANDER TEIXEIRA DE MATTOS. *Twentieth Edition*. Fcap. 8vo. Deckle Edges. 3s. 6d. net. Also Fcap. 8vo. Paper covers, 1s. net.

Mahaffy (J. P.), Litt.D. A HISTORY OF THE EGYPT OF THE PTOLEMIES. Illustrated. *Cr. 8vo*. 6s.

Maitland (F. W.), M.A., LL.D. ROMAN CANON LAW IN THE CHURCH OF ENGLAND. *Royal 8vo*. 7s. 6d.

Marett (R. R.), M.A., Fellow and Tutor of Exeter College, Oxford. THE THRESHOLD OF RELIGION. Cr. 8vo. 3s. 6d. net.

Marriott (Charles). A SPANISH HOLIDAY. Illustrated. *Demy 8vo*. 7s. 6d. net.

Marriott (J. A. R.) M.A. THE LIFE AND TIMES OF LORD FALKLAND. Illustrated. *Second Edition*. Demy 8vo. 7s. 6d. net.

Masefield (John). SEA LIFE IN NELSON'S TIME. Illustrated. *Cr. 8vo*. 3s. 6d. net.

A SAILOR'S GARLAND. Selected and Edited. *Second Edition*. Cr. 8vo. 3s. 6d. net.

AN ENGLISH PROSE MISCELLANY. Selected and Edited. *Cr. 8vo*. 6s.

Masterman (C. F. G.), M.A., M.P. TENNYSON AS A RELIGIOUS TEACHER. *Second Edition*. Cr. 8vo. 6s.

THE CONDITION OF ENGLAND. *Fourth Edition*. Cr. 8vo. 6s.

Mayne (Ethel Colburn). ENCHANTERS OF MEN. Illustrated. *Demy 8vo*. 10s. 6d. net.

Meakin (Annette M. B.), Fellow of the Anthropological Institute. WOMAN IN TRANSITION. *Cr. 8vo*. 6s.

GALICIA: THE SWITZERLAND OF SPAIN. Illustrated. *Demy 8vo*. 12s. 6d. net.

Medley (D. J.), M.A., Professor of History in the University of Glasgow. ORIGINAL ILLUSTRATIONS OF ENGLISH CONSTITUTIONAL HISTORY, COMPRISING A SELECTED NUMBER OF THE CHIEF CHARTERS AND STATUTES. *Cr. 8vo*. 7s. 6d. net.

Methuen (A. M. S.), M.A. THE TRAGEDY OF SOUTH AFRICA. Cr. 8vo. 2s. net.

ENGLAND'S RUIN: DISCUSSED IN FOURTEEN LETTERS TO A PROTECTIONIST. *Ninth Edition*. Cr. 8vo. 3d. net.

Meynell (Everard). COROT AND HIS FRIENDS. Illustrated. *Demy 8vo*. 10s. 6d. net.

Miles (Eustace), M.A. LIFE AFTER LIFE: OR, THE THEORY OF REINCARNATION. *Cr. 8vo*. 2s. 6d. net.

THE POWER OF CONCENTRATION: How TO ACQUIRE IT. *Third Edition*. Cr. 8vo. 3s. 6d. net.

Millais (J. G.). THE LIFE AND LETTERS OF SIR JOHN EVERETT MILLAIS, President of the Royal Academy. Illustrated. *New Edition*. Demy 8vo. 7s. 6d. net.

Milne (J. G.), M.A. A HISTORY OF EGYPT UNDER ROMAN RULE. Illustrated. *Cr. 8vo*. 6s.

Mitton (G. E.). JANE AUSTEN AND HER TIMES. Illustrated. *Second and Cheaper Edition. Large Cr. 8vo. 6s.*

Moffat (Mary M.). QUEEN LOUISA OF PRUSSIA. Illustrated. *Fourth Edition. Cr. 8vo. 6s.*

Money (L. G. Chiozza). RICHES AND POVERTY. *Tenth Edition. Demy 8vo. 5s. net.* Also *Crown 8vo. 1s. net.*
MONEY'S FISCAL DICTIONARY, 1910. *Demy 8vo. Second Edition. 5s. net.*

Moore (T. Sturge). ART AND LIFE. Illustrated. *Cr. 8vo. 5s. net.*

Moorhouse (E. Hallam). NELSON'S LADY HAMILTON. Illustrated. *Second Edition. Demy 8vo. 7s. 6d. net.*

Morgan (J. H.), M.A. THE HOUSE OF LORDS AND THE CONSTITUTION. With an Introduction by the LORD CHANCELLOR. *Cr. 8vo. 1s. net.*

Morton (A. Anderson). See Brodrick (M.).

Norway (A. H.). NAPLES. PAST AND PRESENT. Illustrated. *Third Edition. Cr. 8vo. 6s.*

Oman (C. W. C.), M.A., Fellow of All Souls', Oxford. A HISTORY OF THE ART OF WAR IN THE MIDDLE AGES. Illustrated. *Demy 8vo. 10s. 6d. net.*
ENGLAND BEFORE THE NORMAN CONQUEST. With Maps. *Second Edition. Demy 8vo. 10s. 6d. net.*

Oxford (M. N.), of Guy's Hospital. A HANDBOOK OF NURSING. *Fifth Edition. Cr. 8vo. 3s. 6d.*

Pakes (W. C. C.). THE SCIENCE OF HYGIENE. Illustrated. *Demy 8vo. 15s.*

Parker (Eric). THE BOOK OF THE ZOO; BY DAY AND NIGHT. Illustrated. *Second Edition. Cr. 8vo. 6s.*

Parsons (Mrs. C.). THE INCOMPARABLE SIDDONS. Illustrated. *Demy 8vo. 12s. 6d. net.*

Patmore (K. A.). THE COURT OF LOUIS XIII. Illustrated. *Third Edition. Demy 8vo. 10s. 6d. net.*

Patterson (A. H.). MAN AND NATURE ON TIDAL WATERS. Illustrated. *Cr. 8vo. 6s.*

Petrie (W. M. Flinders), D.C.L., LL.D., Professor of Egyptology at University College. A HISTORY OF EGYPT. Illustrated. *In Six Volumes. Cr. 8vo. 6s. each.*

VOL. I. FROM THE EARLIEST KINGS TO XVITH DYNASTY. *Sixth Edition.*
VOL. II. THE XVIITH AND XVIIITH DYNASTIES. *Fourth Edition.*
VOL. III. XIXTH TO XXXTH DYNASTIES.
VOL. IV. EGYPT UNDER THE PTOLEMAIC DYNASTY. J. P. MAHAFFY, Litt.D.
VOL. V. EGYPT UNDER ROMAN RULE. J. G. MILNE, M.A.
VOL. VI. EGYPT IN THE MIDDLE AGES. STANLEY LANE-POOLE, M.A.
RELIGION AND CONSCIENCE IN ANCIENT EGYPT. Lectures delivered at University College, London. Illustrated. *Cr. 8vo. 2s. 6d.*
SYRIA AND EGYPT, FROM THE TELL EL AMARNA LETTERS. *Cr. 8vo. 2s. 6d.*
EGYPTIAN TALES. Translated from the Papyri. First Series, ivth to xiith Dynasty. Edited by W. M. FLINDERS PETRIE. Illustrated. *Second Edition. Cr. 8vo. 3s. 6d.*
EGYPTIAN TALES. Translated from the Papyri. Second Series, xviiith to xixth Dynasty. Illustrated. *Cr. 8vo. 3s. 6d.*
EGYPTIAN DECORATIVE ART. A Course of Lectures delivered at the Royal Institution. Illustrated. *Cr. 8vo. 3s. 6d.*

Phelps (Ruth S.). SKIES ITALIAN: A LITTLE BREVIARY FOR TRAVELLERS IN ITALY. *Fcap. 8vo. 5s. net.*

Phythian (J. Ernest). TREES IN NATURE, MYTH, AND ART. Illustrated. *Cr. 8vo. 6s.*

Podmore (Frank). MODERN SPIRITUALISM. *Two Volumes. Demy 8vo. 21s. net.*
MESMERISM AND CHRISTIAN SCIENCE: A Short History of Mental Healing. *Second Edition. Demy 8vo. 10s. 6d. net.*

Pollard (Alfred W.). SHAKESPEARE FOLIOS AND QUARTOS. A Study in the Bibliography of Shakespeare's Plays, 1594-1685. Illustrated. *Folio. 21s. net.*

Powell (Arthur E.). FOOD AND HEALTH. *Cr. 8vo. 3s. 6d. net.*

Power (J. O'Connor). THE MAKING OF AN ORATOR. *Cr. 8vo. 6s.*

Price (L. L.), M.A., Fellow of Oriel College, Oxon. A HISTORY OF ENGLISH POLITICAL ECONOMY FROM ADAM SMITH TO ARNOLD TOYNBEE. *Seventh Edition. Cr. 8vo. 2s. 6d.*

Puller-Burry (B.). IN A GERMAN COLONY; or, FOUR WEEKS IN NEW BRITAIN. Illustrated. *Cr. 8vo. 5s. net.*

Pycraft (W. P.). BIRD LIFE. Illustrated. *Demy 8vo. 10s. 6d. net.*

Ragg (Lonsdale), B.D. Oxon. DANTE AND HIS ITALY. Illustrated. *Demy 8vo.* 12s. 6d. *net.*

*****Rappoport (Angelo S.).** HOME LIFE IN RUSSIA. Illustrated. *Demy 8vo.* 10s. 6d. *net.*

Raven-Hill (L.). See Llewellyn (Owen).

Rawlings (Gertrude). COINS AND HOW TO KNOW THEM. Illustrated. *Third Edition. Cr. 8vo.* 5s. *net.*

Rea (Lilian). THE LIFE AND TIMES OF MARIE MADELEINE COUNTESS OF LA FAYETTE. Illustrated. *Demy 8vo.* 10s. 6d. *net.*

Read (C. Stanford), M.B. (Lond.), M.R.C.S., L.R.C.P. FADS AND FEEDING. *Cr. 8vo.* 2s. 6d. *net.*

Rees (J. D.), C.I.E., M.P. THE REAL INDIA. *Second Edition. Demy 8vo.* 10s. 6d. *net.*

Reich (Emil), Doctor Juris. WOMAN THROUGH THE AGES. Illustrated. *Two Volumes. Demy 8vo.* 21s. *net.*

Reid (Archdall), M.B. THE LAWS OF HEREDITY. *Second Edition. Demy 8vo.* 21s. *net.*

Richmond (Wilfrid), Chaplain of Lincoln's Inn. THE CREED IN THE EPISTLES. *Cr. 8vo.* 2s. 6d. *net.*

Roberts (M. E.). See Channer (C. C.).

Robertson (A.), D.D., Lord Bishop of Exeter. REGNUM DEI. (The Bampton Lectures of 1901.) *A New and Cheaper Edition. Demy 8vo.* 7s. 6d. *net.*

Robertson (C. Grant), M.A., Fellow of All Souls' College, Oxford. SELECT STATUTES, CASES, AND CONSTITUTIONAL DOCUMENTS, 1660-1832. *Demy 8vo.* 10s. 6d. *net.*

Robertson (Sir G. S.), K.C.S.I. CHITRAL: THE STORY OF A MINOR SIEGE. Illustrated. *Third Edition. Demy 8vo.* 10s. 6d. *net.*

Roe (Fred). OLD OAK FURNITURE. Illustrated. *Second Edition. Demy 8vo.* 10s. 6d. *net.*

Royde-Smith (N. G.). THE PILLOW BOOK: A GARNER OF MANY MOODS. Collected. *Second Edition. Cr. 8vo.* 4s. 6d. *net.*

POETS OF OUR DAY. Selected, with an Introduction. *Fcap. 8vo.* 5s.

Rumbold (The Right Hon. Sir Horace), Bart., G.C.B., G.C.M.G. THE AUSTRIAN COURT IN THE NINETEENTH CENTURY. Illustrated. *Second Edition. Demy 8vo.* 18s. *net.*

Russell (W. Clark). THE LIFE OF ADMIRAL LORD COLLINGWOOD. Illustrated. *Fourth Edition. Cr. 8vo.* 6s.

St. Francis of Assisi. THE LITTLE FLOWERS OF THE GLORIOUS MESSER, AND OF HIS FRIARS. Done into English, with Notes by WILLIAM HEYWOOD. Illustrated. *Demy 8vo.* 5s. *net.*

'Saki' (H. Munro). REGINALD. *Second Edition. Fcap. 8vo.* 2s. 6d. *net.*
REGINALD IN RUSSIA. *Fcap. 8vo.* 2s. 6d. *net.*

Sanders (Lloyd). THE HOLLAND HOUSE CIRCLE. Illustrated. *Second Edition. Demy 8vo.* 12s. 6d. *net.*

*****Scott (Ernest).** TERRE NAPOLÉON, AND THE EXPEDITION OF DISCOVERY DESPATCHED TO AUSTRALIA BY ORDER OF BONAPARTE, 1800-1804. Illustrated. *Second Edition. Demy 8vo.* 10s. 6d. *net.*

Sélincourt (Hugh de). GREAT RALEGH. Illustrated. *Demy 8vo.* 10s. 6d. *net.*

Selous (Edmund). TOMMY SMITH'S ANIMALS. Illustrated. *Eleventh Edition. Fcap. 8vo.* 2s. 6d.
TOMMY SMITH'S OTHER ANIMALS. Illustrated. *Fifth Edition. Fcap. 8vo.* 2s. 6d.

*****Shafer (Sara A.).** A WHITE PAPER GARDEN. Illustrated. *Demy 8vo.* 7s. 6d. *net.*

Shakespeare (William).
THE FOUR FOLIOS, 1623; 1632; 1664; 1685. Each £4 4s. *net*, or a complete set, £12 12s. *net.*
Folios 2, 3 and 4 are ready.
THE POEMS OF WILLIAM SHAKESPEARE. With an Introduction and Notes by GEORGE WYNDHAM. *Demy 8vo. Buckram, gilt top.* 10s. 6d.

Sharp (A.). VICTORIAN POETS. *Cr. 8vo.* 2s. 6d.

Sidgwick (Mrs. Alfred). HOME LIFE IN GERMANY. Illustrated. *Second Edition. Demy 8vo.* 10s. 6d. *net.*

Sime (John). See Little Books on Art.

Sladen (Douglas). SICILY: The New Winter Resort. Illustrated. *Second Edition. Cr. 8vo.* 5s. *net.*

Smith (Adam). THE WEALTH OF NATIONS. Edited with an Introduction and numerous Notes by EDWIN CANNAN, M.A. *Two Volumes. Demy 8vo.* 21s. *net.*

Smith (Sophia S.). DEAN SWIFT. Illustrated. *Demy 8vo.* 10s. 6d. *net.*

Snell (F. J.). A BOOK OF EXMOOR. Illustrated. *Cr. 8vo.* 6s.

*****Stancliffe.'** GOLF DO'S AND DONT'S. *Second Edition. Fcap. 8vo.* 1s.

General Literature

Stead (Francis H.), M.A. HOW OLD AGE PENSIONS BEGAN TO BE. Illustrated. *Demy 8vo.* 2s. 6d. net.

Stevenson (R. L.). THE LETTERS OF ROBERT LOUIS STEVENSON TO HIS FAMILY AND FRIENDS. Selected and Edited by Sir SIDNEY COLVIN. *Ninth Edition. Two Volumes. Cr. 8vo.* 12s.
VAILIMA LETTERS. With an Etched Portrait by WILLIAM STRANG. *Eighth Edition. Cr. 8vo. Buckram.* 6s.
THE LIFE OF R. L. STEVENSON. See Balfour (G.).

Stevenson (M. I.). FROM SARANAC TO THE MARQUESAS. Being Letters written by Mrs. M. I. STEVENSON during 1887-88. *Cr. 8vo.* 6s. net.
LETTERS FROM SAMOA, 1891-95. Edited and arranged by M. C. BALFOUR. Illustrated. *Second Edition. Cr. 8vo.* 6s. net.

Storr (Vernon F.), M.A., Canon of Winchester. DEVELOPMENT AND DIVINE PURPOSE. *Cr. 8vo.* 5s. net.

Streatfeild (R. A.). MODERN MUSIC AND MUSICIANS. Illustrated. *Second Edition. Demy 8vo.* 7s. 6d. net.

Swanton (E. W.). FUNGI AND HOW TO KNOW THEM. Illustrated. *Cr. 8vo.* 6s. net.

*****Sykes (Ella C.).** PERSIA AND ITS PEOPLE. Illustrated. *Demy 8vo.* 10s. 6d. net.

Symes (J. E.), M.A. THE FRENCH REVOLUTION. *Second Edition. Cr. 8vo.* 2s. 6d.

Tabor (Margaret E.). THE SAINTS IN ART. Illustrated. *Fcap. 8vo.* 3s. 6d. net.

Taylor (A. E.). THE ELEMENTS OF METAPHYSICS. *Second Edition. Demy 8vo.* 10s. 6d. net.

Taylor (John W.). THE COMING OF THE SAINTS. Illustrated. *Demy 8vo.* 7s. 6d. net.

Thibaudeau (A. C.). BONAPARTE AND THE CONSULATE. Translated and Edited by G. K. FORTESCUE, LL.D. Illustrated. *Demy 8vo.* 10s. 6d. net.

Thompson (Francis). SELECTED POEMS OF FRANCIS THOMPSON. With a Biographical Note by WILFRID MEYNELL. With a Portrait in Photogravure. *Seventh Edition. Fcap. 8vo.* 5s. net.

Tileston (Mary W.). DAILY STRENGTH FOR DAILY NEEDS. *Seventeenth Edition. Medium 16mo.* 2s. 6d. net. Also an edition in superior binding, 6s.

Toynbee (Paget), M.A., D. Litt. DANTE IN ENGLISH LITERATURE: FROM CHAUCER TO CARY. *Two Volumes. Demy 8vo.* 21s. net.
See also Oxford Biographies.

Tozer (Basil). THE HORSE IN HISTORY. Illustrated. *Cr. 8vo.* 6s.

Trench (Herbert). DEIRDRE WEDDED, AND OTHER POEMS. *Second and Revised Edition. Large Post 8vo.* 6s.
NEW POEMS. *Second Edition. Large Post 8vo.* 6s.
APOLLO AND THE SEAMAN. *Large Post 8vo. Paper,* 1s. 6d. net; *cloth,* 2s. 6d. net.

Trevelyan (G. M.), Fellow of Trinity College, Cambridge. ENGLAND UNDER THE STUARTS. With Maps and Plans. *Fourth Edition. Demy 8vo.* 10s. 6d. net.

Triggs (Inigo H.), A.R.I.B.A. TOWN PLANNING: PAST, PRESENT, AND POSSIBLE. Illustrated. *Second Edition. Wide Royal 8vo.* 15s. net.

Vaughan (Herbert M.), B.A.(Oxon), F.S.A. THE LAST OF THE ROYAL STUARTS, HENRY STUART, CARDINAL, DUKE OF YORK. Illustrated. *Second Edition. Demy 8vo.* 10s. 6d. net.
THE MEDICI POPES (LEO X. AND CLEMENT VII.). Illustrated. *Demy 8vo.* 15s. net.
THE NAPLES RIVIERA. Illustrated. *Second Edition. Cr. 8vo.* 6s.
*FLORENCE AND HER TREASURES. Illustrated. *Fcap. 8vo.* 5s. net.

Vernon (Hon. W. Warren), M.A. READINGS ON THE INFERNO OF DANTE. With an Introduction by the REV. DR. MOORE. *Two Volumes. Second Edition. Cr. 8vo.* 15s. net.
READINGS ON THE PURGATORIO OF DANTE. With an Introduction by the late DEAN CHURCH. *Two Volumes. Third Edition. Cr. 8vo.* 15s. net.
READINGS ON THE PARADISO OF DANTE. With an Introduction by the BISHOP OF RIPON. *Two Volumes. Second Edition. Cr. 8vo.* 15s. net.

Vincent (J. E.). THROUGH EAST ANGLIA IN A MOTOR CAR. Illustrated. *Cr. 8vo.* 6s.

Waddell (Col. L. A.), LL.D., C.B. LHASA AND ITS MYSTERIES. With a Record of the Expedition of 1903-1904. Illustrated. *Third and Cheaper Edition. Medium 8vo.* 7s. 6d. net.

Wagner (Richard). RICHARD WAGNER'S MUSIC DRAMAS: Interpretations, embodying Wagner's own explanations. By ALICE LEIGHTON CLEATHER and BASIL CRUMP. *In Three Volumes. Fcap. 8vo.* 2s. 6d. each.
   VOL. I.—THE RING OF THE NIBELUNG. *Third Edition.*
   VOL. III.—TRISTAN AND ISOLDE.

Wainemah (Paul). A SUMMER TOUR IN FINLAND. Illustrated. *Demy 8vo. 10s. 6d. net.*

Walkley (A. B.). DRAMA AND LIFE. *Cr. 8vo. 6s.*

Waterhouse (Elizabeth). WITH THE SIMPLE-HEARTED: Little Homilies to Women in Country Places. *Second Edition. Small Pott 8vo. 2s. net.*
COMPANIONS OF THE WAY. Being Selections for Morning and Evening Reading. Chosen and arranged by ELIZABETH WATERHOUSE. *Large Cr. 8vo. 5s. net.*
THOUGHTS OF A TERTIARY. *Second Edition. Small Pott 8vo. 1s. net.*

Watt (Francis). See Henderson (T. F.).

Weigall (Arthur E. P.). A GUIDE TO THE ANTIQUITIES OF UPPER EGYPT: From Abydos to the Sudan Frontier. Illustrated. *Cr. 8vo. 7s. 6d. net.*

Welch (Catharine). THE LITTLE DAUPHIN. Illustrated. *Cr. 8vo. 6s.*

Wells (J.), M.A., Fellow and Tutor of Wadham College. OXFORD AND OXFORD LIFE. *Third Edition. Cr. 8vo. 3s. 6d.*
A SHORT HISTORY OF ROME. *Tenth Edition.* With 3 Maps. *Cr. 8vo. 3s. 6d.*

Westell (W. Percival). THE YOUNG NATURALIST. Illustrated. *Cr. 8vo. 6s.*

Westell (W. Percival), F.L.S., M.B.O.U., and **Cooper (C. S.),** F.R.H.S. THE YOUNG BOTANIST. Illustrated. *Cr. 8vo. 3s. 6d. net.*

***Wheeler (Ethel R.).** FAMOUS BLUE STOCKINGS. Illustrated. *Demy 8vo. 10s. 6d. net.*

Whibley (C.). See Henley (W. E.).

White (George F.), Lieut.-Col. A CENTURY OF SPAIN AND PORTUGAL, 1788-1898. *Demy 8vo. 12s. 6d. net.*

Whitley (Miss). See Dilke (Lady).

Wilde (Oscar). DE PROFUNDIS. *Twelfth Edition. Cr. 8vo. 5s. net.*

THE WORKS OF OSCAR WILDE. *In Twelve Volumes. Fcap. 8vo. 5s. net each volume.*
I. LORD ARTHUR SAVILE'S CRIME AND THE PORTRAIT OF MR. W. H. II. THE DUCHESS OF PADUA. III. POEMS. IV. LADY WINDERMERE'S FAN. V. A WOMAN OF NO IMPORTANCE. VI. AN IDEAL HUSBAND. VII. THE IMPORTANCE OF BEING EARNEST. VIII. A HOUSE OF POMEGRANATES. IX. INTENTIONS. X. DE PROFUNDIS AND PRISON LETTERS. XI. ESSAYS. XII. SALOMÉ, A FLORENTINE TRAGEDY, and LA SAINTE COURTISANE.

Williams (H. Noel). THE WOMEN BONAPARTES. The Mother and three Sisters of Napoleon. Illustrated. *In Two Volumes. Demy 8vo. 24s. net.*
A ROSE OF SAVOY: MARIE ADELÉIDE OF SAVOY, DUCHESSE DE BOURGOGNE, MOTHER OF LOUIS XV. Illustrated. *Second Edition. Demy 8vo. 15s. net.*
*THE FASCINATING DUC DE RICHELIEU: LOUIS FRANÇOIS ARMAND DU PLESSIS, MARÉCHAL DUC DE RICHELIEU. Illustrated. *Demy 8vo. 15s. net.*

Wood (Sir Evelyn), F.M., V.C., G.C.B., G.C.M.G. FROM MIDSHIPMAN TO FIELD-MARSHAL. Illustrated. *Fifth and Cheaper Edition. Demy 8vo. 7s. 6d. net.*
THE REVOLT IN HINDUSTAN. 1857-59. Illustrated. *Second Edition. Cr. 8vo. 6s.*

Wood (W. Birkbeck), M.A., late Scholar of Worcester College, Oxford, and **Edmonds (Major J. E.),** R.E., D.A.Q.M.G. A HISTORY OF THE CIVIL WAR IN THE UNITED STATES. With an Introduction by H. SPENSER WILKINSON. With 24 Maps and Plans. *Third Edition. Demy 8vo. 12s. 6d. net.*

Wordsworth (W.). THE POEMS. With an Introduction and Notes by NOWELL C. SMITH, late Fellow of New College, Oxford. *In Three Volumes. Demy 8vo. 15s. net.*
POEMS BY WILLIAM WORDSWORTH. Selected with an Introduction by STOPFORD A. BROOKE. Illustrated. *Cr. 8vo. 7s. 6d. net.*

Wyatt (Kate M.). See Gloag (M. R.).

Wyllie (M. A.). NORWAY AND ITS FJORDS. Illustrated. *Second Edition. Cr. 8vo. 6s.*

Yeats (W. B.). A BOOK OF IRISH VERSE. *Revised and Enlarged Edition. Cr. 8vo. 3s. 6d.*

Young (Filson). See The Complete Series.

GENERAL LITERATURE 15

PART II.—A SELECTION OF SERIES.

Ancient Cities.

General Editor, B. C. A. WINDLE, D.Sc., F.R.S.

Cr. 8vo. 4s. 6d. net.

With Illustrations by E. H. NEW, and other Artists.

BRISTOL. By Alfred Harvey, M.B.
CANTERBURY. By J. C. Cox, LL.D., F.S.A.
CHESTER. By B. C. A. Windle, D.Sc., F.R.S.
DUBLIN. By S. A. O. Fitzpatrick.

EDINBURGH. By M. G. Williamson, M.A.
LINCOLN. By E. Mansel Sympson, M.A.
SHREWSBURY. By T. Auden, M.A., F.S.A.
WELLS and GLASTONBURY. By T. S. Holmes.

The Antiquary's Books.

General Editor, J. CHARLES COX, LL.D., F.S.A.

Demy 8vo. 7s. 6d. net.

With Numerous Illustrations.

ARCHÆOLOGY AND FALSE ANTIQUITIES. By R. Munro.
BELLS OF ENGLAND, THE. By Canon J. J. Raven. *Second Edition.*
BRASSES OF ENGLAND, THE. By Herbert W. Macklin. *Second Edition.*
CELTIC ART IN PAGAN AND CHRISTIAN TIMES. By J. Romilly Allen.
DOMESDAY INQUEST, THE. By Adolphus Ballard.
ENGLISH CHURCH FURNITURE. By J. C. Cox and A. Harvey. *Second Edition.*
ENGLISH COSTUME. From Prehistoric Times to the End of the Eighteenth Century. By George Clinch.
ENGLISH MONASTIC LIFE. By the Right Rev. Abbot Gasquet. *Fourth Edition.*
ENGLISH SEALS. By J. Harvey Bloom.
FOLK-LORE AS AN HISTORICAL SCIENCE. By Sir G. L. Gomme.

GILDS AND COMPANIES OF LONDON, THE. By George Unwin.
MANOR AND MANORIAL RECORDS, THE. By Nathaniel J. Hone.
MEDIÆVAL HOSPITALS OF ENGLAND, THE. By Rotha Mary Clay.
OLD SERVICE BOOKS OF THE ENGLISH CHURCH. By Christopher Wordsworth, M.A., and Henry Littlehales. *Second Edition.*
PARISH LIFE IN MEDIÆVAL ENGLAND. By the Right Rev. Abbot Gasquet. *Second Edition.*
*PARISH REGISTERS OF ENGLAND, THE. By J. C. Cox.
REMAINS OF THE PREHISTORIC AGE IN ENGLAND. By B. C. A. Windle. *Second Edition.*
ROYAL FORESTS OF ENGLAND, THE. By J. C. Cox, LL.D.
SHRINES OF BRITISH SAINTS. By J. C Wall.

The Arden Shakespeare.

Demy 8vo. 2s. 6d. net each volume.

An edition of Shakespeare in single Plays. Edited with a full Introduction, Textual Notes, and a Commentary at the foot of the page.

ALL'S WELL THAT ENDS WELL.
ANTONY AND CLEOPATRA.
CYMBELINE.
COMEDY OF ERRORS, THE.
HAMLET. *Second Edition.*
JULIUS CAESAR.
KING HENRY V.
KING HENRY VI. PT. I.
KING HENRY VI. PT. II.
KING HENRY VI. PT. III.
KING LEAR.
KING RICHARD III.
LIFE AND DEATH OF KING JOHN, THE.
LOVE'S LABOUR'S LOST.
MACBETH.

MEASURE FOR MEASURE.
MERCHANT OF VENICE, THE.
MERRY WIVES OF WINDSOR, THE.
MIDSUMMER NIGHT'S DREAM, A.
OTHELLO.
PERICLES.
ROMEO AND JULIET.
TAMING OF THE SHREW, THE.
TEMPEST, THE.
TIMON OF ATHENS.
TITUS ANDRONICUS.
TROILUS AND CRESSIDA.
TWO GENTLEMEN OF VERONA, THE.
TWELFTH NIGHT.

Classics of Art.

Edited by Dr. J. H. W. LAING.

With numerous Illustrations. Wide Royal 8vo. Gilt top.

THE ART OF THE GREEKS. By H. B. Walters. 12s. 6d. net.

FLORENTINE SCULPTORS OF THE RENAISSANCE. Wilhelm Bode, Ph.D. Translated by Jessie Haynes. 12s. 6d. net.

*GEORGE ROMNEY. By Arthur B. Chamberlain. 12s. 6d. net.

GHIRLANDAIO. Gerald S. Davies. *Second Edition.* 10s. 6d.

MICHELANGELO. By Gerald S. Davies. 12s. 6d. net.

RUBENS. By Edward Dillon, M.A. 25s. net.

RAPHAEL. By A. P. Oppé. 12s. 6d. net.

TITIAN. By Charles Ricketts. 12s. 6d. net.

TURNER'S SKETCHES AND DRAWINGS. By A. J. Finberg. 12s. 6d. net. *Second Edition.*

VELAZQUEZ. By A. de Beruete. 10s. 6d. net.

The "Complete" Series.

Fully Illustrated. Demy 8vo.

THE COMPLETE COOK. By Lilian Whitling. 7s. 6d. net.

THE COMPLETE CRICKETER. By Albert E. Knight. 7s. 6d. net.

THE COMPLETE FOXHUNTER. By Charles Richardson. 12s. 6d. net. *Second Edition.*

THE COMPLETE GOLFER. By Harry Vardon. 10s. 6d. net. *Tenth Edition.*

THE COMPLETE HOCKEY-PLAYER. By Eustace E. White. 5s. net. *Second Edition.*

THE COMPLETE LAWN TENNIS PLAYER. By A. Wallis Myers. 10s. 6d. net. *Second Edition.*

THE COMPLETE MOTORIST. By Filson Young. 12s. 6d. net. *New Edition* (*Seventh*).

THE COMPLETE MOUNTAINEER. By G. D. Abraham. 15s. net. *Second Edition.*

THE COMPLETE OARSMAN. By R. C. Lehmann, M.P. 10s. 6d. net.

THE COMPLETE PHOTOGRAPHER. By R. Child Bayley. 10s. 6d. net. *Fourth Edition.*

THE COMPLETE RUGBY FOOTBALLER, ON THE NEW ZEALAND SYSTEM. By D. Gallaher and W. J. Stead. 10s. 6d. net. *Second Edition.*

THE COMPLETE SHOT. By G. T. Teasdale Buckell. 12s. 6d. net. *Third Edition.*

The Connoisseur's Library.

With numerous Illustrations. Wide Royal 8vo. Gilt top. 25s. net.

ENGLISH FURNITURE. By F. S. Robinson.

ENGLISH COLOURED BOOKS. By Martin Hardie.

EUROPEAN ENAMELS. By Henry H. Cunynghame, C.B.

GLASS. By Edward Dillon.

GOLDSMITHS' AND SILVERSMITHS' WORK. By Nelson Dawson. *Second Edition.*

*ILLUMINATED MANUSCRIPTS. By J. A. Herbert.

IVORIES. By A. Maskell.

JEWELLERY. By H. Clifford Smith. *Second Edition.*

MEZZOTINTS. By Cyril Davenport.

MINIATURES. By Dudley Heath.

PORCELAIN. By Edward Dillon.

SEALS. By Walter de Gray Birch.

Handbooks of English Church History.

Edited by J. H. BURN, B.D. *Crown 8vo. 2s. 6d. net.*

THE FOUNDATIONS OF THE ENGLISH CHURCH. By J. H. Maude.
THE SAXON CHURCH AND THE NORMAN CONQUEST. By C. T. Cruttwell.
THE MEDIÆVAL CHURCH AND THE PAPACY. By A. C. Jennings.
THE REFORMATION PERIOD. By Henry Gee.
THE STRUGGLE WITH PURITANISM. By Bruce Blaxland.
THE CHURCH OF ENGLAND IN THE EIGHTEENTH CENTURY. By Alfred Plummer.

The Illustrated Pocket Library of Plain and Coloured Books.

Fcap. 8vo. 3s. 6d. net each volume.

WITH COLOURED ILLUSTRATIONS.

OLD COLOURED BOOKS. By George Paston. 2s. net.
THE LIFE AND DEATH OF JOHN MYTTON, ESQ. By Nimrod. *Fifth Edition.*
THE LIFE OF A SPORTSMAN. By Nimrod.
HANDLEY CROSS. By R. S. Surtees. *Third Edition.*
MR. SPONGE'S SPORTING TOUR. By R. S. Surtees.
JORROCKS' JAUNTS AND JOLLITIES. By R. S. Surtees. *Third Edition.*
ASK MAMMA. By R. S. Surtees.
THE ANALYSIS OF THE HUNTING FIELD. By R. S. Surtees.
THE TOUR OF DR. SYNTAX IN SEARCH OF THE PICTURESQUE. By William Combe.
THE TOUR OF DR. SYNTAX IN SEARCH OF CONSOLATION. By William Combe.
THE THIRD TOUR OF DR. SYNTAX IN SEARCH OF A WIFE. By William Combe.
THE HISTORY OF JOHNNY QUAE GENUS. By the Author of 'The Three Tours.'
THE ENGLISH DANCE OF DEATH, from the Designs of T. Rowlandson, with Metrical Illustrations by the Author of 'Doctor Syntax.' *Two Volumes.*
THE DANCE OF LIFE: A Poem. By the Author of 'Dr. Syntax.'
LIFE IN LONDON. By Pierce Egan.
REAL LIFE IN LONDON. By an Amateur (Pierce Egan). *Two Volumes.*
THE LIFE OF AN ACTOR. By Pierce Egan.
THE VICAR OF WAKEFIELD. By Oliver Goldsmith.
THE MILITARY ADVENTURES OF JOHNNY NEWCOMBE. By an Officer.
THE NATIONAL SPORTS OF GREAT BRITAIN. With Descriptions and 50 Coloured Plates by Henry Alken.
THE ADVENTURES OF A POST CAPTAIN. By a Naval Officer.
GAMONIA. By Lawrence Rawstone, Esq.
AN ACADEMY FOR GROWN HORSEMEN. By Geoffrey Gambado, Esq.
REAL LIFE IN IRELAND. By a Real Paddy.
THE ADVENTURES OF JOHNNY NEWCOMBE IN THE NAVY. By Alfred Burton.
THE OLD ENGLISH SQUIRE. By John Careless, Esq.
THE ENGLISH SPY. By Bernard Blackmantle. *Two Volumes. 7s. net.*

WITH PLAIN ILLUSTRATIONS.

THE GRAVE: A Poem. By Robert Blair.
ILLUSTRATIONS OF THE BOOK OF JOB. Invented and engraved by William Blake.
WINDSOR CASTLE. By W. Harrison Ainsworth.
THE TOWER OF LONDON. By W. Harrison Ainsworth.
FRANK FAIRLEGH. By F. E. Smedley.
HANDY ANDY. By Samuel Lover.
THE COMPLEAT ANGLER. By Izaak Walton and Charles Cotton.
THE PICKWICK PAPERS. By Charles Dickens.

Leaders of Religion.

Edited by H. C. BEECHING, M.A., Canon of Westminster. *With Portraits.*
Crown 8vo. 2s. net.

CARDINAL NEWMAN. By R. H. Hutton.
JOHN WESLEY. By J. H. Overton, M.A.
BISHOP WILBERFORCE. By G. W. Daniell, M.A.
CARDINAL MANNING. By A. W. Hutton, M.A.
CHARLES SIMEON. By H. C. G. Moule, D.D.
JOHN KNOX. By F. MacCunn. *Second Edition.*
JOHN HOWE. By R. F. Horton, D.D.
THOMAS KEN. By F. A. Clarke, M.A.
GEORGE FOX, THE QUAKER. By T. Hodgkin, D.C.L. *Third Edition.*

JOHN KEBLE. By Walter Lock, D.D.
THOMAS CHALMERS. By Mrs. Oliphant.
LANCELOT ANDREWES. By R. L. Ottley, D.D. *Second Edition.*
AUGUSTINE OF CANTERBURY. By E. L. Cutts, D.D.
WILLIAM LAUD. By W. H. Hutton, M.A. *Third Edition.*
JOHN DONNE. By Augustus Jessop, D.D.
THOMAS CRANMER. By A. J. Mason, D.D.
BISHOP LATIMER. By R. M. Carlyle and A. J. Carlyle, M.A.
BISHOP BUTLER. By W. A. Spooner, M.A.

The Library of Devotion.

With Introductions and (where necessary) Notes.

Small Pott 8vo, gilt top, cloth, 2s.; leather, 2s. 6d. net.

THE CONFESSIONS OF ST. AUGUSTINE. *Seventh Edition.*
THE IMITATION OF CHRIST. *Sixth Edition.*
THE CHRISTIAN YEAR. *Fourth Edition.*
LYRA INNOCENTIUM. *Second Edition.*
THE TEMPLE. *Second Edition.*
A BOOK OF DEVOTIONS. *Second Edition.*
A SERIOUS CALL TO A DEVOUT AND HOLY LIFE. *Fourth Edition.*
A GUIDE TO ETERNITY.
THE INNER WAY. *Second Edition.*
ON THE LOVE OF GOD.
THE PSALMS OF DAVID.
LYRA APOSTOLICA.
THE SONG OF SONGS.
THE THOUGHTS OF PASCAL. *Second Edition.*
A MANUAL OF CONSOLATION FROM THE SAINTS AND FATHERS.
DEVOTIONS FROM THE APOCRYPHA.
THE SPIRITUAL COMBAT.
THE DEVOTIONS OF ST. ANSELM.
BISHOP WILSON'S SACRA PRIVATA.

GRACE ABOUNDING TO THE CHIEF OF SINNERS.
LYRA SACRA: A Book of Sacred Verse. *Second Edition.*
A DAY BOOK FROM THE SAINTS AND FATHERS.
A LITTLE BOOK OF HEAVENLY WISDOM. A Selection from the English Mystics.
LIGHT, LIFE, and LOVE. A Selection from the German Mystics.
AN INTRODUCTION TO THE DEVOUT LIFE.
THE LITTLE FLOWERS OF THE GLORIOUS MESSER ST. FRANCIS AND OF HIS FRIARS.
DEATH AND IMMORTALITY.
THE SPIRITUAL GUIDE.
DEVOTIONS FOR EVERY DAY IN THE WEEK AND THE GREAT FESTIVALS.
PRECES PRIVATÆ.
HORÆ MYSTICÆ: A Day Book from the Writings of Mystics of Many Nations.

GENERAL LITERATURE

Little Books on Art.

With many Illustrations. Demy 16mo. Gilt top. 2s. 6d. net.

Each volume consists of about 200 pages, and contains from 30 to 40 Illustrations, including a Frontispiece in Photogravure.

ALBRECHT DURER. J. Allen.
ARTS OF JAPAN, THE. E. Dillon.
BOOKPLATES. E. Almack.
BOTTICELLI. Mary L. Bloomer.
BURNE-JONES. F. de Lisle.
CHRISTIAN SYMBOLISM. Mrs. H. Jenner.
CHRIST IN ART. Mrs. H. Jenner.
CLAUDE. E. Dillon.
CONSTABLE. H. W. Tompkins.
COROT. A. Pollard and E. Birnstingl.
ENAMELS. Mrs. N. Dawson.
FREDERIC LEIGHTON. A. Corkran.
GEORGE ROMNEY. G. Paston.
GREEK ART. H. B. Walters.
GREUZE AND BOUCHER. E. F. Pollard.

HOLBEIN. Mrs. G. Fortescue.
ILLUMINATED MANUSCRIPTS. J. W. Bradley.
JEWELLERY. C. Davenport.
JOHN HOPPNER. H. P. K. Skipton.
SIR JOSHUA REYNOLDS. J. Sime.
MILLET. N. Peacock.
MINIATURES. C. Davenport.
OUR LADY IN ART. Mrs. H. Jenner.
RAPHAEL. A. R. Dryhurst. *Second Edition.*
REMBRANDT. Mrs. E. A. Sharp.
TURNER. F. Tyrrell-Gill.
VANDYCK. M. G. Smallwood.
VELASQUEZ. W. Wilberforce and A. R. Gilbert.
WATTS. R. E. D. Sketchley.

The Little Galleries.

Demy 16mo. 2s. 6d. net.

Each volume contains 20 plates in Photogravure, together with a short outline of the life and work of the master to whom the book is devoted.

A LITTLE GALLERY OF REYNOLDS.
A LITTLE GALLERY OF ROMNEY.
A LITTLE GALLERY OF HOPPNER.

A LITTLE GALLERY OF MILLAIS.
A LITTLE GALLERY OF ENGLISH POETS.

The Little Guides.

With many Illustrations by E. H. NEW and other artists, and from photographs.

Small Pott 8vo, gilt top, cloth, 2s. 6d. net; leather, 3s. 6d. net.

The main features of these Guides are (1) a handy and charming form; (2) illustrations from photographs and by well-known artists; (3) good plans and maps; (4) an adequate but compact presentation of everything that is interesting in the natural features, history, archæology, and architecture of the town or district treated.

CAMBRIDGE AND ITS COLLEGES. A. H. Thompson. *Third Edition, Revised.*
ENGLISH LAKES, THE. F. G. Brabant.
ISLE OF WIGHT, THE. G. Clinch.
MALVERN COUNTRY, THE. B. C. A. Windle.
NORTH WALES. A. T. Story.
OXFORD AND ITS COLLEGES. J. Wells. *Ninth Edition.*

SHAKESPEARE'S COUNTRY. B. C. A. Windle. *Third Edition.*
ST. PAUL'S CATHEDRAL. G. Clinch.
WESTMINSTER ABBEY. G. E. Troutbeck. *Second Edition.*

BUCKINGHAMSHIRE. E. S. Roscoe.
CHESHIRE. W. M. Gallichan.

THE LITTLE GUIDES—*continued.*

CORNWALL. A. L. Salmon.
DERBYSHIRE. J. C. Cox.
DEVON. S. Baring-Gould. *Second Edition.*
DORSET. F. R. Heath. *Second Edition.*
ESSEX. J. C. Cox.
HAMPSHIRE. J. C. Cox.
HERTFORDSHIRE. H. W. Tompkins.
KENT. G. Clinch.
KERRY. C. P. Crane.
MIDDLESEX. J. B. Firth.
MONMOUTHSHIRE. G. W. Wade and J. H. Wade.
NORFOLK. W. A. Dutt. *Second Edition, Revised.*
NORTHAMPTONSHIRE. W. Dry.
*NORTHUMBERLAND. J. E. Morris.
NOTTINGHAMSHIRE. L. Guilford.
OXFORDSHIRE. F. G. Brabant.
SOMERSET. G. W. and J. H. Wade.
*STAFFORDSHIRE. C. E. Masefield.
SUFFOLK. W. A. Dutt.
SURREY. F. A. H. Lambert.
SUSSEX. F. G. Brabant. *Third Edition.*
*WILTSHIRE. F. R. Heath.
YORKSHIRE, THE EAST RIDING. J. E. Morris.
YORKSHIRE, THE NORTH RIDING. J. E. Morris.

BRITTANY. S. Baring-Gould.
NORMANDY. C. Scudamore.
ROME. C. G. Ellaby.
SICILY. F. H. Jackson.

The Little Library.

With Introductions, Notes, and Photogravure Frontispieces.

Small Pott 8vo. Gilt top. Each Volume, cloth, 1s. 6d. *net;* leather, 2s. 6d. *net.*

Anon. A LITTLE BOOK OF ENGLISH LYRICS. *Second Edition.*

Austen (Jane). PRIDE AND PREJUDICE. *Two Volumes.*
NORTHANGER ABBEY.

Bacon (Francis). THE ESSAYS OF LORD BACON.

Barham (R. H.). THE INGOLDSBY LEGENDS. *Two Volumes.*

Barnet (Mrs. P. A.). A LITTLE BOOK OF ENGLISH PROSE.

Beckford (William). THE HISTORY OF THE CALIPH VATHEK.

Blake (William). SELECTIONS FROM WILLIAM BLAKE.

Borrow (George). LAVENGRO. *Two Volumes.*
THE ROMANY RYE.

Browning (Robert). SELECTIONS FROM THE EARLY POEMS OF ROBERT BROWNING.

Canning (George). SELECTIONS FROM THE ANTI-JACOBIN: with GEORGE CANNING's additional Poems.

Cowley (Abraham). THE ESSAYS OF ABRAHAM COWLEY.

Crabbe (George). SELECTIONS FROM GEORGE CRABBE.

Craik (Mrs.). JOHN HALIFAX, GENTLEMAN. *Two Volumes.*

Crashaw (Richard). THE ENGLISH POEMS OF RICHARD CRASHAW.

Dante (Alighieri). THE INFERNO OF DANTE. Translated by H. F. CARY.
THE PURGATORIO OF DANTE. Translated by H. F. CARY.
THE PARADISO OF DANTE. Translated by H. F. CARY.

Darley (George). SELECTIONS FROM THE POEMS OF GEORGE DARLEY.

Deane (A. C.). A LITTLE BOOK OF LIGHT VERSE.

Dickens (Charles). CHRISTMAS BOOKS. *Two Volumes.*

Ferrier (Susan). MARRIAGE. *Two Volumes.*
THE INHERITANCE. *Two Volumes.*

Gaskell (Mrs.). CRANFORD.

Hawthorne (Nathaniel). THE SCARLET LETTER.

Henderson (T. F.). A LITTLE BOOK OF SCOTTISH VERSE.

Keats (John). POEMS.

Kinglake (A. W.). EOTHEN. *Second Edition.*

Lamb (Charles). ELIA, AND THE LAST ESSAYS OF ELIA.

Locker (F.). LONDON LYRICS.

Longfellow (H. W.). SELECTIONS FROM LONGFELLOW.

THE LITTLE LIBRARY—*continued*.

Marvell (Andrew). THE POEMS OF ANDREW MARVELL.
Milton (John). THE MINOR POEMS OF JOHN MILTON.
Moir (D. M.). MANSIE WAUCH.
Nichols (J. B. B.). A LITTLE BOOK OF ENGLISH SONNETS.
Rochefoucauld (La). THE MAXIMS OF LA ROCHEFOUCAULD.
Smith (Horace and James). REJECTED ADDRESSES.
Sterne (Laurence). A SENTIMENTAL JOURNEY.
Tennyson (Alfred, Lord). THE EARLY POEMS OF ALFRED, LORD TENNYSON.
IN MEMORIAM.
THE PRINCESS.
MAUD.
Thackeray (W. M.). VANITY FAIR. *Three Volumes.*
PENDENNIS. *Three Volumes.*
ESMOND.
CHRISTMAS BOOKS.
Vaughan (Henry). THE POEMS OF HENRY VAUGHAN.
Walton (Izaak). THE COMPLEAT ANGLER.
Waterhouse (Elizabeth). A LITTLE BOOK OF LIFE AND DEATH. *Thirteenth Edition.*
Wordsworth (W.). SELECTIONS FROM WORDSWORTH.
Wordsworth (W.) and Coleridge (S. T.) LYRICAL BALLADS.

The Little Quarto Shakespeare.

Edited by W. J. CRAIG. With Introductions and Notes.

Pott 16mo. In 40 Volumes. Gilt top. Leather, price 1s. net each volume.
Mahogany Revolving Book Case. 10s. net.

Miniature Library.

Gilt top.

EUPHRANOR: A Dialogue on Youth. By Edward FitzGerald. *Demy 32mo. Leather, 2s. net.*
THE LIFE OF EDWARD, LORD HERBERT OF CHERBURY. Written by himself. *Demy 32mo. Leather, 2s. net.*
POLONIUS: or Wise Saws and Modern Instances. By Edward FitzGerald. *Demy 32mo. Leather, 2s. net.*
THE RUBÁIYÁT OF OMAR KHAYYÁM. By Edward FitzGerald. *Fourth Edition. Leather, 1s. net.*

The New Library of Medicine.

Edited by C. W. SALEEBY, M.D.; F.R.S. Edin. *Demy 8vo.*

CARE OF THE BODY, THE. By F. Cavanagh. *Second Edition. 7s. 6d. net.*
CHILDREN OF THE NATION, THE. By the Right Hon. Sir John Gorst. *Second Edition. 7s. 6d. net.*
CONTROL OF A SCOURGE, THE: or, How Cancer is Curable. By Chas. P. Childe. *7s. 6d. net.*
DISEASES OF OCCUPATION. By Sir Thomas Oliver. *10s. 6d. net.*
DRINK PROBLEM, THE, in its Medico-Sociological Aspects. Edited by T. N. Kelynack. *7s. 6d. net.*
DRUGS AND THE DRUG HABIT. By H. Sainsbury.
FUNCTIONAL NERVE DISEASES. By A. T. Schofield. *7s. 6d. net.*
*HEREDITY, THE LAWS OF. By Archdall Reid. *21s. net.*
HYGIENE OF MIND, THE. By T. S. Clouston. *Fifth Edition. 7s. 6d. net.*
INFANT MORTALITY. By Sir George Newman. *7s. 6d. net.*
PREVENTION OF TUBERCULOSIS (CONSUMPTION), THE. By Arthur Newsholme. *10s. 6d. net.*
AIR AND HEALTH. By Ronald C. Macfie. *7s. 6d. net. Second Edition.*

The New Library of Music.

Edited by ERNEST NEWMAN. *Illustrated. Demy 8vo. 7s. 6d. net.*

HUGO WOLF. By Ernest Newman. Illustrated.

HANDEL. By R. A. Streatfeild. Illustrated. *Second Edition.*

Oxford Biographies.

Illustrated. Fcap. 8vo. Gilt top. Each volume, cloth, 2s. 6d. net; leather, 3s. 6d. net.

DANTE ALIGHIERI. By Paget Toynbee, M.A., D. Litt. *Third Edition.*
GIROLAMO SAVONAROLA By E. L. S. Horsburgh, M.A. *Second Edition.*
JOHN HOWARD. By E. C. S. Gibson, D.D., Bishop of Gloucester.
ALFRED TENNYSON. By A. C. Benson, M.A. *Second Edition.*
SIR WALTER RALEIGH. By I. A Taylor.
ERASMUS. By E. F. H. Capey.

THE YOUNG PRETENDER. By C. S. Terry.
ROBERT BURNS. By T. F. Henderson.
CHATHAM. By A. S. M'Dowall.
FRANCIS OF ASSISI. By Anna M. Stoddart.
CANNING. By W. Alison Phillips.
BEACONSFIELD. By Walter Sichel.
JOHANN WOLFGANG GOETHE. By H. G. Atkins.
FRANÇOIS FENELON. By Viscount St. Cyres.

Romantic History.

Edited by MARTIN HUME, M.A. *Illustrated. Demy 8vo.*

A series of attractive volumes in which the periods and personalities selected are such as afford romantic human interest, in addition to their historical importance.

THE FIRST GOVERNESS OF THE NETHERLANDS, MARGARET OF AUSTRIA. Eleanor E. Tremayne. 10s. 6d. net.
TWO ENGLISH QUEENS AND PHILIP. Martin Hume, M.A. 15s. net.
THE NINE DAYS' QUEEN. Richard Davey. With a Preface by Martin Hume, M.A. *Second Edition.* 10s. 6d. net.

Handbooks of Theology.

THE DOCTRINE OF THE INCARNATION. By R. L. Ottley, D.D. *Fifth Edition, Revised.* Demy 8vo. 12s. 6d.
A HISTORY OF EARLY CHRISTIAN DOCTRINE. By J. F. Bethune-Baker, M.A. *Demy 8vo.* 10s. 6d.
AN INTRODUCTION TO THE HISTORY OF RELIGION. By F. B. Jevons, M.A. Litt. D. *Fifth Edition.* Demy 8vo. 10s. 6d.

AN INTRODUCTION TO THE HISTORY OF THE CREEDS. By A. E. Burn, D.D. *Demy 8vo.* 10s. 6d.
THE PHILOSOPHY OF RELIGION IN ENGLAND AND AMERICA. By Alfred Caldecott, D.D. *Demy 8vo.* 10s. 6d.
THE XXXIX. ARTICLES OF THE CHURCH OF ENGLAND. Edited by E. C. S. Gibson, D.D. *Seventh Edition.* Demy 8vo. 12s. 6d.

The Westminster Commentaries.

General Editor, WALTER LOCK, D.D., Warden of Keble College.

Dean Ireland's Professor of Exegesis in the University of Oxford.

THE ACTS OF THE APOSTLES. Edited by R. B. Rackham, M.A. *Demy 8vo. Fifth Edition.* 10s. 6d.

THE FIRST EPISTLE OF PAUL THE APOSTLE TO THE CORINTHIANS. Edited by H. L. Goudge, M.A. *Third Ed. Demy 8vo.* 6s.

THE BOOK OF EXODUS. Edited by A. H. M'Neile, B.D. With a Map and 3 Plans. *Demy 8vo.* 10s. 6d.

THE BOOK OF EZEKIEL. Edited by H. A. Redpath, M.A., D.Litt. *Demy 8vo.* 10s. 6d.

THE BOOK OF GENESIS. Edited with Introduction and Notes by S. R. Driver, D.D. *Eighth Edition. Demy 8vo.* 10s. 6d.

ADDITIONS AND CORRECTIONS IN THE SEVENTH EDITION OF THE BOOK OF GENESIS. By S. R. Driver, D.D. *Demy 8vo.* 1s.

THE BOOK OF JOB. Edited by E. C. S. Gibson, D.D. *Second Edition. Demy 8vo.* 6s.

THE EPISTLE OF ST. JAMES. Edited with Introduction and Notes by R. J. Knowling, D.D. *Second Edition. Demy 8vo.* 6s.

PART III.—A SELECTION OF WORKS OF FICTION

Albanesi (E. Maria). SUSANNAH AND ONE OTHER. *Fourth Edition. Cr. 8vo.* 6s.
LOVE AND LOUISA. *Second Edition. Cr. 8vo.* 6s.
THE BROWN EYES OF MARY. *Third Edition. Cr. 8vo.* 6s.
I KNOW A MAIDEN. *Third Edition. Cr. 8vo.* 6s.
THE INVINCIBLE AMELIA; OR, THE POLITE ADVENTURESS. *Third Edition. Cr. 8vo.* 3s. 6d.
THE GLAD HEART. *Fifth Edition. Cr. 8vo.* 6s.

Allerton (Mark). SUCH AND SUCH THINGS. *Cr. 8vo.* 6s.

Annesley (Maude). THIS DAY'S MADNESS. *Second Edition. Cr. 8vo.* 6s.

Bagot (Richard). A ROMAN MYSTERY. *Third Edition. Cr. 8vo.* 6s.
THE PASSPORT. *Fourth Edition. Cr. 8vo.* 6s.
ANTHONY CUTHBERT. *Fourth Edition. Cr. 8vo.* 6s.
LOVE'S PROXY. *Cr. 8vo.* 6s.
DONNA DIANA. *Second Edition. Cr. 8vo.* 6s.
CASTING OF NETS. *Twelfth Edition. Cr. 8vo.* 6s.

Bailey (H. C.). STORM AND TREASURE. *Second Edition. Cr. 8vo.* 6s.

Ball (Oona H.) (Barbara Burke). THEIR OXFORD YEAR. Illustrated. *Cr. 8vo.* 6s.

BARBARA GOES TO OXFORD. Illustrated. *Third Edition. Cr. 8vo.* 6s.

Baring-Gould (S.). ARMINELL. *Fifth Edition. Cr. 8vo.* 6s.
IN THE ROAR OF THE SEA. *Seventh Edition. Cr. 8vo.* 6s.
MARGERY OF QUETHER. *Third Edition. Cr. 8vo.* 6s.
THE QUEEN OF LOVE. *Fifth Edition. Cr. 8vo.* 6s.
JACQUETTA. *Third Edition. Cr. 8vo.* 6s.
KITTY ALONE. *Fifth Edition. Cr. 8vo.* 6s.
NOÉMI. Illustrated. *Fourth Edition. Cr. 8vo.* 6s.
THE BROOM-SQUIRE. Illustrated. *Fifth Edition. Cr. 8vo.* 6s.
DARTMOOR IDYLLS. *Cr. 8vo.* 6s.
GUAVAS THE TINNER. Illustrated. *Second Edition. Cr. 8vo.* 6s.
BLADYS OF THE STEWPONEY. Illustrated. *Second Edition. Cr. 8vo.* 6s.
PABO THE PRIEST. *Cr. 8vo.* 6s.
WINEFRED. Illustrated. *Second Edition. Cr. 8vo.* 6s.
ROYAL GEORGIE. Illustrated. *Cr. 8vo.* 6s.
CHRIS OF ALL SORTS. *Cr. 8vo.* 6s.
IN DEWISLAND. *Second Edition. Cr. 8vo.* 6s.
THE FROBISHERS. *Cr. 8vo.* 6s.
DOMITIA. Illustrated. *Second Edition. Cr. 8vo.* 6s.
MRS. CURGENVEN OF CURGENVEN. *Cr. 8vo.* 6s.

Barr (Robert). IN THE MIDST OF ALARMS. *Third Edition. Cr. 8vo.* 6s.
THE COUNTESS TEKLA. *Fifth Edition. Cr. 8vo.* 6s.

THE MUTABLE MANY. *Third Edition.* Cr. 8vo. 6s.

Begbie (Harold). THE CURIOUS AND DIVERTING ADVENTURES OF SIR JOHN SPARROW; OR, THE PROGRESS OF AN OPEN MIND. *Second Edition.* Cr. 8vo. 6s.

Belloc (H.). EMMANUEL BURDEN, MERCHANT. Illustrated. *Second Edition.* Cr. 8vo. 6s.
A CHANGE IN THE CABINET. *Third Edition.* Cr. 8vo. 6s.

Benson (E. F.). DODO: A DETAIL OF THE DAY. *Sixteenth Edition.* Cr. 8vo. 6s.

Birmingham (George A.). THE BAD TIMES. *Second Edition.* Cr. 8vo. 6s.
SPANISH GOLD. *Fifth Edition.* Cr. 8vo. 6s.
THE SEARCH PARTY. *Fourth Edition.* Cr. 8vo. 6s.

Bowen (Marjorie). I WILL MAINTAIN. *Fifth Edition.* Cr. 8vo. 6s.

Bretherton (Ralph Harold). AN HONEST MAN. *Second Edition.* Cr. 8vo. 6s.

Capes (Bernard). WHY DID HE DO IT? *Third Edition.* Cr. 8vo. 6s.

Castle (Agnes and Egerton). FLOWER O' THE ORANGE, and Other Tales. *Third Edition.* Cr. 8vo. 6s.

Clifford (Mrs. W. K.). THE GETTING WELL OF DOROTHY. Illustrated. *Second Edition.* Cr. 8vo. 3s. 6d.

Conrad (Joseph). THE SECRET AGENT: A Simple Tale. *Fourth Ed.* Cr. 8vo. 6s.
A SET OF SIX. *Fourth Edition.* Cr. 8vo. 6s.

Corelli (Marie). A ROMANCE OF TWO WORLDS. *Thirtieth Ed.* Cr. 8vo. 6s.
VENDETTA. *Twenty-eighth Edition.* Cr. 8vo. 6s.
THELMA. *Forty-first Ed.* Cr. 8vo. 6s.
ARDATH: THE STORY OF A DEAD SELF. *Nineteenth Edition.* Cr. 8vo. 6s.
THE SOUL OF LILITH. *Sixteenth Edition.* Cr. 8vo. 6s.
WORMWOOD. *Seventeenth Ed.* Cr. 8vo. 6s.
BARABBAS: A DREAM OF THE WORLD'S TRAGEDY. *Forty-fifth Edition.* Cr. 8vo. 6s.
THE SORROWS OF SATAN. *Fifty-sixth Edition.* Cr. 8vo. 6s.
THE MASTER CHRISTIAN. *Twelfth Edition.* 177th Thousand. Cr. 8vo. 6s.
TEMPORAL POWER: A STUDY IN SUPREMACY. *Second Edition.* 150th Thousand. Cr. 8vo. 6s.
GOD'S GOOD MAN; A SIMPLE LOVE STORY. *Fourteenth Edition.* 152nd Thousand. Cr. 8vo. 6s.
HOLY ORDERS: THE TRAGEDY OF A QUIET LIFE. *Second Edition.* 120th Thousand. Crown 8vo. 6s.
THE MIGHTY ATOM. *Twenty-eighth Edition.* Cr. 8vo. 6s.
BOY: a Sketch. *Twelfth Edition.* Cr. 8vo. 6s.
CAMEOS. *Fourteenth Edition.* Cr. 8vo. 6s.

Cotes (Mrs. Everard). See Duncan (Sara Jeannette).

Crockett (S. R.). LOCHINVAR. Illustrated. *Third Edition.* Cr. 8vo. 6s.
THE STANDARD BEARER. *Second Edition.* Cr. 8vo. 6s.

Croker (Mrs. B. M.). THE OLD CANTONMENT. Cr. 8vo. 6s.
JOHANNA. *Second Edition.* Cr. 8vo. 6s.
THE HAPPY VALLEY. *Fourth Edition.* Cr. 8vo. 6s.
A NINE DAYS' WONDER. *Fourth Edition.* Cr. 8vo. 6s.
PEGGY OF THE BARTONS. *Seventh Edition.* Cr. 8vo. 6s.
ANGEL. *Fifth Edition.* Cr. 8vo. 6s.
KATHERINE THE ARROGANT. *Sixth Edition.* Cr. 8vo. 6s.

Cuthell (Edith E.). ONLY A GUARDROOM DOG. Illustrated. Cr. 8vo. 3s. 6d.

Dawson (Warrington). THE SCAR. *Second Edition.* Cr. 8vo. 6s.
THE SCOURGE. Cr. 8vo. 6s.

Douglas (Theo.). COUSIN HUGH. *Second Edition.* Cr. 8vo. 6s.

Doyle (A. Conan). ROUND THE RED LAMP. *Eleventh Edition.* Cr. 8vo. 6s.

Duncan (Sara Jeannette) (Mrs. Everard Cotes).
A VOYAGE OF CONSOLATION. Illustrated. *Third Edition.* Cr. 8vo. 6s.
COUSIN CINDERELLA. *Second Edition.* Cr. 8vo. 6s.
THE BURNT OFFERING. *Second Edition.* Cr. 8vo. 6s.

Elliot (Robert). THE IMMORTAL CHARLATAN. *Second Edition.* Crown 8vo. 6s.

Fenn (G. Manville). SYD BELTON; or, The Boy who would not go to Sea. Illustrated. *Second Ed.* Cr. 8vo. 3s. 6d.

Findlater (J. H.). THE GREEN GRAVES OF BALGOWRIE. *Fifth Edition.* Cr. 8vo. 6s.
THE LADDER TO THE STARS. *Second Edition.* Cr. 8vo. 6s.

Findlater (Mary). A NARROW WAY. *Third Edition.* Cr. 8vo. 6s.
OVER THE HILLS. *Second Edition.* Cr. 8vo. 6s.
THE ROSE OF JOY. *Third Edition.* Cr. 8vo. 6s.
A BLIND BIRD'S NEST. Illustrated. *Second Edition.* Cr. 8vo. 6s.

Fiction

MARGERY O' THE MILL. *Third Edition. Cr. 8vo. 6s.*
HARDY-ON-THE-HILL. *Third Edition. Cr. 8vo. 6s.*
GALATEA OF THE WHEATFIELD. *Second Edition. Cr. 8vo. 6s.*

Fraser (Mrs. Hugh). THE SLAKING OF THE SWORD. *Second Edition. Cr. 8vo. 6s.*
GIANNELLA. *Second Edition. Cr. 8vo. 6s.*
IN THE SHADOW OF THE LORD. *Third Edition. Cr. 8vo. 6s.*

Fry (B. and C. B.). A MOTHER'S SON. *Fifth Edition. Cr. 8vo. 6s.*

Gerard (Louise). THE GOLDEN CENTIPEDE. *Third Edition. Cr. 8vo. 6s.*

Gibbs (Philip). THE SPIRIT OF REVOLT. *Second Edition. Cr. 8vo. 6s.*

Gissing (George). THE CROWN OF LIFE. *Cr. 8vo. 6s.*

Glendon (George). THE EMPEROR OF THE AIR. *Illustrated. Cr. 8vo. 6s.*

Hamilton (Cosmo). MRS. SKEFFINGTON. *Second Edition. Cr. 8vo. 6s.*

Harraden (Beatrice). IN VARYING MOODS. *Fourteenth Edition. Cr. 8vo. 6s.*
THE SCHOLAR'S DAUGHTER. *Fourth Edition. Cr. 8vo. 6s.*
HILDA STRAFFORD and THE REMITTANCE MAN. *Twelfth Ed. Cr. 8vo. 6s.*
INTERPLAY. *Fifth Edition. Cr. 8vo. 6s.*

Hichens (Robert). THE PROPHET OF BERKELEY SQUARE. *Second Edition. Cr. 8vo. 6s.*
TONGUES OF CONSCIENCE. *Third Edition. Cr. 8vo. 6s.*
FELIX. *Seventh Edition. Cr. 8vo. 6s.*
THE WOMAN WITH THE FAN. *Eighth Edition. Cr. 8vo. 6s.*
BYEWAYS. *Cr. 8vo. 6s.*
THE GARDEN OF ALLAH. *Nineteenth Edition. Cr. 8vo. 6s.*
THE BLACK SPANIEL. *Cr. 8vo. 6s.*
THE CALL OF THE BLOOD. *Seventh Edition. Cr. 8vo. 6s.*
BARBARY SHEEP. *Second Edition. Cr. 8vo. 6s.*

Hilliers (Ashton). THE MASTER-GIRL. *Illustrated. Second Edition. Cr. 8vo. 6s.*

Hope (Anthony). THE GOD IN THE CAR. *Eleventh Edition. Cr. 8vo. 6s.*
A CHANGE OF AIR. *Sixth Edition. Cr. 8vo. 6s.*
A MAN OF MARK. *Seventh Ed. Cr. 8vo. 6s.*
THE CHRONICLES OF COUNT ANTONIO. *Sixth Edition. Cr. 8vo. 6s.*
PHROSO. *Illustrated. Eighth Edition. Cr. 8vo. 6s.*
SIMON DALE. *Illustrated. Eighth Edition. Cr. 8vo. 6s.*
THE KING'S MIRROR. *Fifth Edition. Cr. 8vo. 6s.*

QUISANTE. *Fourth Edition. Cr. 8vo. 6s.*
THE DOLLY DIALOGUES. *Cr. 8vo. 6s.*
A SERVANT OF THE PUBLIC. *Illustrated. Fourth Edition. Cr. 8vo. 6s.*
TALES OF TWO PEOPLE. *Third Edition. Cr. 8vo. 6s.*
THE GREAT MISS DRIVER. *Fourth Edition. Cr. 8vo. 6s.*

Hueffer (Ford Maddox). AN ENGLISH GIRL: A ROMANCE. *Second Edition. Cr. 8vo. 6s.*
MR. APOLLO: A JUST POSSIBLE STORY. *Second Edition. Cr. 8vo. 6s.*

Hutten (Baroness von). THE HALO. *Fifth Edition. Cr. 8vo. 6s.*

Hyne (C. J. Cutcliffe). MR. HORROCKS, PURSER. *Fifth Edition. Cr. 8vo. 6s.*
PRINCE RUPERT, THE BUCCANEER. *Illustrated. Third Edition. Cr. 8vo. 6s.*

Jacobs (W. W.). MANY CARGOES. *Thirty-second Edition. Cr. 8vo. 3s. 6d.*
SEA URCHINS. *Sixteenth Edition. Cr. 8vo. 3s. 6d.*
A MASTER OF CRAFT. *Illustrated. Ninth Edition. Cr. 8vo. 3s. 6d.*
LIGHT FREIGHTS. *Illustrated. Eighth Edition. Cr. 8vo. 3s. 6d.*
THE SKIPPER'S WOOING. *Ninth Edition. Cr. 8vo. 3s. 6d.*
AT SUNWICH PORT. *Illustrated. Tenth Edition. Cr. 8vo. 3s. 6d.*
DIALSTONE LANE. *Illustrated. Seventh Edition. Cr. 8vo. 3s. 6d.*
ODD CRAFT. *Illustrated. Fourth Edition. Cr. 8vo. 3s. 6d.*
THE LADY OF THE BARGE. *Illustrated. Eighth Edition. Cr. 8vo. 3s. 6d.*
SALTHAVEN. *Illustrated. Second Edition. Cr. 8vo. 3s. 6d.*
SAILORS' KNOTS. *Illustrated. Fifth Edition. Cr. 8vo. 3s. 6d.*

James (Henry). THE SOFT SIDE. *Second Edition. Cr. 8vo. 6s.*
THE BETTER SORT. *Cr. 8vo. 6s.*
THE GOLDEN BOWL. *Third Edition. Cr. 8vo. 6s.*

Le Queux (William). THE HUNCHBACK OF WESTMINSTER. *Third Edition. Cr. 8vo. 6s.*
THE CLOSED BOOK. *Third Edition. Cr. 8vo. 6s.*
THE VALLEY OF THE SHADOW. *Illustrated. Third Edition. Cr. 8vo. 6s.*
BEHIND THE THRONE. *Third Edition. Cr. 8vo. 6s.*
THE CROOKED WAY. *Second Edition. Cr. 8vo. 6s.*

Lindsey (William). THE SEVERED MANTLE. *Cr. 8vo. 6s.*

London (Jack). WHITE FANG. *Seventh Edition. Cr. 8vo. 6s.*

Lubbock (Basil). DEEP SEA WARRIORS. Illustrated. *Third Edition.* Cr. 8vo. 6s.

Lucas (St John). THE FIRST ROUND. Cr. 8vo. 6s.

Lyall (Edna). DERRICK VAUGHAN, NOVELIST. 44th Thousand. Cr. 8vo. 3s. 6d.

Maartens (Maarten). THE NEW RELIGION: A Modern Novel. *Third Edition.* Cr. 8vo. 6s.
BROTHERS ALL; More Stories of Dutch Peasant Life. *Third Edition.* Cr. 8vo. 6s.
THE PRICE OF LIS DORIS. *Second Edition.* Cr. 8vo. 6s.

M'Carthy (Justin H.). THE DUKE'S MOTTO. *Fourth Edition.* Cr. 8vo. 6s.

Macnaughtan (S.). THE FORTUNE OF CHRISTINA M'NAB. *Fifth Edition.* Cr. 8vo. 6s.

Malet (Lucas). COLONEL ENDERBY'S WIFE. *Fourth Edition.* Cr. 8vo. 6s.
A COUNSEL OF PERFECTION. *Second Edition.* Cr. 8vo. 6s.
THE WAGES OF SIN. *Sixteenth Edition.* Cr. 8vo. 6s.
THE CARISSIMA. *Fifth Ed.* Cr. 8vo. 6s.
THE GATELESS BARRIER. *Fifth Edition.* Cr. 8vo. 6s.
THE HISTORY OF SIR RICHARD CALMADY. *Seventh Edition.* Cr. 8vo. 6s.

Mann (Mrs. M. E.). THE PARISH NURSE. *Fourth Edition.* Cr. 8vo. 6s.
A SHEAF OF CORN. *Second Edition.* Cr. 8vo. 6s.
THE HEART-SMITER. *Second Edition.* Cr. 8vo. 6s.
AVENGING CHILDREN. *Second Edition.* Cr. 8vo. 6s.

Marsh (Richard). THE COWARD BEHIND THE CURTAIN. Cr. 8vo. 6s.
THE SURPRISING HUSBAND. *Second Edition.* Cr. 8vo. 6s.
A ROYAL INDISCRETION. *Second Edition.* Cr. 8vo. 6s.
LIVE MEN'S SHOES. *Second Edition.* Cr. 8vo. 6s.

Marshall (Archibald). MANY JUNES. *Second Edition.* Cr. 8vo. 6s.
THE SQUIRE'S DAUGHTER. *Third Edition.* Cr. 8vo. 6s.

Mason (A. E. W.). CLEMENTINA. Illustrated. *Sixth Edition.* Cr. 8vo. 6s. and at 2s. net.

Maud (Constance). A DAUGHTER OF FRANCE. *Third Edition.* Cr. 8vo. 6s.

Maxwell (W. B.). VIVIEN. *Ninth Edition.* Cr. 8vo. 6s.
THE RAGGED MESSENGER. *Third Edition.* Cr. 8vo. 6s.
FABULOUS FANCIES. Cr. 8vo. 6s.

THE GUARDED FLAME. *Seventh Edition.* Cr. 8vo. 6s.
ODD LENGTHS. *Second Ed.* Cr. 8vo. 6s.
HILL RISE. *Fourth Edition.* Cr. 8vo. 6s.
THE COUNTESS OF MAYBURY: Between You and I. *Fourth Edition.* Cr. 8vo. 6s.

Meade (L. T.). DRIFT. *Second Edition.* Cr. 8vo. 6s.
RESURGAM. *Second Edition.* Cr. 8vo. 6s.
VICTORY. Cr. 8vo. 6s.
A GIRL OF THE PEOPLE. Illustrated. *Fourth Edition.* Cr. 8vo. 3s. 6d.
HEPSY GIPSY. Illustrated. Cr. 8vo. 2s. 6d.
THE HONOURABLE MISS: A Story of an Old-fashioned Town. Illustrated. *Second Edition.* Cr. 8vo. 3s. 6d.

Mitford (Bertram). THE SIGN OF THE SPIDER. Illustrated. *Seventh Edition.* Cr. 8vo. 3s. 6d.

Molesworth (Mrs.). THE RED GRANGE. Illustrated. *Second Edition.* Cr. 8vo. 3s. 6d.

Montague (C. E.). A HIND LET LOOSE. *Third Edition.* Cr. 8vo. 6s.

Montgomery (K. L.). COLONEL KATE. *Second Edition.* Cr. 8vo. 6s.

Morrison (Arthur). TALES OF MEAN STREETS. *Seventh Edition.* Cr. 8vo. 6s.
A CHILD OF THE JAGO. *Sixth Edition.* Cr. 8vo. 6s.
THE HOLE IN THE WALL. *Fourth Edition.* Cr. 8vo. 6s.
DIVERS VANITIES. Cr. 8vo. 6s.

Nesbit (E.), (Mrs. H. Bland). THE RED HOUSE. Illustrated. *Fifth Edition.* Cr. 8vo. 6s.

Noble (Edward). LORDS OF THE SEA. *Third Edition.* Cr. 8vo. 6s.

Ollivant (Alfred). OWD BOB, THE GREY DOG OF KENMUIR. With a Frontispiece. *Eleventh Ed.* Cr. 8vo. 6s.

Oppenheim (E. Phillips). MASTER OF MEN. *Fourth Edition.* Cr. 8vo. 6s.

Oxenham (John). A WEAVER OF WEBS. Illustrated. *Fourth Ed.* Cr. 8vo. 6s.
THE GATE OF THE DESERT. *Fourth Edition.* Cr. 8vo. 6s.
PROFIT AND LOSS. *Fourth Edition.* Cr. 8vo. 6s.
THE LONG ROAD. *Fourth Edition.* Cr. 8vo. 6s.
THE SONG OF HYACINTH, AND OTHER STORIES. *Second Edition.* Cr. 8vo. 6s.
MY LADY OF SHADOWS. *Fourth Edition.* Cr. 8vo. 6s.

Pain (Barry). THE EXILES OF FALOO. *Second Edition.* Crown 8vo. 6s.

Parker (Gilbert). PIERRE AND HIS PEOPLE. *Sixth Edition.* Cr. 8vo. 6s.

FICTION

MRS. FALCHION. *Fifth Edition. Cr. 8vo. 6s.*
THE TRANSLATION OF A SAVAGE. *Fourth Edition. Cr. 8vo. 6s.*
THE TRAIL OF THE SWORD. Illustrated. *Tenth Edition. Cr. 8vo. 6s.*
WHEN VALMOND CAME TO PONTIAC: The Story of a Lost Napoleon. *Sixth Edition. Cr. 8vo. 6s.*
AN ADVENTURER OF THE NORTH. The Last Adventures of 'Pretty Pierre.' *Fourth Edition. Cr. 8vo. 6s.*
THE SEATS OF THE MIGHTY. Illustrated. *Seventeenth Edition. Cr. 8vo. 6s.*
THE BATTLE OF THE STRONG: a Romance of Two Kingdoms. Illustrated. *Sixth Edition. Cr. 8vo. 6s.*
THE POMP OF THE LAVILETTES. *Third Edition. Cr. 8vo. 3s. 6d.*
NORTHERN LIGHTS. *Fourth Edition. Cr. 8vo. 6s.*

Pasture (Mrs. Henry de la). THE TYRANT. *Fourth Edition. Cr. 8vo. 6s.*

Patterson (J. E.). WATCHERS BY THE SHORE. *Third Edition. Cr. 8vo. 6s.*

Pemberton (Max). THE FOOTSTEPS OF A THRONE. Illustrated. *Fourth Edition. Cr. 8vo. 6s.*
I CROWN THEE KING. Illustrated. *Cr. 8vo. 6s.*
LOVE THE HARVESTER: A STORY OF THE SHIRES. Illustrated.' *Third Edition. Cr. 8vo. 3s. 6d.*
THE MYSTERY OF THE GREEN HEART. *Third Edition. Cr. 8vo. 6s.*

Phillpotts (Eden). LYING PROPHETS. *Third Edition. Cr. 8vo. 6s.*
CHILDREN OF THE MIST. *Fifth Edition. Cr. 8vo. 6s.*
THE HUMAN BOY. With a Frontispiece. *Seventh Edition. Cr. 8vo. 6s.*
SONS OF THE MORNING. *Second Edition. Cr. 8vo. 6s.*
THE RIVER. *Third Edition. Cr. 8vo. 6s.*
THE AMERICAN PRISONER. *Fourth Edition. Cr. 8vo. 6s.*
THE SECRET WOMAN. *Fourth Edition. Cr. 8vo. 6s.*
KNOCK AT A VENTURE. *Third Edition. Cr. 8vo. 6s.*
THE PORTREEVE. *Fourth Edition. Cr. 8vo. 6s.*
THE POACHER'S WIFE. *Second Edition. Cr. 8vo. 6s.*
THE STRIKING HOURS. *Second Edition. Cr. 8vo. 6s.*

Pickthall (Marmaduke). SAÏD THE FISHERMAN. *Eighth Edition. Cr. 8vo. 6s.*

'Q' (A. T. Quiller Couch). THE WHITE WOLF. *Second Edition. Cr. 8vo. 6s.*
THE MAYOR OF TROY. *Fourth Edition. Cr. 8vo. 6s.*
MERRY-GARDEN AND OTHER STORIES. *Cr. 8vo. 6s.*

MAJOR VIGOUREUX. *Third Edition. Cr. 8vo. 6s.*

Querido (Israel). TOIL OF MEN. Translated by F. S. ARNOLD. *Cr. 8vo. 6s.*

Rawson (Maud Stepney). THE ENCHANTED GARDEN. *Fourth Edition. Cr. 8vo. 6s.*
THE EASY GO LUCKIES: OR, ONE WAY OF LIVING. *Second Edition. Cr. 8vo. 6s.*
HAPPINESS. *Second Edition. Cr. 8vo. 6s.*

Rhys (Grace). THE BRIDE. *Second Edition. Cr. 8vo. 6s.*

Ridge (W. Pett). ERB. *Second Edition. Cr. 8vo. 6s.*
A SON OF THE STATE. *Third Edition. Cr. 8vo. 3s. 6d.*
A BREAKER OF LAWS. *Cr. 8vo. 3s. 6d.*
MRS. GALER'S BUSINESS. Illustrated. *Second Edition. Cr. 8vo. 6s.*
THE WICKHAMSES. *Fourth Edition. Cr. 8vo. 6s.*
NAME OF GARLAND. *Third Edition. Cr. 8vo. 6s.*
SPLENDID BROTHER. *Fourth Edition. Cr. 8vo. 6s.*

Ritchie (Mrs. David G.). MAN AND THE CASSOCK. *Second Edition. Cr. 8vo. 6s.*

Roberts (C. G. D.). THE HEART OF THE ANCIENT WOOD. *Cr. 8vo. 3s. 6d.*

Robins (Elizabeth). THE CONVERT. *Third Edition. Cr. 8vo. 6s.*

Rosenkrantz (Baron Palle). THE MAGISTRATE'S OWN CASE. *Cr. 8vo. 6s.*

Russell (W. Clark). MY DANISH SWEETHEART. Illustrated. *Fifth Edition. Cr. 8vo. 6s.*
HIS ISLAND PRINCESS. Illustrated. *Second Edition. Cr. 8vo. 6s.*
ABANDONED. *Second Edition. Cr. 8vo. 6s.*
MASTER ROCKAFELLAR'S VOYAGE. Illustrated. *Fourth Edition. Cr. 8vo. 3s. 6d.*

Sandys (Sydney). JACK CARSTAIRS OF THE POWER HOUSE. Illustrated. *Second Edition. Cr. 8vo. 6s.*

Sergeant (Adeline). THE PASSION OF PAUL MARILLIER. *Cr. 8vo. 6s.*

*****Shakespear (Olivia).** UNCLE HILARY. *Cr. 8vo. 6s.*

Sidgwick (Mrs. Alfred). THE KINSMAN. Illustrated. *Third Edition. Cr. 8vo. 6s.*
THE SEVERINS. *Fourth Edition. Cr. 8vo. 6s.*

Stewart (Newton V.). A SON OF THE EMPEROR: BEING PASSAGES FROM THE LIFE OF ENZIO, KING OF SARDINIA AND CORSICA. *Cr. 8vo. 6s.*

Swayne (Martin Lutrell). THE BISHOP AND THE LADY. *Second Edition. Cr. 8vo. 6s.*

Thurston (E. Temple). MIRAGE. *Fourth Edition. Cr. 8vo. 6s.*

Underhill (Evelyn). THE COLUMN OF DUST. *Cr. 8vo. 6s.*

Vorst (Marie Van). THE SENTIMENTAL ADVENTURES OF JIMMY BULSTRODE. *Cr. 8vo. 6s.*
IN AMBUSH. *Second Edition. Cr. 8vo. 6s.*

Waineman (Paul). THE WIFE OF NICHOLAS FLEMING. *Cr. 8vo. 6s.*

Watson (H. B. Marriott). TWISTED EGLANTINE. Illustrated. *Third Edition. Cr. 8vo. 6s.*
THE HIGH TOBY. *Third Edition. Cr. 8vo. 6s.*
A MIDSUMMER DAY'S DREAM. *Third Edition. Cr. 8vo. 6s.*
THE CASTLE BY THE SEA. *Third Edition. Cr. 8vo. 6s.*
THE PRIVATEERS. Illustrated. *Second Edition. Cr. 8vo. 6s.*
A POPPY SHOW: BEING DIVERS AND DIVERSE TALES. *Cr. 8vo. 6s.*
THE FLOWER OF THE HEART. *Third Edition. Cr. 8vo. 6s.*

Webling (Peggy). THE STORY OF VIRGINIA PERFECT. *Third Edition. Cr. 8vo. 6s.*
*THE SPIRIT OF MIRTH. *Cr. 8vo. 6s.*

Wells (H. G.). THE SEA LADY. *Cr. 8vo. 6s. Also Medium 8vo. 6d.*

Weyman (Stanley). UNDER THE RED ROBE. Illustrated. *Twenty-third Edition. Cr. 8vo. 6s.*

Whitby (Beatrice). THE RESULT OF AN ACCIDENT. *Second Edition. Cr. 8vo. 6s.*

White (Edmund). THE HEART OF HINDUSTAN. *Second Edition. Cr. 8vo. 6s.*

White (Percy). LOVE AND THE WISE MEN. *Third Edition. Cr. 8vo. 6s.*

Williamson (Mrs. C. N.). THE ADVENTURE OF PRINCESS SYLVIA. *Second Edition. Cr. 8vo. 6s.*

Williamson (C. N. and A. M.). THE LIGHTNING CONDUCTOR: The Strange Adventures of a Motor Car. Illustrated. *Seventeenth Edition. Cr. 8vo. 6s. Also Cr. 8vo. 1s. net.*
THE PRINCESS PASSES: A Romance of a Motor. Illustrated. *Ninth Edition. Cr. 8vo. 6s.*
MY FRIEND THE CHAUFFEUR. Illustrated. *Tenth Edition. Cr. 8vo. 6s.*
LADY BETTY ACROSS THE WATER. *Eleventh Edition. Cr. 8vo. 6s.*
THE CAR OF DESTINY AND ITS ERRAND IN SPAIN. Illustrated. *Fifth Edition. Cr. 8vo. 6s.*
THE BOTOR CHAPERON. Illustrated. *Sixth Edition. Cr. 8vo. 6s.*
SCARLET RUNNER. Illustrated. *Third Edition. Cr. 8vo. 6s.*
SET IN SILVER. Illustrated. *Third Edition. Cr. 8vo. 6s.*
LORD LOVELAND DISCOVERS AMERICA. *Second Edition. Cr. 8vo. 6s.*

Wyllarde (Dolf). THE PATHWAY OF THE PIONEER (Nous Autres). *Fourth Edition. Cr. 8vo. 6s.*

Books for Boys and Girls.

Illustrated. Crown 8vo. 3s. 6d.

THE GETTING WELL OF DOROTHY. By Mrs. W. K. Clifford. *Second Edition.*
ONLY A GUARD-ROOM DOG. By Edith E. Cuthell.
MASTER ROCKAFELLAR'S VOYAGE. By W. Clark Russell. *Fourth Edition.*
SYD BELTON: Or, the Boy who would not go to Sea. By G. Manville Fenn. *Second Edition.*
THE RED GRANGE. By Mrs. Molesworth. *Second Edition.*

A GIRL OF THE PEOPLE. By L. T. Meade. *Fourth Edition.*
HEPSY GIPSY. By L. T. Meade. *2s. 6d.*
THE HONOURABLE MISS. By L. T. Meade. *Second Edition.*
THERE WAS ONCE A PRINCE. By Mrs. M. E. Mann.
WHEN ARNOLD COMES HOME. By Mrs. M. E. Mann.

The Novels of Alexandre Dumas.

Medium 8vo.   Price 6d.   Double Volumes, 1s.

ACTÉ.
THE ADVENTURES OF CAPTAIN PAMPHILE.
AMAURY.
THE BIRD OF FATE.
THE BLACK TULIP.
THE CASTLE OF EPPSTEIN.
CATHERINE BLUM.
CÉCILE.
THE CHATELET.
THE CHEVALIER D'HARMENTAL. (Double volume.)
CHICOT THE JESTER.
THE COMTE DE MONTGOMERY.
CONSCIENCE.
THE CONVICT'S SON.
THE CORSICAN BROTHERS; and OTHO THE ARCHER.
CROP-EARED JACQUOT.
DOM GORENFLOT.
THE FATAL COMBAT.
THE FENCING MASTER.
FERNANDE.
GABRIEL LAMBERT.
GEORGES.
THE GREAT MASSACRE.
HENRI DE NAVARRE.
HÉLÈNE DE CHAVERNY.
THE HOROSCOPE.
LOUISE DE LA VALLIÈRE. (Double volume.)
THE MAN IN THE IRON MASK. (Double volume.)
MAÎTRE ADAM.
THE MOUTH OF HELL.
NANON. (Double volume.)
OLYMPIA.
PAULINE; PASCAL BRUNO; and BONTEKOE.
PÈRE LA RUINE.
THE PRINCE OF THIEVES.
THE REMINISCENCES OF ANTONY.
ROBIN HOOD.
SAMUEL GELB.
THE SNOWBALL AND THE SULTANETTA.
SYLVANDIRE.
THE TAKING OF CALAIS.
TALES OF THE SUPERNATURAL.
TALES OF STRANGE ADVENTURE.
TALES OF TERROR.
THE THREE MUSKETEERS. (Double volume.)
THE TRAGEDY OF NANTES.
TWENTY YEARS AFTER. (Double volume.)
THE WILD-DUCK SHOOTER.
THE WOLF-LEADER.

Methuen's Sixpenny Books.

Medium 8vo.

Albanesi (E. Maria). LOVE AND LOUISA.
I KNOW A MAIDEN.
Anstey (F.). A BAYARD OF BENGAL.
Austen (J.). PRIDE AND PREJUDICE.
Bagot (Richard). A ROMAN MYSTERY.
CASTING OF NETS.
DONNA DIANA.
Balfour (Andrew). BY STROKE OF SWORD.
Baring-Gould (S.). FURZE BLOOM.
CHEAP JACK ZITA.
KITTY ALONE.
URITH.
THE BROOM SQUIRE.
IN THE ROAR OF THE SEA.
NOÉMI.
A BOOK OF FAIRY TALES. Illustrated.
LITTLE TU'PENNY.
WINEFRED.
THE FROBISHERS.
THE QUEEN OF LOVE.

ARMINELL.
BLADYS OF THE STEWPONEY.

Barr (Robert). JENNIE BAXTER.
IN THE MIDST OF ALARMS.
THE COUNTESS TEKLA.
THE MUTABLE MANY.

Benson (E. F.). DODO.
THE VINTAGE.

Brontë (Charlotte). SHIRLEY.

Brownell (C. L.). THE HEART OF JAPAN.

Burton (J. Bloundelle). ACROSS THE SALT SEAS.

Caffyn (Mrs.). ANNE MAULEVERER.

Capes (Bernard). THE LAKE OF WINE.

Clifford (Mrs. W. K.). A FLASH OF SUMMER.
MRS. KEITH'S CRIME.

Corbett (Julian). A BUSINESS IN GREAT WATERS.

Croker (Mrs. B. M.). ANGEL.
A STATE SECRET.
PEGGY OF THE BARTONS.
JOHANNA.

Dante (Alighieri). THE DIVINE COMEDY (Cary).

Doyle (A. Conan). ROUND THE RED LAMP.

Duncan (Sara Jeannette). A VOYAGE OF CONSOLATION.
THOSE DELIGHTFUL AMERICANS.

Eliot (George). THE MILL ON THE FLOSS.

Findlater (Jane H.). THE GREEN GRAVES OF BALGOWRIE.

Gallon (Tom). RICKERBY'S FOLLY.

Gaskell (Mrs.). CRANFORD.
MARY BARTON.
NORTH AND SOUTH.

Gerard (Dorothea). HOLY MATRIMONY.
THE CONQUEST OF LONDON.
MADE OF MONEY.

Gissing (G.). THE TOWN TRAVELLER.
THE CROWN OF LIFE.

Glanville (Ernest). THE INCA'S TREASURE.
THE KLOOF BRIDE.

Gleig (Charles). BUNTER'S CRU

Grimm (The Brothers). GR FAIRY TALES.

Hope (Anthony). A MAN OF MA
A CHANGE OF AIR.
THE CHRONICLES OF CO ANTONIO.
PHROSO.
THE DOLLY DIALOGUES.

Hornung (E. W.). DEAD MEN NO TALES.

Ingraham (J. H.). THE THRON DAVID.

Le Queux (W.). THE HUNCH OF WESTMINSTER.

Levett-Yeats (S. K.). THE TRAI WAY.
ORRAIN.

Linton (E. Lynn). THE TRUE TORY OF JOSHUA DAVIDSON

Lyall (Edna). DERRICK VAUGH

Malet (Lucas). THE CARISSIMA
A COUNSEL OF PERFECTION.

Mann (Mrs. M. E.). MRS. P HOWARD.
A LOST ESTATE.
THE CEDAR STAR.
ONE ANOTHER'S BURDENS.
THE PATTEN EXPERIMENT.
A WINTER'S TALE.

Marchmont (A. W.). MISER H LEY'S SECRET.
A MOMENT'S ERROR.

Marryat (Captain). PETER SIM JACOB FAITHFUL.

March (Richard). A METAMORPI
THE TWICKENHAM PEERAGE.
THE GODDESS.
THE JOSS.

Mason (A. E. W.). CLEMENTIN

Mathers (Helen). HONEY.
GRIFF OF GRIFFITHSCOURT.
SAM'S SWEETHEART.
THE FERRYMAN.

Meade (Mrs. L. T.). DRIFT.

Miller (Esther). LIVING LIES.

Mitford (Bertram). THE SIGN C SPIDER.

Montresor (F. F.). THE ALIEN.

orrison (Arthur). THE HOLE IN THE WALL.
sbit (E.). THE RED HOUSE.
rris (W. E.). HIS GRACE.
LES INGILBY.
IE CREDIT OF THE COUNTY.
RD LEONARD THE LUCKLESS.
ATTHEW AUSTEN.
ARISSA FURIOSA.
phant (Mrs.). THE LADY'S WALK.
ROBERT'S FORTUNE.
E PRODIGALS.
E TWO MARYS.
penhelm (E. P.). MASTER OF MEN
ker (Gilbert). THE POMP OF THE LAVILETTES.
EN VALMOND CAME TO PONTIAC.
E TRAIL OF THE SWORD.
iberton (Max). THE FOOTSTEPS OF A THRONE.
ROWN THEE KING.
lpotts (Eden). THE HUMAN BOY.
LDREN OF THE MIST.
POACHER'S WIFE.
E RIVER.
(A. T. Quiller Couch). THE HITE WOLF.
re (W. Pett). A SON OF THE STATE.
T PROPERTY.
RGE and THE GENERAL.

ERB.
Russell (W. Clark). ABANDONED.
A MARRIAGE AT SEA.
MY DANISH SWEETHEART.
HIS ISLAND PRINCESS.
Sergeant (Adeline). THE MASTER OF BEECHWOOD.
BALBARA'S MONEY.
THE YELLOW DIAMOND.
THE LOVE THAT OVERCAME.
Sidgwick (Mrs. Alfred). THE KINSMAN.
Surtees (R. S.). HANDLEY CROSS.
MR. SPONGE'S SPORTING TOUR.
ASK MAMMA.
Walford (Mrs. L. B.). MR. SMITH.
COUSINS.
THE BABY'S GRANDMOTHER.
TROUBLESOME DAUGHTERS.
Wallace (General Lew). BEN-HUR.
THE FAIR GOD.
Watson (H. B. Marriott). THE ADVENTURERS.
*CAPTAIN FORTUNE.
Weekes (A. B.). PRISONERS OF WAR.
Wells (H. G.). THE SEA LADY.
White (Percy). A PASSIONATE PILGRIM.

www.ingramcontent.com/pod-product-compliance
Lightning Source LLC
Chambersburg PA
CBHW021349230426
43666CB00006B/452